Python Parallel Programming Cookbook

Master efficient parallel programming to build powerful applications using Python

Giancarlo Zaccone

BIRMINGHAM - MUMBAI

Python Parallel Programming Cookbook

First published: August 2015

Production reference: 1210815

Published by Packt Publishing Ltd.
Livery Place
35 Livery Street
Birmingham B3 2PB, UK.

ISBN 978-1-78528-958-3

www.packtpub.com

Credits

Author
Giancarlo Zaccone

Reviewers
Aditya Atluri
Ravi Chityala
Mike Galloy
Ludovic Gasc

Commissioning Editor
Sarah Crofton

Acquisition Editor
Meeta Rajani

Content Development Editor
Rashmi Suvarna

Technical Editor
Mrunmayee Patil

Copy Editor
Neha Vyas

Project Coordinator
Judie Jose

Proofreader
Safis Editing

Indexer
Mariammal Chettiyar

Graphics
Sheetal Aute
Disha Haria
Jason Monterio
Abhinash Sahu

Production Coordinator
Conidon Miranda

Cover Work
Conidon Miranda

About the Author

Giancarlo Zaccone has more than 10 years of experience in managing research projects, both in scientific and industrial domains. He worked as a researcher at the National Research Council (CNR), where he was involved in a few parallel numerical computing and scientific visualization projects.

He currently works as a software engineer at a consulting company, developing and maintaining software systems for space and defense applications.

Giancarlo holds a master's degree in physics from the University of Naples Federico II and has completed a second-level postgraduate master's program in scientific computing from the Sapienza University of Rome.

You can know more about him at https://it.linkedin.com/in/giancarlozaccone.

About the Reviewers

Aditya Atluri is a graduate student who focuses on computer graphics and GPUs. He also develops hardware using FPGAs, HDLs, and other software to leverage maximum performance for current applications using C++ and Python. His areas of interest are compilers, drivers, physically based rendering, and real-time rendering. His current focus is on making a contribution to MESA (the open source graphics driver stack for Linux), where he will implement OpenGL extensions for the AMD backend. He has developed Urutu, a compiler that translate high-level abstraction code (Python) to GPU by retaining the thread-level parallelism. For this, he is supported by NVIDIA with research grant. He is also working on Vulpes, a C++ STL library for Mac and iOS GPUs, which is built on Metal API.

Ravi Chityala is a senior engineer at Elekta Inc. He has more than 12 years of experience in image processing and scientific computing. He is also a part time instructor at the University of California, Santa Cruz Extension, San Jose, CA, where he teaches advanced Python to programmers. He began using Python as a scripting tool and fell in love with the language's simplicity, power, and expressiveness. He now uses it for web development, scientific prototyping and computing, and he uses it as a glue to automate the process. He combined his experience in image processing and his love for Python and coauthored the book *Image Acquisition and Processing using Python*, published by CRC Press.

Mike Galloy is a software developer who focuses on high-performance computing and visualization in scientific programming. He works mostly on IDL, but occasionally uses C, CUDA, and Python. He currently works for the National Center for Atmospheric Research (NCAR) at the Mauna Loa Solar Observatory. Previously, he worked for Tech-X Corporation, where he was the main developer for GPULib, a library of IDL bindings for GPU-accelerated computation routines. He is the creator and main developer of the open source projects, IDLdoc, mgunit, and rIDL, as well as the author of the book *Modern IDL*.

Ludovic Gasc is a senior software developer and engineer at Eyepea and ALLOcloud, a highly renowned open source VoIP and unified communications company in Europe.

Over the last 5 years, he has developed redundant distributed systems for the telecom sector that are based on Python, AsyncIO, PostgreSQL, and Redis.

You can contact him on his blog at `http://www.gmludo.eu`.

He is also the creator of the blog *API-Hour: Write efficient network daemons (HTTP, SSH) with ease*. For more information, visit `http://www.api-hour.io`.

www.PacktPub.com

Support files, eBooks, discount offers, and more

For support files and downloads related to your book, please visit www.PacktPub.com.

Did you know that Packt offers eBook versions of every book published, with PDF and ePub files available? You can upgrade to the eBook version at www.PacktPub.com and as a print book customer, you are entitled to a discount on the eBook copy. Get in touch with us at service@packtpub.com for more details.

At www.PacktPub.com, you can also read a collection of free technical articles, sign up for a range of free newsletters and receive exclusive discounts and offers on Packt books and eBooks.

https://www2.packtpub.com/books/subscription/packtlib

Do you need instant solutions to your IT questions? PacktLib is Packt's online digital book library. Here, you can search, access, and read Packt's entire library of books.

Why Subscribe?

- ▸ Fully searchable across every book published by Packt
- ▸ Copy and paste, print, and bookmark content
- ▸ On demand and accessible via a web browser

Free Access for Packt account holders

If you have an account with Packt at www.PacktPub.com, you can use this to access PacktLib today and view 9 entirely free books. Simply use your login credentials for immediate access.

Table of Contents

Preface

The study of computer science should cover not only the principles on which computational processing is based, but should also reflect the current state of knowledge of these fields. Today, the technology requires that professionals from all branches of computer science know both the software and hardware whose interaction at all levels is the key to understanding the basics of computational processing.

For this reason, in this book, a special focus is given on the relationship between hardware architectures and software.

Until recently, programmers could rely on the work of the hardware designers, compilers, and chip manufacturers to make their software programs faster or more efficient without the need for changes.

This era is over. So now, if a program is to run faster, it must become a parallel program.

Although the goal of many researchers is to ensure that programmers are not aware of the parallel nature of the hardware for which they write their programs, it will take many years before this actually becomes possible. Nowadays, most programmers need to thoroughly understand the link between hardware and software so that the programs can be run efficiently on modern computer architectures.

To introduce the concepts of parallel programming, the Python programming language has been adopted. Python is fun and easy to use, and its popularity has grown steadily in recent years. Python was developed more than 10 years ago by Guido van Rossum, who derived Python's syntax simplicity and ease of use largely from ABC, which is a teaching language that was developed in the 80s.

In addition to this specific context, Python was created to solve real-life problems, and it borrows a wide variety of typical characteristics of programming languages, such as C ++, Java, and Scheme. This is one of its most remarkable features, which has led to its broad appeal among professional software developers, the scientific research industry, and computer science educators. One of the reasons why Python is liked so much is because it provides the best balance between the practical and conceptual approaches. It is an interpreted language, so you can start doing things immediately without getting lost in the problems of compilation and linking. Python also provides an extensive software library that can be used in all sorts of tasks ranging from the Web, graphics, and of course, parallel computing. This practical aspect is a great way to engage readers and allow them to carry out projects that are important in this book.

This book contains a wide variety of examples that are inspired by many situations, and these offer you the opportunity to solve real-life problems. This book examines the principles of software design for parallel architectures, insisting on the importance of clarity of the programs and avoiding the use of complex terminology in favor of clear and direct examples. Each topic is presented as part of a complete, working Python program, which is followed by the output of the program in question.

The modular organization of the various chapters provides a proven path to move from the simplest arguments to the most advanced ones, but this is also suitable for those who only want to learn a few specific issues.

I hope that the settings and content of this book are able to provide you with a useful contribution for your better understanding and dissemination of parallel programming techniques.

What this book covers

Chapter 1, Getting Started with Parallel Computing and Python, gives you an overview of parallel programming architectures and programming models. This chapter introduces the Python programming language, the characteristics of the language, its ease of use and learning, extensibility, and richness of software libraries and applications. It also shows you how to make Python a valuable tool for any application, and also, of course, for parallel computing.

Chapter 2, Thread-based Parallelism, discusses thread parallelism using the threading Python module. Through complete programming examples, you will learn how to synchronize and manipulate threads to implement your multithreading applications.

Chapter 3, Process-based Parallelism, will guide through the process-based approach to parallelize a program. A complete set of examples will show you how to use the multiprocessing Python module. Also, this chapter will explain how to perform communication through processes, using the message passing parallel programming paradigm via the mpi4py Python module.

Chapter 4, Asynchronous Programming, explains the asynchronous model for concurrent programming. In some ways, it is simpler than the threaded one because there is a single instruction stream and tasks explicitly relinquish control instead of being suspended arbitrarily. This chapter will show you how to use the Python asyncio module to organize each task as a sequence of smaller steps that must be executed in an asynchronous manner.

Chapter 5, Distributed Python, introduces you to distributed computing. It is the process of aggregating several computing units logically and may even be geographically distributed to collaboratively run a single computational task in a transparent and coherent way. This chapter will present some of the solutions proposed by Python for the implementation of these architectures using the OO approach, Celery, SCOOP, and remote procedure calls, such as Pyro4 and RPyC. It will also include different approaches, such as PyCSP, and finally, Disco, which is the Python version of the MapReduce algorithm.

Chapter 6, GPU Programming with Python, describes the modern Graphics Processing Units (GPUs) that provide breakthrough performance for numerical computing at the cost of increased programming complexity. In fact, the programming models for GPUs require the programmer to manually manage the data transfer between a CPU and GPU. This chapter will teach you, through the programming examples and use cases, how to exploit the computing power provided by the GPU cards, using the powerful Python modules: PyCUDA, NumbaPro, and PyOpenICL.

What you need for this book

All the examples of this book can be tested in a Windows 7 32-bit machine. Also, a Linux environment will be useful.

The Python versions needed to run the examples are:

- Python 3.3 (for the first five chapters)
- Python 2.7 (only for *Chapter 6, GPU Programming with Python*)

The following modules (all of which are freely downloadable) are required:

- mpich-3.1.4
- pip 6.1.1
- mpi4py1.3.1
- asyncio 3.4.3
- Celery 3.1.18
- Numpy 1.9.2
- Flower 0.8.32 (optional)
- SCOOP 0.7.2

- ▸ Pyro 4.4.36
- ▸ PyCSP 0.9.0
- ▸ DISCO 0.5.2
- ▸ RPyC 3.3.0
- ▸ PyCUDA 2015.1.2
- ▸ CUDA Toolkit 4.2.9 (at least)
- ▸ NVIDIA GPU SDK 4.2.9 (at least)
- ▸ NVIDIA GPU driver
- ▸ Microsoft Visual Studio 2008 C++ Express Edition (at least)
- ▸ Anaconda Python Distribution
- ▸ NumbaPro compiler
- ▸ PyOpenCL 2015.1
- ▸ Win32 OpenCL Driver 15.1 (at least)

Who this book is for

This book is intended for software developers who want to use parallel programming techniques to write powerful and efficient code. After reading this book, you will be able to master the basics and the advanced features of parallel computing. The Python programming language is easy to use and allows nonexperts to deal with and easily understand the topics exposed in this book.

Sections

This book contains the following sections:

Getting ready

This section tells us what to expect in the recipe and describes how to set up any software or any preliminary settings needed for the recipe.

How to do it...

This section characterizes the steps that are to be followed to "cook" the recipe.

How it works...

This section usually consists a brief and detailed explanation of what happened in the previous section.

There's more...

This section consists of additional information about the recipe in order to make the reader more anxious about the recipe.

See also

This section may contain references to the recipe.

Conventions

In this book, you will find a number of styles of text that distinguish between different kinds of information. Here are some examples of these styles, and an explanation of their meaning.

Code words in text, database table names, folder names, filenames, file extensions, pathnames, dummy URLs, user input, and Twitter handles are shown as follows: "To execute this first example, we need the program `helloPythonWithThreads.py`."

A block of code is set as follows:

```
print ("Hello Python Parallel Cookbook!!")
closeInput = raw_input("Press ENTER to exit")
print "Closing calledProcess"
```

When we wish to draw your attention to a particular part of a code block, the relevant lines or items are set in bold:

```
@asyncio.coroutine
def factorial(number):
do Something

@asyncio.coroutine
```

Any command-line input or output is written as follows:

```
C:\>mpiexec -n 4 python virtualTopology.py
```

New terms and important words are shown in bold. Words that you see on the screen, in menus or dialog boxes for example, appear in the text like this: "Open an admin Command Prompt by right-clicking on the command prompt icon and select Run as administrator."

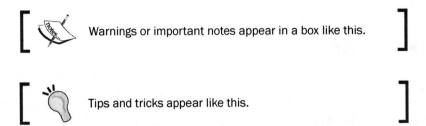

Warnings or important notes appear in a box like this.

Tips and tricks appear like this.

Reader feedback

Feedback from our readers is always welcome. Let us know what you think about this book—what you liked or may have disliked. Reader feedback is important for us to develop titles that you really get the most out of.

To send us general feedback, simply send an e-mail to feedback@packtpub.com, and mention the book title via the subject of your message.

If there is a topic that you have expertise in and you are interested in either writing or contributing to a book, see our author guide on www.packtpub.com/authors.

Customer support

Now that you are the proud owner of a Packt book, we have a number of things to help you to get the most from your purchase.

Downloading the example code

You can download the example code files for all Packt books you have purchased from your account at http://www.packtpub.com. If you purchased this book elsewhere, you can visit http://www.packtpub.com/support and register to have the files e-mailed directly to you.

Errata

Although we have taken every care to ensure the accuracy of our content, mistakes do happen. If you find a mistake in one of our books—maybe a mistake in the text or the code—we would be grateful if you would report this to us. By doing so, you can save other readers from frustration and help us improve subsequent versions of this book. If you find any errata, please report them by visiting http://www.packtpub.com/submit-errata, selecting your book, clicking on the errata submission form link, and entering the details of your errata. Once your errata are verified, your submission will be accepted and the errata will be uploaded on our website, or added to any list of existing errata, under the Errata section of that title. Any existing errata can be viewed by selecting your title from http://www.packtpub.com/support.

Piracy

Piracy of copyright material on the Internet is an ongoing problem across all media. At Packt, we take the protection of our copyright and licenses very seriously. If you come across any illegal copies of our works, in any form, on the Internet, please provide us with the location address or website name immediately so that we can pursue a remedy.

Please contact us at copyright@packtpub.com with a link to the suspected pirated material.

We appreciate your help in protecting our authors, and our ability to bring you valuable content.

Questions

You can contact us at questions@packtpub.com if you are having a problem with any aspect of the book, and we will do our best to address it.

1
Getting Started with Parallel Computing and Python

In this chapter, we will cover the following recipes:

- ▶ What is parallel computing?
- ▶ The parallel computing memory architecture
- ▶ Memory organization
- ▶ Parallel programming models
- ▶ How to design a parallel program
- ▶ How to evaluate the performance of a parallel program
- ▶ Introducing Python
- ▶ Python in a parallel world
- ▶ Introducing processes and threads
- ▶ Start working with processes and Python
- ▶ Start working with threads and Python

Introduction

This chapter gives you an overview of parallel programming architectures and programming models. These concepts are useful for inexperienced programmers who have approached parallel programming techniques for the first time. This chapter can be a basic reference for the experienced programmers. The dual characterization of parallel systems is also presented in this chapter. The first characterization is based on the architecture of the system and the second characterization is based on parallel programming paradigms. Parallel programming will always be a challenge for programmers. This programming-based approach is further described in this chapter, when we present the design procedure of a parallel program. The chapter ends with a brief introduction of the Python programming language. The characteristics of the language, ease of use and learning, and extensibility and richness of software libraries and applications make Python a valuable tool for any application and also, of course, for parallel computing. In the final part of the chapter, the concepts of threads and processes are introduced in relation to their use in the language. A typical way to solve a problem of a large-size is to divide it into smaller and independent parts in order to solve all the pieces simultaneously. A parallel program is intended for a program that uses this approach, that is, the use of multiple processors working together on a common task. Each processor works on its section (the independent part) of the problem. Furthermore, a data information exchange between processors could take place during the computation. Nowadays, many software applications require more computing power. One way to achieve this is to increase the clock speed of the processor or to increase the number of processing cores on the chip. Improving the clock speed increases the heat dissipation, thereby decreasing the performance per watt and moreover, this requires special equipment for cooling. Increasing the number of cores seems to be a feasible solution, as power consumption and dissipation are way under the limit and there is no significant gain in performance.

To address this problem, computer hardware vendors decided to adopt multi-core architectures, which are single chips that contain two or more processors (cores). On the other hand, the GPU manufactures also introduced hardware architectures based on multiple computing cores. In fact, today's computers are almost always present in multiple and heterogeneous computing units, each formed by a variable number of cores, for example, the most common multi-core architectures.

Therefore, it became essential for us to take advantage of the computational resources available, to adopt programming paradigms, techniques, and instruments of parallel computing.

The parallel computing memory architecture

Based on the number of instructions and data that can be processed simultaneously, computer systems are classified into four categories:

- ▸ **Single instruction, single data (SISD)**
- ▸ **Single instruction, multiple data (SIMD)**
- ▸ **Multiple instruction, single data (MISD)**
- ▸ **Multiple instruction, multiple data (MIMD)**

This classification is known as Flynn's taxonomy.

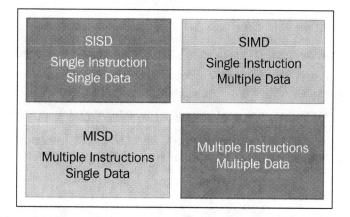

SISD

The SISD computing system is a uniprocessor machine. It executes a single instruction that operates on a single data stream. In SISD, machine instructions are processed sequentially.

In a clock cycle, the CPU executes the following operations:

- ▸ **Fetch**: The CPU fetches the data and instructions from a memory area, which is called a register.
- ▸ **Decode**: The CPU decodes the instructions.
- ▸ **Execute**: The instruction is carried out on the data. The result of the operation is stored in another register.

Once the execution stage is complete, the CPU sets itself to begin another CPU cycle.

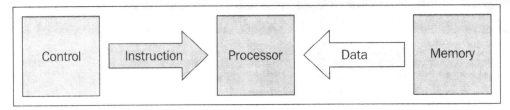

The SISD architecture schema

The algorithms that run on these types of computers are sequential (or serial), since they do not contain any parallelism. Examples of SISD computers are hardware systems with a single CPU.

The main elements of these architectures (Von Neumann architectures) are:

- **Central memory unit**: This is used to store both instructions and program data
- **CPU**: This is used to get the instruction and/or data from the memory unit, which decodes the instructions and sequentially implements them
- **The I/O system**: This refers to the input data and output data of the program

The conventional single processor computers are classified as SISD systems. The following figure specifically shows which areas of a CPU are used in the stages of fetch, decode, and execute:

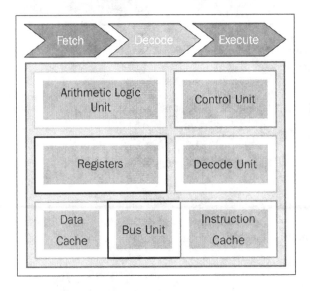

CPU's components in the fetch-decode-execute phase

MISD

In this model, *n* processors, each with their own control unit, share a single memory unit. In each clock cycle, the data received from the memory is processed by all processors simultaneously, each in accordance with the instructions received from its control unit. In this case, the parallelism (instruction-level parallelism) is obtained by performing several operations on the same piece of data. The types of problems that can be solved efficiently in these architectures are rather special, such as those regarding data encryption; for this reason, the computer MISD did not find space in the commercial sector. MISD computers are more of an intellectual exercise than a practical configuration.

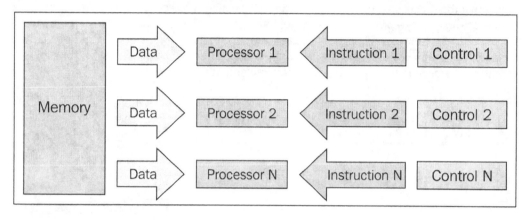

The MISD architecture scheme

SIMD

A SIMD computer consists of *n* identical processors, each with its own local memory, where it is possible to store data. All processors work under the control of a single instruction stream; in addition to this, there are *n* data streams, one for each processor. The processors work simultaneously on each step and execute the same instruction, but on different data elements. This is an example of data-level parallelism. The SIMD architectures are much more versatile than MISD architectures. Numerous problems covering a wide range of applications can be solved by parallel algorithms on SIMD computers. Another interesting feature is that the algorithms for these computers are relatively easy to design, analyze, and implement. The limit is that only the problems that can be divided into a number of subproblems (which are all identical, each of which will then be solved contemporaneously, through the same set of instructions) can be addressed with the SIMD computer. With the supercomputer developed according to this paradigm, we must mention the Connection Machine (1985 Thinking Machine) and MPP (NASA - 1983). As we will see in *Chapter 6, GPU Programming with Python*, the advent of modern **graphics processor unit** (**GPU**), built with many SIMD embedded units has lead to a more widespread use of this computational paradigm.

MIMD

This class of parallel computers is the most general and more powerful class according to Flynn's classification. There are *n* processors, *n* instruction streams, and *n* data streams in this. Each processor has its own control unit and local memory, which makes MIMD architectures more computationally powerful than those used in SIMD. Each processor operates under the control of a flow of instructions issued by its own control unit; therefore, the processors can potentially run different programs on different data, solving subproblems that are different and can be a part of a single larger problem. In MIMD, architecture is achieved with the help of the parallelism level with threads and/or processes. This also means that the processors usually operate asynchronously. The computers in this class are used to solve those problems that do not have a regular structure that is required by the model SIMD. Nowadays, this architecture is applied to many PCs, supercomputers, and computer networks. However, there is a counter that you need to consider: asynchronous algorithms are difficult to design, analyze, and implement.

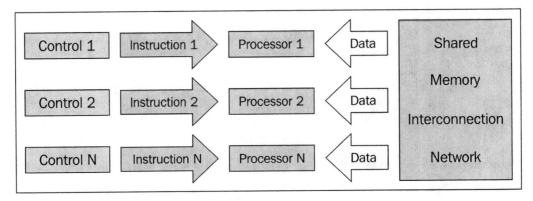

The MIMD architecture scheme

Memory organization

Another aspect that we need to consider to evaluate a parallel architecture is memory organization or rather, the way in which the data is accessed. No matter how fast the processing unit is, if the memory cannot maintain and provide instructions and data at a sufficient speed, there will be no improvement in performance. The main problem that must be overcome to make the response time of the memory compatible with the speed of the processor is the memory cycle time, which is defined as the time that has elapsed between two successive operations. The cycle time of the processor is typically much shorter than the cycle time of the memory. When the processor starts transferring data (to or from the memory), the memory will remain occupied for the entire time of the memory cycle: during this period, no other device (I/O controller, processor, or even the processor itself that made the request) can use the memory because it will be committed to respond to the request.

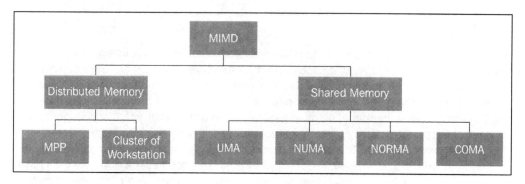

The memory organization in MIMD architecture

Solutions to the problem of access memory resulted in a dichotomy of MIMD architectures. In the first type of system, known as the shared memory system, there is high virtual memory and all processors have equal access to data and instructions in this memory. The other type of system is the distributed memory model, wherein each processor has a local memory that is not accessible to other processors. The difference between shared memory and distributed memory lies in the structure of the virtual memory or the memory from the perspective of the processor. Physically, almost every system memory is divided into distinct components that are independently accessible. What distinguishes a shared memory from a distributed memory is the memory access management by the processing unit. If a processor were to execute the instruction load R0, i, which means load in the R0 register the contents of the memory location i, the question now is what should happen? In a system with shared memory, the i index is a global address and the memory location i is the same for each processor. If two processors were to perform this instruction at the same time, they would load the same information in their registers R0. In a distributed memory system, i is a local address. If two processors were to load the statement R0 at the same time, different values may end up in the respective register's R0, since, in this case, the memory cells are allotted one for each local memory. The distinction between shared memory and distributed memory is very important for programmers because it determines the way in which different parts of a parallel program must communicate. In a system, shared memory is sufficient to build a data structure in memory and go to the parallel subroutine, which are the reference variables of this data structure. Moreover, a distributed memory machine must make copies of shared data in each local memory. These copies are created by sending a message containing the data to be shared from one processor to another. A drawback of this memory organization is that sometimes, these messages can be very large and take a relatively long transfer time.

Shared memory

The schema of a shared memory multiprocessor system is shown in the following figure. The physical connections here are quite simple. The bus structure allows an arbitrary number of devices that share the same channel. The bus protocols were originally designed to allow a single processor, and one or more disks or tape controllers to communicate through the shared memory here. Note that each processor has been associated with a cache memory, as it is assumed that the probability that a processor needs data or instructions present in the local memory is very high. The problem occurs when a processor modifies data stored in the memory system that is simultaneously used by other processors. The new value will pass from the processor cache that has been changed to shared memory; later, however, it must also be passed to all the other processors, so that they do not work with the obsolete value. This problem is known as the problem of cache coherency, a special case of the problem of memory consistency, which requires hardware implementations that can handle concurrency issues and synchronization similar to those having thread programming.

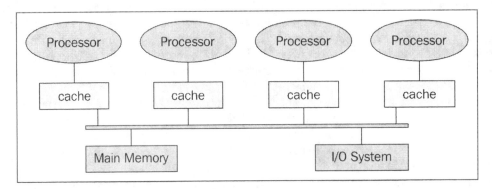

The shared memory architecture schema

The main features of shared memory systems are:

▶ The memory is the same for all processors, for example, all the processors associated with the same data structure will work with the same logical memory addresses, thus accessing the same memory locations.

▶ The synchronization is made possible by controlling the access of processors to the shared memory. In fact, only one processor at a time can have access to the memory resources.

- A shared memory location must not be changed from a task while another task accesses it.

- Sharing data is fast; the time required for the communication between two tasks is equal to the time for reading a single memory location (it is depending on the speed of memory access).

The memory access in shared memory systems are as follows:

- **Uniform memory access (UMA)**: The fundamental characteristic of this system is the access time to the memory that is constant for each processor and for any area of memory. For this reason, these systems are also called as **symmetric multiprocessor (SMP)**. They are relatively simple to implement, but not very scalable; the programmer is responsible for the management of the synchronization by inserting appropriate controls, semaphores, locks, and so on in the program that manages resources.

- **Non-uniform memory access (NUMA)**: These architectures divide the memory area into a high-speed access area that is assigned to each processor and a common area for the data exchange, with slower access. These systems are also called as **Distributed Shared Memory Systems (DSM)**. They are very scalable, but complex to develop.

- **No remote memory access (NORMA)**: The memory is physically distributed among the processors (local memory). All local memories are private and can only access the local processor. The communication between the processors is through a communication protocol used for exchange of messages, the message-passing protocol.

- **Cache only memory access (COMA)**: These systems are equipped with only cache memories. While analyzing NUMA architectures, it was noticed that these architectures kept the local copies of the data in the cache and that these data were stored as duplication in the main memory. This architecture removes duplicates and keeps only the cache memories, the memory is physically distributed among the processors (local memory). All local memories are private and can only access the local processor. The communication between the processors is through a communication protocol for exchange of messages, the message-passing protocol.

Distributed memory

In a system with distributed memory, the memory is associated with each processor and a processor is only able to address its own memory. Some authors refer to this type of system as "multicomputer", reflecting the fact that the elements of the system are themselves small complete systems of a processor and memory, as you can see in the following figure:

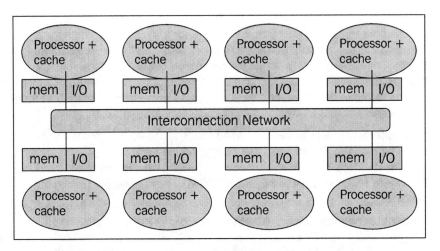

The distributed memory architecture scheme

This kind of organization has several advantages. At first, there are no conflicts at the level of the communication bus or switch. Each processor can use the full bandwidth of their own local memory without any interference from other processors. Secondly, the lack of a common bus means that there is no intrinsic limit to the number of processors, the size of the system is only limited by the network used to connect the processors. Thirdly, there are no problems of cache coherency. Each processor is responsible for its own data and does not have to worry about upgrading any copies. The main disadvantage is that the communication between processors is more difficult to implement. If a processor requires data in the memory of another processor, the two processors should necessarily exchange messages via the message-passing protocol. This introduces two sources of slowdown; to build and send a message from one processor to another takes time, and also, any processor should be stopped in order to manage the messages received from other processors. A program designed to work on a distributed memory machine must be organized as a set of independent tasks that communicate via messages.

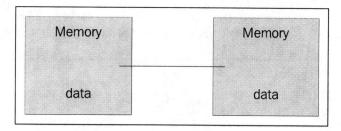

Basic message passing

The main features of distributed memory systems are as follows:

- Memory is physically distributed between processors; each local memory is directly accessible only by its processor.

- Synchronization is achieved by moving data (even if it's just the message itself) between processors (communication).

- The subdivision of data in the local memories affects the performance of the machine—it is essential to make a subdivision accurate, so as to minimize the communication between the CPUs. In addition to this, the processor that coordinates these operations of decomposition and composition must effectively communicate with the processors that operate on the individual parts of data structures.

- The message-passing protocol is used so that the CPU's can communicate with each other through the exchange of data packets. The messages are discrete units of information; in the sense that they have a well-defined identity, so it is always possible to distinguish them from each other.

Massively parallel processing

MPP machines are composed of hundreds of processors (which can be as large as hundreds of thousands in some machines) that are connected by a communication network. The fastest computers in the world are based on these architectures; some example systems of these architectures are: Earth Simulator, Blue Gene, ASCI White, ASCI Red, and ASCI Purple and Red Storm.

A cluster of workstations

These processing systems are based on classical computers that are connected by communication networks. The computational clusters fall into this classification.

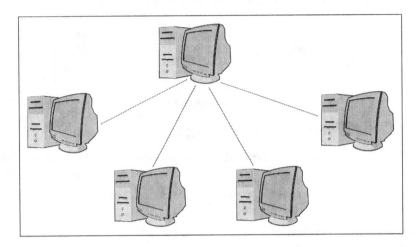

An example of a cluster of workstation architecture

In a cluster architecture, we define a node as a single computing unit that takes part in the cluster. For the user, the cluster is fully transparent—all the hardware and software complexity is masked and data and applications are made accessible as if they were all from a single node.

Here, we've identified three types of clusters:

- **The fail-over cluster**: In this, the node's activity is continuously monitored, and when one stops working, another machine takes over the charge of those activities. The aim is to ensure a continuous service due to the redundancy of the architecture.

- **The load balancing cluster**: In this system, a job request is sent to the node that has less activity. This ensures that less time is taken to complete the process.

- **The high-performance computing cluster**: In this, each node is configured to provide extremely high performance. The process is also divided in multiple jobs on multiple nodes. The jobs are parallelized and will be distributed to different machines.

The heterogeneous architecture

The introduction of GPU accelerators in the homogeneous world of supercomputing has changed the nature of how supercomputers were both used and programmed previously. Despite the high performance offered by GPUs, they cannot be considered as an autonomous processing unit as they should always be accompanied by a combination of CPUs. The programming paradigm, therefore, is very simple; the CPU takes control and computes in a serial manner, assigning to the graphic accelerator the tasks that are computationally very expensive and have a high degree of parallelism. The communication between a CPU and GPU can take place not only through the use of a high-speed bus, but also through the sharing of a single area of memory for both physical or virtual. In fact, in the case where both the devices are not equipped with their own memory areas, it is possible to refer to a common memory area using the software libraries provided by the various programming models, such as CUDA and OpenCL. These architectures are called heterogeneous architectures, wherein applications can create data structures in a single address space and send a job to the device hardware appropriate for the resolution of the task. Several processing tasks can operate safely on the same regions to avoid data consistency problems, thanks to the atomic operations. So, despite the fact that the CPU and GPU do not seem to work efficiently together, with the use of this new architecture, we can optimize their interaction with and performance of parallel applications.

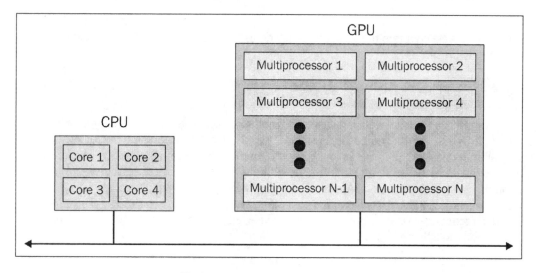

The heterogeneous architecture scheme

Parallel programming models

Parallel programming models exist as an abstraction of hardware and memory architectures. In fact, these models are not specific and do not refer to particular types of machines or memory architectures. They can be implemented (at least theoretically) on any kind of machines. Compared to the previous subdivisions, these programming models are made at a higher level and represent the way in which the software must be implemented to perform a parallel computation. Each model has its own way of sharing information with other processors in order to access memory and divide the work.

There is no better programming model in absolute terms; the best one to apply will depend very much on the problem that a programmer should address and resolve. The most widely used models for parallel programming are:

- ▸ The shared memory model
- ▸ The multithread model
- ▸ The distributed memory/message passing model
- ▸ The data parallel model

In this recipe, we will give you an overview of these models. A more accurate description will be in the next chapters that will introduce you to the appropriate Python module that implements these.

The shared memory model

In this model the tasks share a single shared memory area, where the access (reading and writing data) to shared resources is asynchronous. There are mechanisms that allow the programmer to control the access to the shared memory, for example, locks or semaphores. This model offers the advantage that the programmer does not have to clarify the communication between tasks. An important disadvantage in terms of performance is that it becomes more difficult to understand and manage data locality; keeping data local to the processor that works on it conserves memory accesses, cache refreshes, and bus traffic that occur when multiple processors use the same data.

The multithread model

In this model, a process can have multiple flows of execution, for example, a sequential part is created and subsequently, a series of tasks are created that can be executed parallelly. Usually, this type of model is used on shared memory architectures. So, it will be very important for us to manage the synchronization between threads, as they operate on shared memory, and the programmer must prevent multiple threads from updating the same locations at the same time. The current generation CPUs are multithreaded in software and hardware. Posix threads are the classic example of the implementation of multithreading on software. The Intel Hyper-threading technology implements multithreading on hardware by switching between two threads when one is stalled or waiting on I/O. Parallelism can be achieved from this model even if the data alignment is nonlinear.

The message passing model

The message passing model is usually applied in the case where each processor has its own memory (distributed memory systems). More tasks can reside on the same physical machine or on an arbitrary number of machines. The programmer is responsible for determining the parallelism and data exchange that occurs through the messages. The implementation of this parallel programming model requires the use of (ad hoc) software libraries to be used within the code. Numerous implementations of message passing model were created: some of the examples are available since the 1980s, but only from the mid-90s, was created to standardized model, coming to a de facto standard called MPI (the message passing interface). The MPI model is designed clearly with distributed memory, but being models of parallel programming, multiplatform can also be used with a shared memory machine.

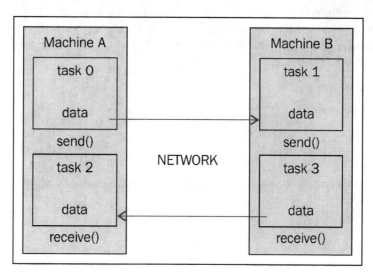

The message passing paradigm model

The data parallel model

In this model, we have more tasks that operate on the same data structure, but each task operates on a different portion of data. In the shared memory architecture, all tasks have access to data through shared memory and distributed memory architectures, where the data structure is divided and resides in the local memory of each task. To implement this model, a programmer must develop a program that specifies the distribution and alignment of data. The current generation GPUs operates high throughout with the data aligned.

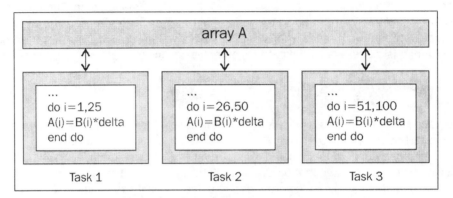

The data parallel paradigm model

How to design a parallel program

The design of algorithms that exploit parallelism is based on a series of operations, which must necessarily be carried out for the program to perform the job correctly without producing partial or erroneous results. The macro operations that must be carried out for a correct parallelization of an algorithm are:

- Task decomposition
- Task assignment
- Agglomeration
- Mapping

Task decomposition

In this first phase, the software program is split into tasks or a set of instructions that can then be executed on different processors to implement parallelism. To do this subdivision, there are two methods that are used:

- **Domain decomposition**: Here, the data of the problems is decomposed; the application is common to all the processors that work on a different portion of data. This methodology is used when we have a large amount of data that must be processed.
- **Functional decomposition**: In this case, the problem is split into tasks, where each task will perform a particular operation on all the available data.

Task assignment

In this step, the mechanism by which the task will be distributed among the various processes is specified. This phase is very important because it establishes the distribution of workload among the various processors. The load balance is crucial here; in fact, all processors must work with continuity, avoiding an idle state for a long time. To perform this, the programmer takes into account the possible heterogeneity of the system that tries to assign more tasks to better performing processors. Finally, for greater efficiency of parallelization, it is necessary to limit communication as much as possible between processors, as they are often the source of slowdowns and consumption of resources.

Agglomeration

Agglomeration is the process of combining smaller tasks with larger ones in order to improve performance. If the previous two stages of the design process partitioned the problem into a number of tasks that greatly exceed the number of processors available, and if the computer is not specifically designed to handle a huge number of small tasks (some architectures, such as GPUs, handle this fine and indeed benefit from running millions or even billions of tasks), then the design can turn out to be highly inefficient. Commonly, this is because tasks have to be communicated to the processor or thread so that they compute the said task. Most communication has costs that are not only proportional with the amount of data transferred, but also incur a fixed cost for every communication operation (such as the latency which is inherent in setting up a TCP connection). If the tasks are too small, this fixed cost can easily make the design inefficient.

Mapping

In the mapping stage of the parallel algorithm design process, we specify where each task is to be executed. The goal is to minimize the total execution time. Here, you must often make tradeoffs, as the two main strategies often conflict with each other:

▶ The tasks that communicate frequently should be placed in the same processor to increase locality

▶ The tasks that can be executed concurrently should be placed in different processors to enhance concurrency

This is known as the mapping problem, and it is known to be NP-complete. As such, no polynomial time solutions to the problem in the general case exist. For tasks of equal size and tasks with easily identified communication patterns, the mapping is straightforward (we can also perform agglomeration here to combine tasks that map to the same processor.) However, if the tasks have communication patterns that are hard to predict or the amount of work varies per task, it is hard to design an efficient mapping and agglomeration scheme. For these types of problems, load balancing algorithms can be used to identify agglomeration and mapping strategies during runtime. The hardest problems are those in which the amount of communication or the number of tasks changes during the execution of the program. For these kind of problems, dynamic load balancing algorithms can be used, which run periodically during the execution.

Dynamic mapping

There exists many load balancing algorithms for various problems, both global and local. Global algorithms require global knowledge of the computation being performed, which often adds a lot of overhead. Local algorithms rely only on information that is local to the task in question, which reduces overhead compared to global algorithms, but are usually worse at finding an optimal agglomeration and mapping. However, the reduced overhead may reduce the execution time even though the mapping is worse by itself. If the tasks rarely communicate other than at the start and end of the execution, a task-scheduling algorithm is often used that simply maps tasks to processors as they become idle. In a task-scheduling algorithm, a task pool is maintained. Tasks are placed in this pool and are taken from it by workers.

There are three common approaches in this model, which are explained next.

Manager/worker

This is the basic dynamic mapping scheme in which all the workers connect to a the centralized manager. The manager repeatedly sends tasks to the workers and collects the results. This strategy is probably the best for a relatively small number of processors. The basic strategy can be improved by fetching tasks in advance so that communication and computation overlap each other.

Hierarchical manager/worker

This is the variant of a manager/worker that has a semi-distributed layout; workers are split into groups, each with their own manager. These group managers communicate with the central manager (and possibly, among themselves as well), while workers request tasks from the group managers. This spreads the load among several managers and can, as such, handle a larger amount of processors if all workers request tasks from the same manager.

Decentralize

In this scheme, everything is decentralized. Each processor maintains its own task pool and communicates with the other processors in order to request tasks. How the processors choose other processors to request tasks varies and is determined on the basis of the problem.

How to evaluate the performance of a parallel program

The development of parallel programming created the need of performance metrics and a software tool to evaluate the performance of a parallel algorithm in order to decide whether its use is convenient or not. Indeed, the focus of parallel computing is to solve large problems in a relatively short time. The factors that contribute to the achievement of this objective are, for example, the type of hardware used, the degree of parallelism of the problem, and which parallel programming model is adopted. To facilitate this, analysis of basic concepts was introduced, which compares the parallel algorithm obtained from the original sequence. The performance is achieved by analyzing and quantifying the number of threads and/or the number of processes used.

To analyze this, a few performance indexes are introduced: speedup, efficiency, and scaling.

The limitations of a parallel computation are introduced by the Ahmdal's law to evaluate the degree of the efficiency of parallelization of a sequential algorithm we have the Gustafson's law.

Speedup

Speedup is the measure that displays the benefit of solving a problem in parallel. It is defined as the ratio of the time taken to solve a problem on a single processing element, TS, to the time required to solve the same problem on p identical processing elements, Tp.

$$S = \frac{T_S}{T_P}$$

We denote speedup by $S = \frac{T_S}{T_P}$. We have a linear speedup, where if $S=p$, it means that the speed of execution increases with the number of processors. Of course, this is an ideal case. While the speedup is absolute when T_S is the execution time of the best sequential algorithm, the speedup is relative when T_S is the execution time of the parallel algorithm for a single processor.

Let's recap these conditions:

- $S = p$ is linear or ideal speedup
- $S < p$ is real speedup
- $S > p$ is superlinear speedup

Efficiency

In an ideal world, a parallel system with p processing elements can give us a speedup equal to p. However, this is very rarely achieved. Usually, some time is wasted in either idling or communicating. Efficiency is a performance metric estimating how well-utilized the processors are in solving a task, compared to how much effort is wasted in communication and synchronization.

We denote it by E and can define it as $E = \dfrac{S}{p} = \dfrac{T_S}{pT_P}$. The algorithms with linear speedup have the value of $E = 1$; in other cases, the value of E is less than 1. The three cases are identified as follows:

- When $E = 1$, it is a linear case
- When $E < 1$, it is a real case
- When $E << 1$, it is a problem that is parallelizable with low efficiency

Scaling

Scaling is defined as the ability to be efficient on a parallel machine. It identifies the computing power (speed of execution) in proportion with the number of processors. By increasing the size of the problem and at the same time the number of processors, there will be no loss in terms of performance. The scalable system, depending on the increments of the different factors, may maintain the same efficiency or improve it.

Amdahl's law

Amdahl's law is a widely used law used to design processors and parallel algorithms. It states that the maximum speedup that can be achieved is limited by the serial component of the program: $S = \dfrac{1}{1-P}$, where $1 - P$ denotes the serial component (not parallelized) of a program. This means that for, as an example, a program in which 90 percent of the code can be made parallel, but 10 percent must remain serial, the maximum achievable speedup is 9 even for an infinite number of processors.

Gustafson's law

Gustafson's law is based on the following considerations:

- ▸ While increasing the dimension of a problem, its sequential parts remain constant
- ▸ While increasing the number of processors, the work required on each of them still remains the same

This states that $S(P) = P - \alpha\,(P - 1)$, where P is the number of processors, S is the speedup, and α is the non-parallelizable fraction of any parallel process. This is in contrast to Amdahl's law, which takes the single-process execution time to be the fixed quantity and compares it to a shrinking per process parallel execution time. Thus, Amdahl's law is based on the assumption of a fixed problem size; it assumes that the overall workload of a program does not change with respect to the machine size (that is, the number of processors). Gustafson's law addresses the deficiency of Amdahl's law, which does not take into account the total number of computing resources involved in solving a task. It suggests that the best way to set the time allowed for the solution of a parallel problem is to consider all the computing resources and on the basis of this information, it fixes the problem.

Introducing Python

Python is a powerful, dynamic, and interpreted programming language that is used in a wide variety of applications. Some of its features include:

- ▸ A clear and readable syntax
- ▸ A very extensive standard library, where through additional software modules, we can add data types, functions, and objects
- ▸ Easy-to-learn rapid development and debugging; the development of Python code in Python can be up to 10 times faster than the C/C++ code
- ▸ Exception-based error handling
- ▸ A strong introspection functionality
- ▸ Richness of documentation and software community

Python can be seen as a glue language. Using Python, better applications can be developed because different kinds of programmers can work together on a project. For example, when building a scientific application, C/C++ programmers can implement efficient numerical algorithms, while scientists on the same project can write Python programs that test and use those algorithms. Scientists don't have to learn a low-level programming language and a C/C++ programmer doesn't need to understand the science involved.

You can read more about this from `https://www.python.org/doc/essays/omg-darpa-mcc-position`.

Getting ready

Python can be downloaded from `https://www.python.org/downloads/`.

Although you can create Python programs with Notepad or TextEdit, you'll notice that it's much easier to read and write code using an **Integrated Development Environment** (**IDE**).

There are many IDEs that are designated specifically for Python, including IDLE (`http://www.python.org/idle`), PyCharm (`https://www.jetbrains.com/pycharm/`), and Sublime Text, (`http://www.sublimetext.com/`).

How to do it...

Let's take a look at some examples of the very basic code to get an idea of the features of Python. Remember that the symbol `>>>` denotes the Python shell:

- Operations with integers:

  ```
  >>> # This is a comment
  >>> width = 20
  >>> height = 5*9
  >>> width * height
  900
  ```

  Only for this first example, we will see how the code appears in the Python shell:

```
Python Shell

File  Edit  Shell  Debug  Options  Windows  Help

Python 3.3.0 (v3.3.0:bd8afb90ebf2, Sep 29 2012, 10:55:48) [MSC v.1600 32 bit (Intel)]
 on win32
Type "copyright", "credits" or "license()" for more information.
>>> #This is a comment
>>> width = 20
>>> height = 5*9
>>> width * height
900
>>>
                                                              Ln: 8 Col: 4
```

Let's see the other basic examples:

- Complex numbers:
```
>>> a=1.5+0.5j
>>> a.real
1.5
>>> a.imag
0.5
>>> abs(a)   # sqrt(a.real**2 + a.imag**2)
5.0
```

- Strings manipulation:
```
>>> word = 'Help' + 'A'
>>> word
'HelpA'
>>> word[4]
'A'
>>> word[0:2]
'He'
>>> word[-1]      # The last character
'A'
```

- Defining lists:
```
>>> a = ['spam', 'eggs', 100, 1234]
>>> a[0]
'spam'
>>> a[3]
1234
>>> a[-2]
100
>>> a[1:-1]
['eggs', 100]
>>> len(a)
4
```

- ▸ The `while` loop:

```
# Fibonacci series:
>>> while b < 10:
...         print b
...         a, b = b, a+b
...
1
1
2
3
5
8
```

- ▸ The `if` command:

  First we use the `input()` statement to insert an integer:

```
>>>x = int(input("Please enter an integer here: "))
Please enter an integer here:
```

  Then we implement the `if` condition on the number inserted:

```
>>>if x < 0:
...         print ('the number is negative')
...elif x == 0:
...         print ('the number is zero')
...elif x == 1:
...         print ('the number is one')
...else:
...         print ('More')
...
```

- ▸ The `for` loop:

```
>>> # Measure some strings:
... a = ['cat', 'window', 'defenestrate']
>>> for x in a:
...         print (x, len(x))
...
cat 3
window 6
defenestrate 12
```

- Defining functions:

```
>>> def fib(n):     # write Fibonacci series up to n
...     """Print a Fibonacci series up to n."""
...     a, b = 0, 1
...     while b < n:
...         print (b),
...         a, b = b, a+b
...
>>> # Now call the function we just defined:
... fib(2000)
1 1 2 3 5 8 13 21 34 55 89 144 233 377 610 987 1597
```

- Importing modules:

```
>>> import math
>>> math.sin(1)
0.8414709848078965

>>> from math import *
>>> log(1)
0.0
```

- Defining classes:

```
>>> class Complex:
...     def __init__(self, realpart, imagpart):
...         self.r = realpart
...         self.i = imagpart
...
>>> x = Complex(3.0, -4.5)
>>> x.r, x.i
(3.0, -4.5)
```

Python in a parallel world

To be an interpreted language, Python is fast, and if speed is critical, it easily interfaces with extensions written in faster languages, such as C or C++. A common way of using Python is to use it for the high-level logic of a program; the Python interpreter is written in C and is known as CPython. The interpreter translates the Python code in an intermediate language called Python bytecode, which is analogous to an assembly language, but contains a high level of instruction. While a Python program runs, the so-called evaluation loop translates Python bytecode into machine-specific operations. The use of interpreter has advantages in code programming and debugging, but the speed of a program could be a problem. A first solution is provided by third-party packages, where a programmer writes a C module and then imports it from Python. Another solution is the use of a Just-in-Time Python compiler, which is an alternative to CPython, for example, the PyPy implementation optimizes code generation and the speed of a Python program. In this book, we will examine a third approach to the problem; in fact, Python provides ad hoc modules that could benefit from parallelism. The description of many of these modules, in which the parallel programming paradigm falls, will be discussed in subsequent chapters.

However, in this chapter, we will introduce the two fundamental concepts of threads and processes and how they are addressed in the Python programming language.

Introducing processes and threads

A process is an executing instance of an application, for example, double-clicking on the Internet browser icon on the desktop will start a process than runs the browser. A thread is an active flow of control that can be activated in parallel with other threads within the same process. The term "flow control" means a sequential execution of machine instructions. Also, a process can contain multiple threads, so starting the browser, the operating system creates a process and begins executing the primary threads of that process. Each thread can execute a set of instructions (typically, a function) independently and in parallel with other processes or threads. However, being the different active threads within the same process, they share space addressing and then the data structures. A thread is sometimes called a lightweight process because it shares many characteristics of a process, in particular, the characteristics of being a sequential flow of control that is executed in parallel with other control flows that are sequential. The term "light" is intended to indicate that the implementation of a thread is less onerous than that of a real process. However, unlike the processes, multiple threads may share many resources, in particular, space addressing and then the data structures.

Let's recap:

- ▸ A process can consist of multiple parallel threads.

- ▸ Normally, the creation and management of a thread by the operating system is less expensive in terms of CPU's resources than the creation and management of a process. Threads are used for small tasks, whereas processes are used for more heavyweight tasks—basically, the execution of applications.

- ▸ The threads of the same process share the address space and other resources, while processes are independent of each other.

Before examining in detail the features and functionality of Python modules for the management of parallelism via threads and processes, let's first look at how the Python programming language works with these two entities.

Start working with processes in Python

On common operating systems, each program runs in its own process. Usually, we start a program by double-clicking on the icon's program or selecting it from a menu. In this recipe, we simply demonstrate how to start a single new program from inside a Python program. A process has its own space address, data stack, and other auxiliary data to keep track of the execution; the OS manages the execution of all processes, managing the access to the computational resources of the system via a scheduling procedure.

Getting ready

In this first Python application, you'll simply get the Python language installed.

 Refer to `https://www.python.org/` to get the latest version of Python.

How to do it...

To execute this first example, we need to type the following two programs:

- ▸ `called_Process.py`
- ▸ `calling_Process.py`

You can use the Python IDE (3.3.0) to edit these files:

The code for the `called_Process.py` file is as shown:

```
print ("Hello Python Parallel Cookbook!!")
closeInput = raw_input("Press ENTER to exit")
print "Closing calledProcess"
```

The code for the `calling_Process.py` file is as shown:

```
##The following modules must be imported
import os
import sys


##this is the code to execute
program = "python"
print("Process calling")
arguments = ["called_Process.py"]


##we call the called_Process.py script
os.execvp(program, (program,) + tuple(arguments))
print("Good Bye!!")
```

To run the example, open the `calling_Process.py` program with the Python IDE and then press the *F5* button on the keyboard.

You will see the following output in the Python shell:

At same time, the OS prompt displays the following:

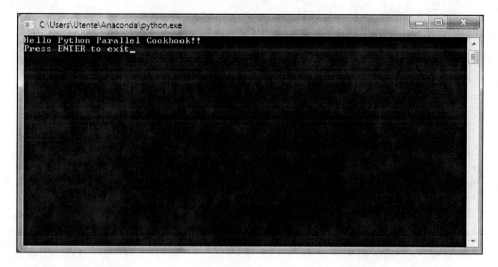

We have two processes running to close the OS prompt; simply press the *Enter* button on the keyboard to do so.

How it works...

In the preceding example, the execvp function starts a new process, replacing the current one. Note that the "Good Bye" message is never printed. Instead, it searches for the program called_Process.py along the standard path, passes the contents of the second argument tuple as individual arguments to that program, and runs it with the current set of environment variables. The instruction input() in called_Process.py is only used to manage the closure of OS prompt. In the recipe dedicated to process-based parallelism, we will finally see how to manage a parallel execution of more processes via the multiprocessing Python module.

Start working with threads in Python

As mentioned briefly in the previous section, thread-based parallelism is the standard way of writing parallel programs. However, the Python interpreter is not fully thread-safe. In order to support multithreaded Python programs, a global lock called the **Global Interpreter Lock** (**GIL**) is used. This means that only one thread can execute the Python code at the same time; Python automatically switches to the next thread after a short period of time or when a thread does something that may take a while. The GIL is not enough to avoid problems in your own programs. Although, if multiple threads attempt to access the same data object, it may end up in an inconsistent state.

In this recipe, we simply show you how to create a single thread inside a Python program.

How to do it...

To execute this first example, we need the program `helloPythonWithThreads.py`:

```python
## To use threads you need import Thread using the following code:
from threading import Thread


##Also we use the sleep function to make the thread "sleep"
from time import sleep


## To create a thread in Python you'll want to make your class work as a
thread.
## For this, you should subclass your class from the Thread class
class CookBook(Thread):
    def __init__(self):
        Thread.__init__(self)
        self.message = "Hello Parallel Python CookBook!!\n"


##this method prints only the message
    def print_message(self):
        print (self.message)


##The run method prints ten times the message
    def run(self):
        print ("Thread Starting\n")
        x=0
        while (x < 10):
            self.print_message()
            sleep(2)
            x += 1
        print ("Thread Ended\n")



#start the main process
print ("Process Started")
```

```
# create an instance of the HelloWorld class
hello_Python = CookBook()

# print the message...starting the thread
hello_Python.start()

#end the main process
print ("Process Ended")
```

To run the example, open the `calling_Process.py` program with the Python IDE and then press the *F5* button on the keyboard.

You will see the following output in the Python shell:

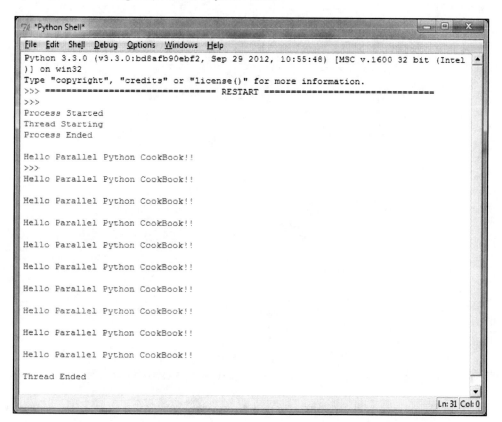

How it works...

While the main program has reached the end, the thread continues printing its message every two seconds. This example demonstrates what threads are—a subtask doing something in a parent process.

A key point to make when using threads is that you must always make sure that you never leave any thread running in the background. This is very bad programming and can cause you all sorts of pain when you work on bigger applications.

2
Thread-based Parallelism

In this chapter, we will cover the following recipes:

- How to use the Python threading module
- How to define a thread
- How to determine the current thread
- How to use a thread in a subclass
- Thread synchronization with Lock and RLock
- Thread synchronization with semaphores
- Thread synchronization with a condition
- Thread synchronization with an event
- How to use the `with` statement
- Thread communication using a queue
- Evaluating the performance of multithread applications
- The criticality of multithreaded programming

Introduction

Currently, the most widely used programming paradigm for the management of concurrence in software applications is based on multithreading. Generally, an application is made by a single process that is divided into multiple independent threads, which represent activities of different types that run parallel and compete with each other.

Although such a style of programming can lead to disadvantages of use and problems that need to be solved, modern applications with the mechanism of multithreading are still used quite widely.

Practically, all the existing operating systems support multithreading, and in almost all programming languages, there are mechanisms that you can use to implement concurrent applications through the use of threads.

Therefore, multithreaded programming is definitely a good choice to achieve concurrent applications. However, it is not the only choice available—there are several other alternatives, some of which, inter alia, perform better on the definition of thread.

A thread is an independent execution flow that can be executed parallelly and concurrently with other threads in the system. Multiple threads can share data and resources, taking advantage of the so-called space of shared information. The specific implementation of threads and processes depends on the operating system on which you plan to run the application, but, in general, it can be stated that a thread is contained inside a process and that different threads in the same process conditions share some resources. In contrast to this, different processes do not share their own resources with other processes.

Each thread appears to be mainly composed of three elements: program counter, registers, and stack. Shared resources with other threads of the same process essentially include data and operating system resources. Similar to what happens to the processes, even the threads have their own state of execution and can synchronize with each other. The states of execution of a thread are generally called ready, running, and blocked. A typical application of a thread is certainly parallelization of an application software, especially, to take advantage of modern multi-core processors, where each core can run a single thread. The advantage of threads over the use of processes lies in the performance, as the context switch between processes turns out to be much heavier than the switch context between threads that belong to the same process.

Multithreaded programming prefers a communication method between threads using the space of shared information. This choice requires that the major problem that is to be addressed by programming with threads is related to the management of that space.

Using the Python threading module

Python manages a thread via the `threading` package that is provided by the Python standard library. This module provides some very interesting features that make the threading-based approach a whole lot easier; in fact, the threading module provides several synchronization mechanisms that are very simple to implement.

The major components of the threading module are:

- The thread object
- The Lock object
- The RLock object
- The semaphore object
- The condition object
- The event object

In the following recipes, we examine the features offered by the threading library with different application examples. For the examples that follow, we will refer to the Python distribution 3.3 (even though Python 2.7 could be used).

How to define a thread

The simplest way to use a thread is to instantiate it with a target function and then call the `start()` method to let it begin its work. The Python module threading has the `Thread()` method that is used to run processes and functions in a different thread:

```
class threading.Thread(group=None,
                       target=None,
                       name=None,
                       args=(),
                       kwargs={})
```

In the preceding code:

- `group`: This is the value of `group` that should be `None`; this is reserved for future implementations
- `target`: This is the function that is to be executed when you start a thread activity
- `name`: This is the name of the thread; by default, a unique name of the form `Thread-N` is assigned to it

- ▸ `args`: This is the tuple of arguments that are to be passed to a target
- ▸ `kwargs`: This is the dictionary of keyword arguments that are to be used for the target function

It is useful to spawn a thread and pass arguments to it that tell it what work to do. This example passes a number, which is the thread number, and then prints out the result.

How to do it...

Let's see how to define a thread with the threading module, for this, a few lines of code are necessary:

```python
import threading

def function(i):
    print ("function called by thread %i\n"   %i)
    return

threads = []
for i in range(5):
    t = threading.Thread(target=function , args=(i,))
    threads.append(t)
    t.start()
    t.join()
```

The output of the preceding code should be, as follows:

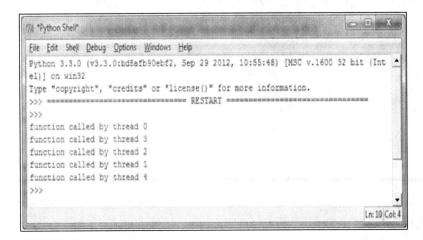

We should also point out that the output could be achieved in a different manner; in fact, multiple threads might print the result back to `stdout` at the same time, so the output order cannot be predetermined.

How it works...

To import the threading module, we simply use the Python command:

```
import threading
```

In the main program, we instantiate a thread, using the `Thread` object with a target function called `function`. Also, we pass an argument to the function that will be included in the output message:

```
t = threading.Thread(target=function , args=(i,))
```

The thread does not start running until the `start()` method is called, and that `join()` makes the calling thread wait until the thread has finished the execution:

```
t.start()
t.join()
```

How to determine the current thread

Using arguments to identify or name the thread is cumbersome and unnecessary. Each `Thread` instance has a name with a default value that can be changed as the thread is created. Naming threads is useful in server processes with multiple service threads that handle different operations.

How to do it...

To determine which thread is running, we create three target functions and import the `time` module to introduce a suspend execution of two seconds:

```
import threading
import time

def first_function():
    print (threading.currentThread().getName()+\
            str(' is Starting \n'))
    time.sleep(2)
    print (threading.currentThread().getName()+\
            str( ' is Exiting \n'))
    return

def second_function():
    print (threading.currentThread().getName()+\
            str(' is Starting \n'))
    time.sleep(2)
```

```
        print (threading.currentThread().getName()+\
                str( ' is Exiting \n'))
        return

    def third_function():
        print (threading.currentThread().getName()+\
                str(' is Starting \n'))
        time.sleep(2)
        print (threading.currentThread().getName()+\
                str( ' is Exiting \n'))
        return


    if __name__ == "__main__":

        t1 = threading.Thread\
            (name='first_function', target=first_function)
        t2 = threading.Thread\
            (name='second_function', target=second_function)
        t3 = threading.Thread\
            (name='third_function',target=third_function)

        t1.start()
        t2.start()
        t3.start()
```

The output of this should be, as follows:

How it works...

We instantiate a thread with a target function. Also, we pass the name that is to be printed and if it is not defined, the default name will be used:

```
t1 = threading.Thread(name='first_function', target=first_function)
t2 = threading.Thread(name='second_function', target=second_function)
t3 = threading.Thread(target=third_function)
```

Then, we call the `start()` and `join()` methods on them:

```
t1.start()
t2.start()
t3.start()
t1.join()
t2.join()
t3.join()
```

How to use a thread in a subclass

To implement a new thread using the threading module, you have to do the following:

▶ Define a new subclass of the `Thread` class

▶ Override the `_init_(self [,args])` method to add additional arguments

▶ Then, you need to override the `run(self [,args])` method to implement what the thread should do when it is started

Once you have created the new `Thread` subclass, you can create an instance of it and then start a new thread by invoking the `start()` method, which will, in turn, call the `run()` method.

How to do it...

To implement a thread in a subclass, we define the `myThread` class. It has two methods that must be overridden with the thread's arguments:

```
import threading
import time

exitFlag = 0

class myThread (threading.Thread):
    def __init__(self, threadID, name, counter):
        threading.Thread.__init__(self)
        self.threadID = threadID
```

```
            self.name = name
            self.counter = counter
        def run(self):
            print ("Starting " + self.name)
            print_time(self.name, self.counter, 5)
            print ("Exiting " + self.name)

    def print_time(threadName, delay, counter):
        while counter:
            if exitFlag:
                thread.exit()
            time.sleep(delay)
            print ("%s: %s" %\
                    (threadName, time.ctime(time.time())))
            counter -= 1

# Create new threads
thread1 = myThread(1, "Thread-1", 1)
thread2 = myThread(2, "Thread-2", 2)

# Start new Threads
thread1.start()
thread2.start()
print ("Exiting Main Thread")
```

When the previous code is executed, it produces the following result:

How it works...

The threading module is the preferred form for creating and managing threads. Each thread is represented by a class that extends the Thread class and overrides its run() method. Then, this method becomes the starting point of the thread. In the main program, we create several objects of the myThread type; the execution of the thread begins when the start() method is called. Calling the constructor of the Thread class is mandatory—using it, we can redefine some properties of the thread as the name or group of the thread. The thread is placed in the active state of the call to start() and remains there until it ends the run() method or you throw an unhandled exception to it. The program ends when all the threads are terminated.

The join() command just handles the termination of threads.

Thread synchronization with Lock and RLock

When two or more operations belonging to concurrent threads try to access the shared memory and at least one of them has the power to change the status of the data without a proper synchronization mechanism a race condition can occur and it can produce invalid code execution and bugs and unexpected behavior. The easiest way to get around the race conditions is the use of a lock. The operation of a lock is simple; when a thread wants to access a portion of shared memory, it must necessarily acquire a lock on that portion prior to using it. In addition to this, after completing its operation, the thread must release the lock that was previously obtained so that a portion of the shared memory is available for any other threads that want to use it. In this way, it is evident that the impossibility of incurring races is critical as the need of the lock for the thread requires that at a given instant, only a given thread can use this part of the shared memory. Despite their simplicity, the use of a lock works. However, in practice, we can see how this approach can often lead the execution to a bad situation of deadlock. A deadlock occurs due to the acquisition of a lock from different threads; it is impossible to proceed with the execution of operations since the various locks between them block access to the resources.

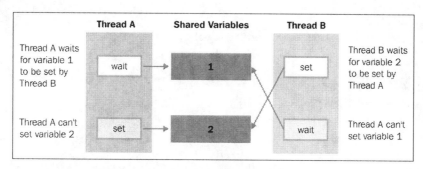

Deadlock

For the sake of simplicity, let's think of a situation wherein there are two concurrent threads (**Thread A** and **Thread B**) who have at their disposal resources **1** and **2**. Suppose **Thread A** requires resource **1** and **Thread B** requires resource **2**. In this case, both threads require their own lock and up to this point, everything proceeds smoothly. Imagine, however, that subsequently, before releasing the lock, **Thread A** requires a lock on resource **2** and **Thread B** requires a lock on resource **1,** which is now necessary for both the processes. Since both resources are locked, the two threads are blocked and waiting each other until the occupied resource is released. This situation is the most emblematic example of the occurrence of a deadlock situation. As said, therefore, showing the use of locks to ensure synchronization so that you can access the shared memory on one hand is a working solution, but, on the other hand, it is potentially destructive in certain cases.

In this recipe, we describe the Python threading synchronization mechanism called `lock()`. It allows us to restrict the access of a shared resource to a single thread or a single type of thread at a time. Before accessing the shared resource of the program, the thread must acquire the lock and must then allow any other threads access to the same resource.

How to do it...

The following example demonstrates how you can manage a thread through the mechanism of `lock()`. In this code, we have two functions: `increment()` and `decrement()`, respectively. The first function increments the value of the shared resource, while the second function decrements the value, where each function is inserted in a suitable thread. In addition to this, each function has a loop in which the increase or decrease is repeated. We want to make sure, through the proper management of the shared resources, that the result of the execution is equal to the value of the shared variable that is initialized to zero.

The sample code is shown, as follows, where each feature within the sample code is properly commented:

```
import threading

shared_resource_with_lock      = 0
shared_resource_with_no_lock      = 0
COUNT = 100000
shared_resource_lock = threading.Lock()


####LOCK MANAGEMENT##
def increment_with_lock():
    global shared_resource_with_lock
    for i in range(COUNT):
```

```python
        shared_resource_lock.acquire()
        shared_resource_with_lock += 1
        shared_resource_lock.release()

def decrement_with_lock():
    global shared_resource_with_lock
    for i in range(COUNT):
        shared_resource_lock.acquire()
        shared_resource_with_lock -= 1
        shared_resource_lock.release()

####NO LOCK MANAGEMENT ##
def increment_without_lock():
    global shared_resource_with_no_lock
    for i in range(COUNT):
        shared_resource_with_no_lock += 1

def decrement_without_lock():
    global shared_resource_with_no_lock
    for i in range(COUNT):
        shared_resource_with_no_lock -= 1

####the Main program
if __name__ == "__main__":
    t1 = threading.Thread(target = increment_with_lock)
    t2 = threading.Thread(target = decrement_with_lock)
    t3 = threading.Thread(target = increment_without_lock)
    t4 = threading.Thread(target = decrement_without_lock)
    t1.start()
    t2.start()
    t3.start()
    t4.start()
    t1.join()
    t2.join()
    t3.join()
    t4.join()
    print ("the value of shared variable with lock management is %s"\
            %shared_resource_with_lock)
    print ("the value of shared variable with race condition is %s"\
            %shared_resource_with_no_lock)
```

This is the result that you get after a single run:

```
Python Shell                                                              _  □  X

File  Edit  Shell  Debug  Options  Windows  Help
Python 3.3.0 (v3.3.0:bd8afb90ebf2, Sep 29 2012, 10:55:48) [MSC v.1600 32 bit (Intel)] on win32
Type "copyright", "credits" or "license()" for more information.
>>> ================================ RESTART ================================
>>>
the value of shared variable with lock management is 0
the value of shared variable without lock management is -28050
>>> |

                                                                       Ln: 7 Col: 4
```

As you can see, we have the correct result with the appropriate management and lock instructions. Note again that the result for the shared variable without lock management could differ from the result shown.

How it works...

In the main method, we have the following procedures:

```
t1 = threading.Thread(target = increment_with_lock)

t2 = threading.Thread(target = decrement_with_lock)
```

For thread starting, use:

```
t1.start()
t2.start()
```

For thread joining, use:

```
t1.join()
t2.join()
```

In the `increment_with_lock()` and `decrement_with_lock()` functions, you can see how to use lock management. When you need to access the resource, call `acquire()` to hold the lock (this will wait for the lock to be released, if necessary) and call `release()` to release it:

```
shared_resource_lock.acquire()
shared_resource_with_lock -= 1
shared_resource_lock.release()
```

Let's recap:

- ▸ Locks have two states: locked and unlocked
- ▸ We have two methods that are used to manipulate the locks: `acquire()` and `release()`

The following are the rules:

- ▸ If the state is unlocked, a call to `acquire()` changes the state to locked
- ▸ If the state is locked, a call to `acquire()` blocks until another thread calls `release()`
- ▸ If the state is unlocked, a call to `release()` raises a `RuntimeError` exception
- ▸ If the state is locked, a call to `release()` changes the state to unlocked

There's more...

Despite their theoretical smooth running, the locks are not only subject to harmful situations of deadlock, but also have many other negative aspects for the application as a whole. This is a conservative approach which, by its nature, often introduces unnecessary overhead; it also limits the scalability of the code and its readability. Furthermore, the use of a lock is decidedly in conflict with the possible need to impose the priority of access to the memory shared by the various processes. Finally, from a practical point of view, an application containing a lock presents considerable difficulties when searching for errors (debugging). In conclusion, it would be appropriate to use alternative methods to ensure synchronized access to shared memory and avoid race conditions.

Thread synchronization with RLock

If we want only the thread that acquires a lock to release it, we must use a `RLock()` object. Similar to the `Lock()` object, the `RLock()` object has two methods: `acquire()` and `release()`. `RLock()` is useful when you want to have a thread-safe access from outside the class and use the same methods from inside the class.

How to do it...

In the sample code, we introduced the `Box` class, which has the methods `add()` and `remove()`, respectively, that provide us access to the `execute()` method so that we can perform the action of adding or deleting an item, respectively. Access to the `execute()` method is regulated by `RLock()`:

```
import threading
import time
```

```python
class Box(object):
    lock = threading.RLock()
    def __init__(self):
        self.total_items = 0
    def execute(self,n):
        Box.lock.acquire()
        self.total_items += n
        Box.lock.release()
    def add(self):
        Box.lock.acquire()
        self.execute(1)
        Box.lock.release()
    def remove(self):
        Box.lock.acquire()
        self.execute(-1)
        Box.lock.release()


## These two functions run n in separate
## threads and call the Box's methods

def adder(box,items):
    while items > 0:
        print ("adding 1 item in the box\n")
        box.add()
        time.sleep(5)
        items -= 1

def remover(box,items):
    while items > 0:
        print ("removing 1 item in the box")
        box.remove()
        time.sleep(5)
        items -= 1

## the main program build some
## threads and make sure it works
if __name__ == "__main__":
    items = 5
    print ("putting %s items in the box " % items)
    box = Box()
    t1 = threading.Thread(target=adder,args=(box,items))
    t2 = threading.Thread(target=remover,args=(box,items))
    t1.start()
    t2.start()
```

```
t1.join()
t2.join()
print ("%s items still remain in the box " % box.total_items)
```

How it works...

In the main program, we repeated what was written in the preceding example; the two threads `t1` and `t2` are with the associated functions `adder()` and `remover()`. The functions are active when the number of items is greater than zero. The call to `RLock()` is carried out inside the `Box` class:

```
class Box(object):
    lock = threading.RLock()
```

The two functions `adder()` and `remover()` interact with the items of the `Box` class, respectively, and call the `Box` class methods: `add()` and `remove()`. In each method call, a resource is captured and then released. As for the object `lock()`, `RLock()` owns the `acquire()` and `release()` methods to acquire and release the resource; then for each method, we have the following function calls:

```
        Box.lock.acquire()
    #...do something
        Box.lock.release()
```

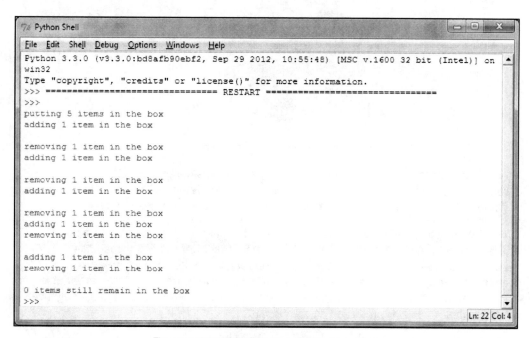

The execution result of the RLock() object's example

Thread synchronization with semaphores

Invented by E. Dijkstra and used for the first time in the operating system, a semaphore is an abstract data type managed by the operating system, used to synchronize the access by multiple threads to shared resources and data. Essentially, a semaphore is constituted of an internal variable that identifies the number of concurrent access to a resource to which it is associated.

Also, in the threading module, the operation of a semaphore is based on the two functions `acquire()` and `release()`, as explained:

▶ Whenever a thread wants to access a resource that is associated with a semaphore, it must invoke the `acquire()` operation, which decreases the internal variable of the semaphore and allows access to the resource if the value of this variable appears to be non-negative. If the value is negative, the thread would be suspended and the release of the resource by another thread will be placed on hold.

▶ Whenever a thread has finished using the data or shared resource, it must release the resource through the `release()` operation. In this way, the internal variable of the semaphore is incremented, and the first waiting thread in the semaphore's queue will have access to the shared resource.

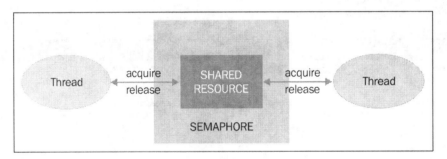

Thread synchronization with semaphores

Although at first glance the mechanism of semaphores does not present obvious problems, it works properly only if the wait and signal operations are performed in atomic blocks. If not, or if one of the two operations is stopped, this could arise unpleasant situations.

Suppose that two threads execute simultaneously, the operation waits on a semaphore, whose internal variable has the value 1. Also assume that after the first thread has the semaphore decremented from 1 to 0, the control goes to the second thread, which decrements the light from 0 to -1 and waits as the negative value of the internal variable. At this point, with the control that returns to the first thread, the semaphore has a negative value and therefore, the first thread also waits.

Therefore, despite the semaphore having access to a thread, the fact that the wait operation was not performed in atomic terms has led to a solution of the stall.

Getting ready

The next code describes the problem, where we have two threads, `producer()` and `consumer()` that share a common resource, which is the item. The task of `producer()` is to generate the item while the `consumer()` thread's task is to use the item produced.

If the item has not yet produced the `consumer()` thread, it has to wait. As soon as the item is produced, the `producer()` thread notifies the consumer that the resource should be used.

How to do it...

In the following example, we use the consumer-producer model to show you the synchronization via semaphores. When the producer creates an item, it releases the semaphore. Also, the consumer acquires it and consumes the shared resource. The synchronization process done via the semaphores is shown in the following code:

```
###Using a Semaphore to synchronize threads

import threading
import time
import random

##The optional argument gives the initial value for the internal
##counter;
##it defaults to 1.
##If the value given is less than 0, ValueError is raised.
semaphore = threading.Semaphore(0)

def consumer():
    print ("consumer is waiting.")
    ##Acquire a semaphore
    semaphore.acquire()
    ##The consumer have access to the shared resource
    print ("Consumer notify : consumed item number %s " %item)


def producer():
    global item
    time.sleep(10)
    ##create a random item
    item = random.randint(0,1000)
    print ("producer notify : produced item number %s" %item)
```

```
##Release a semaphore, incrementing the internal counter by one.
##When it is zero on entry and another thread is waiting for it
##to become larger than zero again, wake up that thread.
semaphore.release()


#Main program
if __name__ == '__main__':
    for i in range (0,5) :
        t1 = threading.Thread(target=producer)
        t2 = threading.Thread(target=consumer)
        t1.start()
        t2.start()
        t1.join()
        t2.join()
    print ("program terminated")
```

This is the result that we get after five runs:

```
Python Shell

File   Edit   Shell   Debug   Options   Windows   Help
Python 3.3.0 (v3.3.0:bd8afb90ebf2, Sep 29 2012, 10:55:48) [MSC v.1600 32 bit (Intel)]
on win32
Type "copyright", "credits" or "license()" for more information.
>>> ============================== RESTART ==============================
>>>
consumer is waiting.
producer notify : producted item number 193
Consumer notify : consumed item number 193
consumer is waiting.
producer notify : producted item number 631
Consumer notify : consumed item number 631
consumer is waiting.
producer notify : producted item number 770
Consumer notify : consumed item number 770
consumer is waiting.
producer notify : producted item number 688
Consumer notify : consumed item number 688
consumer is waiting.
producer notify : producted item number 16
Consumer notify : consumed item number 16
program terminated
>>>
                                                                        Ln: 21 Col: 4
```

How it works...

Initializing a semaphore to 0, we obtain a so-called semaphore event whose sole purpose is to synchronize the computation of two or more threads. Here, a thread must necessarily make use of data or common resources simultaneously:

```
semaphore = threading.Semaphore(0)
```

This operation is very similar to that described in the lock mechanism of the lock. The `producer()` thread creates the item and after that, frees the resource by calling:

```
semaphore.release()
```

The semaphore's `release()` method increments the counter and then notifies the other thread. Similarly, the `consumer()` method acquires the data by:

```
semaphore.acquire()
```

If the semaphore's counter is equal to 0, it blocks the condition's `acquire()` method until it gets notified by a different thread. If the semaphore's counter is greater than 0, it decrements the value.

Finally, the acquired data is then printed on the standard output:

```
print ("Consumer notify : consumed item number %s " %item)
```

There's more...

A particular use of semaphores is the mutex. A mutex is nothing but a semaphore with an internal variable initialized to the value 1, which allows the realization of mutual exclusion in access to data and resources.

Semaphores are still commonly used in programming languages that are multithreaded; however, using them you can run into situations of deadlock. For example, there is a deadlock situation created when the thread `t1` executes a wait on the semaphore `s1`, while the `t2` thread executes a wait on the semaphore `s1`, and then `t1`, and then executes a wait on `s2` and `t2`, and then executes a wait on `s1`.

Thread synchronization with a condition

A condition identifies a change of state in the application. This is a synchronization mechanism where a thread waits for a specific condition and another thread notifies that this condition has taken place. Once the condition takes place, the thread acquires the lock to get exclusive access to the shared resource.

Getting ready

A good way to illustrate this mechanism is by looking again at a producer/consumer problem. The class producer writes to a buffer as long as it is not full, and the class consumer takes the data from the buffer (eliminating them from the latter), as long as the buffer is full. The class producer will notify the consumer that the buffer is not empty, while the consumer will report to the producer that the buffer is not full.

How to do it...

To show you the condition mechanism, we will again use the consumer producer model:

```
from threading import Thread, Condition
import time

items = []
condition = Condition()

class consumer(Thread):
  def __init__(self):
    Thread.__init__(self)

  def consume(self):
    global condition
    global items

    condition.acquire()
    if len(items) == 0:
      condition.wait()
      print("Consumer notify : no item to consume")
    items.pop()
    print("Consumer notify : consumed 1 item")
    print("Consumer notify : items to consume are "\
                  + str(len(items)))
```

```
        condition.notify()
        condition.release()

    def run(self):
        for i in range(0,20):
            time.sleep(10)
            self.consume()


class producer(Thread):
    def __init__(self):
        Thread.__init__(self)

    def produce(self):
        global condition
        global items

        condition.acquire()
        if len(items) == 10:
            condition.wait()
            print("Producer notify : items producted are "\
                                    + str(len(items)))
            print("Producer notify : stop the production!!")
        items.append(1)
        print("Producer notify : total items producted "\
                        + str(len(items)))
        condition.notify()
        condition.release()

    def run(self):
        for i in range(0,20):
            time.sleep(5)
            self.produce()

if __name__ == "__main__":
        producer = producer()
        consumer = consumer()
        producer.start()
        consumer.start()
        producer.join()
        consumer.join()
```

This is the result that we get after a single run:

How it works...

The class consumer acquires the shared resource that is modeled through the list `items[]`:

```
condition.acquire()
```

If the length of the list is equal to 0, the consumer is placed in a waiting state:

```
if len(items) == 0:
    condition.wait()
```

Otherwise, it makes a `pop` operation from the items list:

```
items.pop()
```

So, the consumer's state is notified to the producer and the shared resource is released:

```
condition.notify()
condition.release()
```

The class producer acquires the shared resource and then it verifies that the list is completely full (in our example, we place the maximum number of items, 10, that can be contained in the items list). If the list is full, then the producer is placed in the wait state until the list is consumed:

```
condition.acquire()
if len(items) == 10:
    condition.wait()
```

If the list is not full, a single item is added. The state is notified and the resource is released:

```
condition.notify()
condition.release()
```

There's more...

It's interesting to see the Python internals for the condition synchronizations mechanism. The internal class `_Condition` creates a `RLock()` object if no existing lock is passed to the class's constructor. Also, the lock will be managed when `acquire()` and `released()` are called:

```
class _Condition(_Verbose):
    def __init__(self, lock=None, verbose=None):
        _Verbose.__init__(self, verbose)
        if lock is None:
            lock = RLock()
        self.__lock = lock
```

Thread synchronization with an event

Events are objects that are used for communication between threads. A thread waits for a signal while another thread outputs it. Basically, an event object manages an internal flag that can be set to `true` with the `set()` method and reset to `false` with the `clear()` method. The `wait()` method blocks until the flag is `true`.

How to do it...

To understand the thread synchronization through the event object, let's take a look again at the producer/consumer problem:

```python
import time
from threading import Thread, Event
import random

items = []
event = Event()

class consumer(Thread):
    def __init__(self, items, event):
        Thread.__init__(self)
        self.items = items
        self.event = event

    def run(self):
        while True:
            time.sleep(2)
            self.event.wait()
            item = self.items.pop()
            print ('Consumer notify : %d popped from list by %s'\
                    %(item, self.name))


class producer(Thread):
    def __init__(self, integers, event):
        Thread.__init__(self)
        self.items = items
        self.event = event

    def run(self):
        global item
        for i in range(100):
            time.sleep(2)
            item = random.randint(0, 256)
            self.items.append(item)
            print ('Producer notify : item N° %d appended \
                    to list by %s'\
                    % (item, self.name))
            print ('Producer notify : event set by %s'\
                    % self.name)
```

```
                    self.event.set()
                    print ('Produce notify : event cleared by %s \n'\
                            % self.name)
                    self.event.clear()


    if __name__ == '__main__':
        t1 = producer(items, event)
        t2 = consumer(items, event)
        t1.start()
        t2.start()
        t1.join()
            t2.join()
```

This is the output that we get when we run the program. The `t1` thread appends a value to the list and then sets the event to notify the consumer. The consumer's call to `wait()` stops blocking and the integer is retrieved from the list.

How it works...

The `producer` class is initialized with the list of items and the `Event()` function. Unlike the example with condition objects, the item list is not global, but it is passed as a parameter:

```
class consumer(Thread):
    def __init__(self, items, event):
        Thread.__init__(self)
        self.items = items
        self.event = event
```

In the run method for each item that is created, the `producer` class appends it to the list of items and then notifies the event. There are two steps that you need to take for this and the first step is as follows:

```
self.event.set()
```

The second step is:

```
self.event.clear()
```

The `consumer` class is initialized with the list of items and the `Event()` function.

In the run method, the consumer waits for a new item to consume. When the item arrives, it is popped from the item list:

```
def run(self):
    while True:
        time.sleep(2)
        self.event.wait()
        item = self.items.pop()
        print ('Consumer notify : %d popped from list by %s' %
            (item, self.name))
```

All the operations between the `producer` and the `consumer` classes can be easily resumed with the help of the following schema:

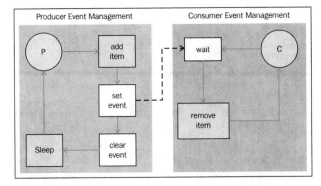

Thread synchronization with event objects

Using the with statement

Python's `with` statement was introduced in Python 2.5. It's useful when you have two related operations that must be executed as a pair with a block of code in between. Also, with the `with` statement, you can allocate and release some resource exactly where you need it; for this reason, the `with` statement is called a context manager. In the threading module, all the objects provided by the `acquire()` and `release()` methods may be used in a `with` statement block.

So the following objects can be used as context managers for a `with` statement:

- Lock
- RLock
- Condition
- Semaphore

Getting ready

In this example, we simply test all the objects using the `with` statement.

How to do it...

This example shows the basic use of the `with` statement. We have a set with the most important synchronization primitives. So, we test them by calling each one with the `with` statement:

```python
import threading
import logging

logging.basicConfig(level=logging.DEBUG,
                    format='(%(threadName)-10s) %(message)s',)

def threading_with(statement):
    with statement:
        logging.debug('%s acquired via with'  %statement)

def threading_not_with(statement):
    statement.acquire()
    try:
        logging.debug('%s acquired directly' %statement )
    finally:
        statement.release()
```

```
if __name__ == '__main__':

#let's create a test battery
    lock = threading.Lock()
    rlock = threading.RLock()
    condition = threading.Condition()
    mutex = threading.Semaphore(1)
    threading_synchronization_list = \
        [lock, rlock, condition, mutex]

#in the for cycle we call the threading_with
# e threading_no_with function
    for statement in threading_synchronization_list :
        t1 = threading.Thread(target=threading_with,
            args=(statement,))
        t2 = threading.Thread(target=threading_not_with,
            args=(statement,))
        t1.start()
        t2.start()
        t1.join()
        t2.join()
```

The output shows the use of the `with` statement for each function and also where it is not used:

How it works...

In the main program, we have defined a list, `threading_synchronization_list`, of thread communication directives that are to be tested:

```
lock = threading.Lock()
rlock = threading.RLock()
condition = threading.Condition()
mutex = threading.Semaphore(1)
threading_synchronization_list = \

    [lock, rlock, condition, mutex]
```

After defining them, we pass each object in the `for` cycle:

```
for statement in threading_synchronization_list :
        t1 = threading.Thread(target=threading_with,
            args=(statement,))
        t2 = threading.Thread(target=threading_not_with,
            args=(statement,))
```

Finally, we have two target functions, in which the `threading_with` tests the `with` statement:

```
def threading_with(statement):
    with statement:
        logging.debug('%s acquired via with'  %statement)
```

There's more...

In the following example we have used the Python support for logging, as we can see:

```
logging.basicConfig(level=logging.DEBUG,
                    format='(%(threadName)-10s) %(message)s',)
```

It embeds the thread name in every log message using the formatter code's `%(threadName)s` statement. The logging module is thread-safe, so the messages from different threads are kept distinct in the output.

Thread communication using a queue

As discussed earlier, threading can be complicated when threads need to share data or resources. As we saw, the Python threading module provides many synchronization primitives, including semaphores, condition variables, events, and locks. While these options exist, it is considered a best practice to instead concentrate on using the module queue. Queues are much easier to deal with and make threaded programming considerably safer, as they effectively funnel all access to a resource of a single thread and allow a cleaner and more readable design pattern.

We will simply consider these four queue methods:

- ▶ `put ()`: This puts an item in the queue
- ▶ `get ()`: This removes and returns an item from the queue
- ▶ `task_done ()`: This needs to be called each time an item has been processed
- ▶ `join ()`: This blocks until all items have been processed

How to do it...

In this example, we will see how to use the threading module with the queue module. Also, we have two entities here that try to share a common resource, a queue. The code is as follows:

```python
from threading import Thread, Event
from queue import Queue
import time
import random


class producer(Thread):
    def __init__(self, queue):
        Thread.__init__(self)
        self.queue = queue

    def run(self) :
        for i in range(10):
```

```python
            item = random.randint(0, 256)
            self.queue.put(item)
            print ('Producer notify: item N°%d appended to queue by %s
                \n'\
                % (item, self.name))
            time.sleep(1)


class consumer(Thread):
    def __init__(self, queue):
        Thread.__init__(self)
        self.queue = queue

    def run(self):
        while True:
            item = self.queue.get()
            print ('Consumer notify : %d popped from queue by %s'\
                % (item, self.name))
            self.queue.task_done()


if __name__ == '__main__':
        queue = Queue()
        t1 = producer(queue)
        t2 = consumer(queue)
        t3 = consumer(queue)
        t4 = consumer(queue)
        t1.start()
        t2.start()
        t3.start()
        t4.start()
        t1.join()
        t2.join()
        t3.join()
        t4.join()
```

After running the code, you should have an output similar to this:

How it works...

First, the `producer` class. We don't need to pass the integers list because we use the queue to store the integers that are generated:

```
class producer(Thread):
    def _init__(self, queue):
        Thread._init__(self)
        self.queue = queue
```

The thread in the `producer` class generates integers and puts them in the queue in a
`for` loop:

```
def run(self) :
        for i in range(100):
            item = random.randint(0, 256)
            self.queue.put(item)
```

The producer uses `Queue.put(item[, block[, timeout]])` to insert data into the
queue. It has the logic to acquire the lock before inserting data in a queue.

There are two possibilities:

▸ If optional args `block` is `true` and `timeout` is `None` (this is the default case that
we used in the example), it is necessary for us to block until a free slot is available.
If timeout is a positive number, it blocks at most `timeout` seconds and raises the
full exception if no free slot is available within that time.

▸ If the block is `false`, put an item in the queue if a free slot is immediately available;
otherwise, raise the full exception (timeout is ignored in this case). Here, `put()`
checks whether the queue is full and then calls `wait()` internally and after this, the
producer starts waiting.

Next is the `consumer` class. The thread gets the integer from the queue and indicates that
it is done working on it using `task_done()`:

```
def run(self):
        while True:
            item = self.queue.get()
            self.queue.task_done()
```

The consumer uses `Queue.get([block[, timeout]])` and acquires the lock before
removing data from the queue. If the queue is empty, it puts the consumer in a waiting state.

Finally, in the main, we create the `t` thread for the producer and three threads, `t1`, `t2`, and `t3`
for the `consumer` class:

```
if __name__ == '__main__':
        queue = Queue()
        t = producer(queue)
        t1 = consumer(queue)
        t2 = consumer(queue)
        t3 = consumer(queue)
```

```
t.start()
t1.start()
t2.start()
t3.start()

t.join()
t1.join()
t2.join()
t3.join()
```

All the operations between the `producer` class and the `consumer` class can easily be resumed with the following schema:

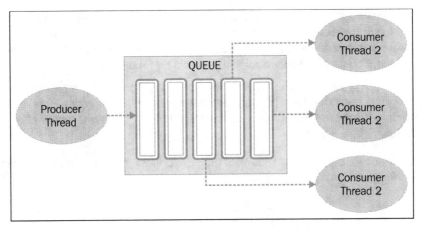

Thread synchronization with the queue module

Evaluating the performance of multithread applications

In this recipe, we will verify the impact of the GIL, evaluating the performance of a multithread application. The GIL, as described in the previous chapter, is the lock introduced by the CPython interpreter. The GIL prevents parallel execution of multiple threads in the interpreter. Before being executed each thread must wait for the GIL to release the thread that is running. In fact, the interpreter forces the executing thread to acquire the GIL before it accesses anything on the interpreter itself as the stack and instances of Python objects. This is precisely the purpose of GIL—it prevents concurrent access to Python objects from different threads. The GIL then protects the memory of the interpreter and makes the garbage work in the right manner. The fact is that the GIL prevents the programmer from improving the performance by executing threads in parallel. If we remove the GIL from the CPython interpreter, the threads would be executed in parallel. The GIL does not prevent a process from running on a different processor, it simply allows only one thread at a time to turn inside the interpreter.

How to do it...

The next code is a simple tool that is used to evaluate the performance of a multithreaded application. Each test calls a function only once in a hundred loop iterations. Then, we will see the fastest among the hundred calls. In the `for` loop, we call the `non_threaded` and `threaded` functions. Also, we iterate the tests that increase the number of calls and threads. We will try with 1, 2, 3, 4, and 8 at the end of calls threads. In the non-threaded execution, we simply call the function sequentially the same number of times corresponding to those threads that we would use. To keep things simple, all the measurements of the speed of execution are provided by the Python's module timer.

This module is designed to evaluate the performance of pieces of Python code, which are generally single statements.

The code is as follows:

```python
from threading import Thread

class threads_object(Thread):
  def run(self):
    function_to_run()

class nothreads_object(object):
  def run(self):
    function_to_run()

def non_threaded(num_iter):
  funcs = []
  for i in range(int(num_iter)):
    funcs.append(nothreads_object())
  for i in funcs:
    i.run()

def threaded(num_threads):
  funcs = []
  for i in range(int(num_threads)):
    funcs.append(threads_object())
  for i in funcs:
    i.start()
  for i in funcs:
    i.join()

def function_to_run():
    pass
```

```
def show_results(func_name, results):
  print ("%-23s %4.6f seconds" % (func_name, results))


if __name__ == "__main__":
    import sys
    from timeit import Timer

    repeat = 100
    number = 1
    num_threads = [ 1, 2, 4, 8]

     print ('Starting tests')
    for i in num_threads:
        t = Timer("non_threaded(%s)"\
                    % i, "from __main__ import non_threaded")
        best_result =\
                    min(t.repeat(repeat=repeat, number=number))
        show_results("non_threaded (%s iters)"\
                % i, best_result)

        t = Timer("threaded(%s)"\
                    % i, "from __main__ import threaded")
        best_result = \
                    min(t.repeat(repeat=repeat, number=number))
        show_results("threaded (%s threads)"\
                    % i, best_result)


    print ('Iterations complete')
```

How it works...

We performed a total of three tests and for each head, we used a different function, changing the function code `function_to_run()` defined in the sample code.

The machine used for these tests is a Core 2 Duo CPU – 2.33Ghz.

The first test

In this test, we simply evaluate the empty function:

```
def function_to_run():
    pass
```

It will show us the overhead associated with each mechanism that we are testing:

If we look at the results, we see how the thread calls are more expensive than the calls without threads. In particular, we also note how the cost of adding the thread is proportional to their number; in our example, we have four threads with 0.0007143 seconds, while with eight threads, we employ 0.001397 seconds.

The second test

A typical example of threaded applications is the processing of numbers. Let's take a simple method to calculate the brute force of the Fibonacci sequence; note that there is no sharing of the state here, just try to include more tasks that generate sequences of numbers:

```
def function_to_run():
    a, b = 0, 1
    for i in range(10000):
        a, b = b, a + b
```

This is the output:

As we can see from the output, we get no advantage by increasing the number of threads. The function is executed in Python and because of the overhead for creating threads and GIL, the multithreaded example can never be faster than the non-threaded example. Again, let's remember that the GIL allows only one thread at a time to access the interpreter.

The third test

The following test consists in reading 1,000 times a block of data (1Kb) from the test.dat file. The function tested is as follows:

```
def function_to_run():
    fh=open("C:\\CookBookFileExamples\\test.dat","rb")
    size = 1024
    for i in range(1000):
        fh.read(size)
```

These are the results of the test:

```
Python Shell                                                    [-][□][X]
File  Edit  Shell  Debug  Options  Windows  Help
Python 3.3.0 (v3.3.0:bd8afb90ebf2, Sep 29 2012, 10:55:48) [MSC v.1600 32 bit (Intel
)] on win32
Type "copyright", "credits" or "license()" for more information.
>>> ============================== RESTART ==============================
>>>
Starting tests
non_threaded (1 iters)    0.074713 seconds
threaded (1 threads)      0.074958 seconds
non_threaded (2 iters)    0.150131 seconds
threaded (2 threads)      0.082746 seconds
non_threaded (4 iters)    0.301600 seconds
threaded (4 threads)      0.168953 seconds
non_threaded (8 iters)    0.604644 seconds
threaded (8 threads)      0.353848 seconds
Iterations complete
>>> |
                                                            Ln: 15 Col: 4
```

We have begun to see a better result in the multithreading case. In particular, we've noted how the threaded execution is half time-consuming if we compare it with the `non_threaded` one. Let's remember that in real life, we would not use threads as a benchmark. Typically, we would put the threads in a queue, pull them out, and perform other tasks. Having multiple threads that execute the same function although useful in certain cases, is not a common use case for a concurrent program, unless it divides the data in the input.

The fourth test

In the final example, we use `urllib.request`, a Python module for fetching URL's. This module based on the `socket` module, is written in C and is thread-safe.

The following script tries to get to the `https://www.packtpub.com/` main page and simply read the first 1k bytes of it:

```python
def function_to_run():
    import urllib.request
    for i in range(10):
        with urllib.request.urlopen("https://www.packtpub.com/")as f:
            f.read(1024)
```

The following is the result of the preceding code:

```
7% Python Shell
File  Edit  Shell  Debug  Options  Windows  Help
Python 3.3.0 (v3.3.0:bd8afb90ebf2, Sep 29 2012, 10:55:48) [MSC v.1600 32 bit (In
tel)] on win32
Type "copyright", "credits" or "license()" for more information.
>>> ================================ RESTART ================================
>>>
Starting tests
non_threaded (1 iters)   3.133642 seconds
threaded (1 threads)     3.159739 seconds
non_threaded (2 iters)   6.626534 seconds
threaded (2 threads)     3.383511 seconds
non_threaded (4 iters)   13.403415 seconds
threaded (4 threads)     3.732269 seconds
non_threaded (8 iters)   26.904945 seconds
threaded (8 threads)     4.927647 seconds
Iterations complete
>>>
                                                              Ln: 15  Col: 4
```

As you can see, during the I/O, the GIL is released. The multithreading execution becomes faster than the single-threaded execution. Since many applications perform a certain amount of work in the I/O, the GIL does not prevent a programmer from creating a multithreading work that concurrently increases the speed of execution.

There's more...

Let's remember that you do not add threads to speed up the startup time of an application, but to add support to the concurrence. For example, it's useful to create a pool of threads once and then reuse the worker. This allows us to split a big dataset and run the same function on different parts (the producer/consumer model). So, although it is not the norm for concurrent applications, these tests are designed to be simple. Is the GIL an obstacle for those who work on pure Python and try to exploit multi-core hardware architectures? Yes it does. While threads are a language construct, the CPython interpreter is the bridge between the threads and operating system. This is why Jython, IronPython, and others interpreters do not possess GIL, as it was simply not necessary and it has not been reimplemented in the interpreter.

3
Process-based Parallelism

In this chapter, we will cover the following recipes:

- ▸ Using the `multiprocessing` Python module
- ▸ How to spawn a process
- ▸ How to name a process
- ▸ How to run a process in the background
- ▸ How to kill a process
- ▸ How to use a process in a subclass
- ▸ How to exchange objects between processes
- ▸ Using a queue to exchange objects
- ▸ Using pipes to exchange objects
- ▸ How to synchronize processes
- ▸ How to manage a state between processes
- ▸ How to use a process pool
- ▸ Using the `mpi4py` Python module
- ▸ Point-to-point communication
- ▸ Avoiding deadlock problems
- ▸ Collective communication using `broadcast`
- ▸ Collective communication using a `scatter` function

- ▸ Collective communication using a `gather` function
- ▸ Collective communication using `AlltoAll`
- ▸ Reduction operation
- ▸ How to optimize the communication

Introduction

In the previous chapter, we saw how to use threads to implement concurrent applications. This section will examine the process-based approach. In particular, the focus is on two libraries: the Python `multiprocessing` module and the Python `mpi4py` module.

The Python `multiprocessing` library, which is part of the standard library of the language, implements the shared memory programming paradigm, that is, the programming of a system that consists of one or more processors that have access to a common memory.

The Python library `mpi4py` implements the programming paradigm called message passing. It is expected that there are no shared resources (and this is also called shared nothing) and that all communications take place through the messages that are exchanged between the processes.

For these features, it is in contrast with the techniques of communication that provide memory sharing and the use of lock or similar mechanisms to achieve mutual exclusion. In a message passing code, the processes are connected via the communication primitives of the types `send()` and `receive()`.

In the introduction of the Python multiprocessing docs, it is clearly mentioned that all the functionality within this package requires the main module to be importable to the children (`https://docs.python.org/3.3/library/multiprocessing.html`).

The `__main__` module is not importable to the children in IDLE, even if you run the script as a file with IDLE. To get the correct result, we will run all the examples from the Command Prompt:

```
python multiprocessing_example.py
```

Here, `multiprocessing_example.py` is the script's name. For the examples described in this chapter, we will refer to the Python distribution 3.3 (even though Python 2.7 could be used).

How to spawn a process

The term "spawn" means the creation of a process by a parent process. The parent process can of course continue its execution asynchronously or wait until the child process ends its execution. The multiprocessing library of Python allows the spawning of a process through the following steps:

1. Build the object process.

2. Call its `start()` method. This method starts the process's activity.

3. Call its `join()` method. It waits until the process has completed its work and exited.

How to do it...

This example shows you how to create a series (five) of processes. Each process is associated with the function `foo(i)`, where `i` is the ID associated with the process that contains it:

```
#Spawn a Process: Chapter 3: Process Based Parallelism
import multiprocessing

def foo(i):
    print ('called function in process: %s' %i)
    return

if __name__ == '__main__':
    Process_jobs = []
    for i in range(5):
        p = multiprocessing.Process(target=foo, args=(i,))
        Process_jobs.append(p)
        p.start()
        p.join()
```

To run the process and display the results, let's open the Command Prompt, preferably in the folder containing the example file (named `spawn_a_process.py`), and then type the following command:

```
python spawn_a_process.py
```

We obtain the following output using this command:

```
C:\Python CookBook\ Chapter 3 - Process Based Parallelism\Example Codes
Chapter 3>python spawn_a_process.py
called function in process: 0
called function in process: 1
called function in process: 2
called function in process: 3
called function in process: 4
```

How it works...

As explained in the introduction section of this recipe, to create the object process, we must first import the multiprocessing module with the following command:

```
import multiprocessing
```

Then, we create the object process in the main program:

```
p = multiprocessing.Process(target=foo, args=(i,))
```

Further, we call the `start()` method:

```
p.start()
```

The object process has for argument the function to which the child process is associated (in our case, the function is called `foo()`). We also pass an argument to the function that takes into account the process in which the associated function is situated. Finally, we call the `join()` method on the process created:

```
p.join()
```

Without `p.join()`, the child process will sit idle and not be terminated, and then, you must manually kill it.

There's more...

This reminds us once again of the importance of instantiating the `Process` object within the main section:

```
if __name__ == '__main__':
```

This is because the child process created imports the script file where the target function is contained. Then, by instantiating the process object within this block, we prevent an infinite recursive call of such instantiations. A valid workaround is used to define the target function in a different script, and then imports it to the namespace. So for our first example, we could have:

```
import multiprocessing
import target_function

if __name__ == '__main__':
    Process_jobs = []
    for i in range(5):
        p = multiprocessing.Process    \
            (target=target_function.function,args=(i,))
        Process_jobs.append(p)
        p.start()
        p.join()
```

Here, `target_function.py` is as shown:

```
#target_function.py

def function(i):
    print ('called function in process: %s' %i)
    return
```

The output is always similar to that shown in the preceding example.

How to name a process

In the previous example, we identified the processes and how to pass a variable to the target function. However, it is very useful to associate a name to the processes as debugging an application requires the processes to be well marked and identifiable.

How to do it...

The procedure to name a process is similar to that described for the threading library (see the recipe *How to determine the current thread* in *Chapter 2, Thread-based Parallelism*, of the present book.)

In the main program, we create a process with a name and a process without a name. Here, the common target is the `foo()` function:

```python
#Naming a Process: Chapter 3: Process Based Parallelism
import multiprocessing
import time

def foo():
    name = multiprocessing.current_process().name
    print ("Starting %s \n" %name)
    time.sleep(3)
    print ("Exiting %s \n" %name)

if __name__ == '__main__':
    process_with_name = \
                    multiprocessing.Process\
                    (name='foo_process',\
                     target=foo)
    process_with_name.daemon = True
    process_with_default_name = \
                            multiprocessing.Process\
                            (target=foo)
    process_with_name.start()
    process_with_default_name.start()
```

To run the process, open the Command Prompt and type the following command:

python naming_process.py

This is the result that we get after using the preceding command:

C:\Python CookBook\Chapter 3 - Process Based Parallelism\Example Codes Chapter 3>python naming_process.py

Starting foo_process

Starting Process-2

Exiting foo_process

Exiting Process-2

How it works...

The operation is similar to the procedure used for naming a thread. To name a process, we should provide an argument with the object's name:

```
process_with_name = multiprocessing.Process
            (name='foo_function', target=foo)
```

In this case, we called the `foo_function` process. If the process child wants to know which its parent process is, it must use the following statement:

```
name = multiprocessing.current_process().name
```

This statement will provide the name of the parent process.

How to run a process in the background

Running a process in background is a typical mode of execution of laborious processes that do not require your presence or intervention, and this course may be concurrent to the execution of other programs. The Python multiprocessing module allows us, through the daemonic option, to run background processes.

How to do it...

To run a background process, simply follow the given code:

```
import multiprocessing
import time

def foo():
    name = multiprocessing.current_process().name
    print ("Starting %s \n" %name)
    time.sleep(3)
    print ("Exiting %s \n" %name)


if __name__ == '__main__':
    background_process = multiprocessing.Process\
                    (name='background_process',\
                     target=foo)
    background_process.daemon = True
```

```
NO_background_process = multiprocessing.Process\
                            (name='NO_background_process',\
                             target=foo)

NO_background_process.daemon = False

background_process.start()
NO_background_process.start()
```

To run the script from the Command Prompt, type the following command:

python background_process.py

The final output of this command is as follows:

C:\Python CookBook\ Chapter 3 - Process Based Parallelism\Example Codes Chapter 3>python background_process.py

Starting NO_background_process

Exiting NO_background_process

How it works...

To execute the process in background, we set the daemon parameter:

background_process.daemon = True

The processes in the no-background mode have an output, so the daemonic process ends automatically after the main program ends to avoid the persistence of running processes.

There's more...

Note that a daemonic process is not allowed to create child processes. Otherwise, a daemonic process would leave its children orphaned if it gets terminated when its parent process exits. Additionally, these are not Unix daemons or services, they are normal processes that will be terminated (and not joined) if non-daemonic processes have exited.

How to kill a process

It's possible to kill a process immediately using the `terminate()` method. Also, we use the `is_alive()` method to keep track of whether the process is alive or not.

How to do it...

In this example, a process is created with the target function `foo()`. After the start, we kill it with the `terminate()` function:

```python
#kill a Process: Chapter 3: Process Based Parallelism
import multiprocessing
import time

def foo():
    print ('Starting function')
    time.sleep(0.1)
    print ('Finished function')

if __name__ == '__main__':
    p = multiprocessing.Process(target=foo)
    print ('Process before execution:', p, p.is_alive())
    p.start()
    print ('Process running:', p, p.is_alive())
    p.terminate()
    print ('Process terminated:', p, p.is_alive())
    p.join()
    print ('Process joined:', p, p.is_alive())
    print ('Process exit code:', p.exitcode)
```

The following is the output we get when we use the preceding command:

```
76 Python Shell
File  Edit  Shell  Debug  Options  Windows  Help
Python 3.3.0 (v3.3.0:bd8afb90ebf2, Sep 29 2012, 10:55:48) [MSC v.1600 32 bit (Int
el)] on win32
Type "copyright", "credits" or "license()" for more information.
>>> ============================== RESTART ==================================
>>>
Process before execution: <Process(Process-1, initial)> False
Process running: <Process(Process-1, started)> True
Process terminated: <Process(Process-1, stopped[SIGTERM])> True
Process joined: <Process(Process-1, stopped[SIGTERM])> False
Process exit code: -15
>>> |
                                                                     Ln: 10 Col: 4
```

How it works...

We create the process and then monitor its lifetime by the `is_alive()` method. Then, we finish it with a call to `terminate()`:

p.terminate()

Finally, we verify the status code when the process is finished, and read the attribute of the `ExitCode` process. The possible values of `ExitCode` are, as follows:

- ▶ `== 0`: This means that no error was produced
- ▶ `> 0`: This means that the process had an error and exited that code
- ▶ `< 0`: This means that the process was killed with a signal of *-1 * ExitCode*

For our example, the output value of the `ExitCode` code is equal to `-15`. The negative value `-15` indicates that the child was terminated by an interrupt signal identified by the number 15.

How to use a process in a subclass

To implement a custom subclass and process, we must:

- ▶ Define a new subclass of the `Process` class
- ▶ Override the `_init_(self [,args])` method to add additional arguments
- ▶ Override the `run(self [,args])` method to implement what `Process` should when it is started

Once you have created the new `Process` subclass, you can create an instance of it and then start by invoking the `start()` method, which will in turn call the `run()` method.

How to do it...

We will rewrite the first example in this manner:

```python
#Using a process in a subclass Chapter 3: Process Based #Parallelism

import multiprocessing

class MyProcess(multiprocessing.Process):
    def run(self):
        print ('called run method in process: %s' %self.name)
        return

if __name__ == '__main__':
    jobs = []
    for i in range(5):
        p = MyProcess ()
        jobs.append(p)
        p.start()
        p.join()
```

To run the script from the Command Prompt, type the following command:

python subclass_process.py

The result of the preceding command is as follows:

```
C:\Python CookBook\Chapter 3 - Process Based Parallelism\Example Codes
Chapter 3>python subclass_process.py

called run method in process: MyProcess-1
called run method in process: MyProcess-2
called run method in process: MyProcess-3
called run method in process: MyProcess-4
called run method in process: MyProcess-5
```

How it works...

Each Process subclass could be represented by a class that extends the Process class and overrides its run() method. This method is the starting point of Process:

```python
class MyProcess (multiprocessing.Process):
    def run(self):
        print ('called run method in process: %s' %self.name)
        return
```

In the main program, we create several objects of the type `MyProcess()`. The execution of the thread begins when the `start()` method is called:

```
p = MyProcess()
p.start()
```

The `join()` command just handles the termination of processes.

How to exchange objects between processes

The development of parallel applications has the need for the exchange of data between processes. The multiprocessing library has two communication channels with which it can manage the exchange of objects: queues and pipes.

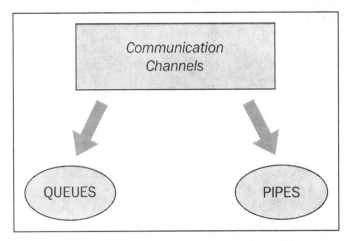

Communication channels in the multiprocessing module

Using queue to exchange objects

As explained before, it is possible for us to share data with the queue data structure.

A queue returns a process shared queue, is thread and process safe, and any serializable object (Python serializes an object using the pickable module) can be exchanged through it.

How to do it...

In the following example, we show you how to use a queue for a producer-consumer problem. The `producer` class creates the item and queues and then, the `consumer` class provides the facility to remove the inserted item:

```python
import multiprocessing
import random
import time

class producer(multiprocessing.Process):
    def __init__(self, queue):
        multiprocessing.Process.__init__(self)
        self.queue = queue

    def run(self) :
        for i in range(10):
            item = random.randint(0, 256)
            self.queue.put(item)
            print ("Process Producer : item %d appended to queue %s"\
                    % (item,self.name))
            time.sleep(1)
            print ("The size of queue is %s"\
                    % self.queue.qsize())

class consumer(multiprocessing.Process):
    def __init__(self, queue):
        multiprocessing.Process.__init__(self)
        self.queue = queue

    def run(self):
        while True:
            if (self.queue.empty()):
                print("the queue is empty")
                break
            else :
                time.sleep(2)
                item = self.queue.get()
                print ('Process Consumer : item %d popped from by %s \n'\
                        % (item, self.name))
                time.sleep(1)
```

```
if __name__ == '__main__':
        queue = multiprocessing.Queue()
        process_producer = producer(queue)
        process_consumer = consumer(queue)
        process_producer.start()
        process_consumer.start()
        process_producer.join()
        process_consumer.join()
```

This is the output that we get after the execution:

```
C:\Python CookBook\Chapter 3 - Process Based Parallelism\Example Codes
Chapter 3>python using_queue.py
Process Producer : item 69 appended to queue producer-1
The size of queue is 1
Process Producer : item 168 appended to queue producer-1
The size of queue is 2
Process Consumer : item 69 popped from by consumer-2
Process Producer : item 235 appended to queue producer-1
The size of queue is 2
Process Producer : item 152 appended to queue producer-1
The size of queue is 3
Process Producer : item 213 appended to queue producer-1
Process Consumer : item 168 popped from by consumer-2
The size of queue is 3
Process Producer : item 35 appended to queue producer-1
The size of queue is 4
Process Producer : item 218 appended to queue producer-1
The size of queue is 5
Process Producer : item 175 appended to queue producer-1
Process Consumer : item 235 popped from by consumer-2
The size of queue is 5
Process Producer : item 140 appended to queue producer-1
The size of queue is 6
Process Producer : item 241 appended to queue producer-1
The size of queue is 7
Process Consumer : item 152 popped from by consumer-2
Process Consumer : item 213 popped from by consumer-2
```

```
Process Consumer : item 35 popped from by consumer-2
Process Consumer : item 218 popped from by consumer-2
Process Consumer : item 175 popped from by consumer-2
Process Consumer : item 140 popped from by consumer-2
Process Consumer : item 241 popped from by consumer-2
the queue is empty
```

How it works...

The multiprocessing class has its `Queue` object instantiated in the main program:

```
if __name__ == '__main__':
        queue = multiprocessing.Queue()
```

Then, we create the two processes, `producer` and `consumer`, with the `Queue` object as an attribute:

```
        process_producer = producer(queue)
        process_consumer = consumer(queue)
```

The process producer is responsible for entering 10 items in the queue using its `put()` method:

```
for i in range(10):
            item = random.randint(0, 256)
            self.queue.put(item)
```

The process consumer has the task of removing the items from the queue (using the `get` method) and verifying that the queue is not empty. If this happens, the flow inside the `while` loop ends with a `break` statement:

```
def run(self):
        while True:
            if (self.queue.empty()):
                print("the queue is empty")
                break
            else :
                time.sleep(2)
                item = self.queue.get()
                print ('Process Consumer : item %d popped from by %s
    \n'\
                        % (item, self.name))
                time.sleep(1)
```

There's more...

A queue has the `JoinaleQueue` subclass. It has the following two additional methods:

- ▸ `task_done()`: This indicates that a task is complete, for example, after the `get()` method is used to fetch items from the queue. So, it must be used only by queue consumers.
- ▸ `join()`: This blocks the processes until all the items in the queue have been achieved and processed.

Using pipes to exchange objects

The second communication channel is the pipe data structure.

A pipe does the following:

- ▸ Returns a pair of connection objects connected by a pipe
- ▸ In this, every object has send/receive methods to communicate between processes

How to do it...

Here is a simple example with pipes. We have one process pipe the gives out numbers from 0 to 9 and another process that takes the numbers and squares them:

```
import multiprocessing


def create_items(pipe):
    output_pipe, _ = pipe
    for item in range(10):
        output_pipe.send(item)
    output_pipe.close()

def multiply_items(pipe_1, pipe_2):
    close, input_pipe = pipe_1
    close.close()
    output_pipe, _ = pipe_2
    try:
        while True:
            item = input_pipe.recv()
            output_pipe.send(item * item)
    except EOFError:
        output_pipe.close()
```

```
if __name__== '__main__':

#First process pipe with numbers from 0 to 9
    pipe_1 = multiprocessing.Pipe(True)
    process_pipe_1 = \
                multiprocessing.Process\
                (target=create_items, args=(pipe_1,))
    process_pipe_1.start()

#second pipe,
    pipe_2 = multiprocessing.Pipe(True)
    process_pipe_2 = \
                multiprocessing.Process\
                (target=multiply_items, args=(pipe_1, pipe_2,))
    process_pipe_2.start()

    pipe_1[0].close()
    pipe_2[0].close()

    try:
        while True:

            print (pipe_2[1].recv())
    except EOFError:
        print("End")
```

The output obtained is as follows:

How it works...

Let's remember that the `pipe()` function returns a pair of connection objects connected by a two way pipe. In the example, `out_pipe` contains the numbers from 0 to 9, generated by the target function `create_items()`:

```
def create_items(pipe):
    output_pipe, _ = pipe
    for item in range(10):
        output_pipe.send(item)
    output_pipe.close()
```

In the second process, we have two pipes: the input pipe and final output pipe that contains the results:

```
process_pipe_2 = multiprocessing.Process(target=multiply_items,
                    args=(pipe_1, pipe_2,))
```

These are finally printed as:

```
try:
        while True:
            print (pipe_2[1].recv())
except EOFError:
        print ("End")
```

How to synchronize processes

Multiple processes can work together to perform a given task. Usually, they share data. It is important that the access to shared data by various processes does not produce inconsistent data. Processes that cooperate by sharing data must therefore act in an orderly manner in order to access that data. Synchronization primitives are quite similar to those encountered for the library and threading.

They are as follows:

▶ **Lock**: This object can be in one of the states: locked and unlocked. A lock object has two methods, `acquire()` and `release()`, to manage the access to a shared resource.

▶ **Event**: This realizes simple communication between processes, one process signals an event and the other processes wait for it. An `Event` object has two methods, `set()` and `clear()`, to manage its own internal flag.

▶ **Condition**: This object is used to synchronize parts of a workflow, in sequential or parallel processes. It has two basic methods, `wait()` is used to wait for a condition and `notify_all()` is used to communicate the condition that was applied.

▶ **Semaphore**: This is used to share a common resource, for example, to support a fixed number of simultaneous connections.

▶ **RLock**: This defines the recursive `lock` object. The methods and functionality for RLock are the same as the `Threading` module.

▶ **Barrier**: This divides a program into phases as it requires all of the processes to reach it before any of them proceeds. Code that is executed after a barrier cannot be concurrent with the code executed before the barrier.

How to do it...

The example here shows the use of `barrier()` to synchronize two processes. We have four processes, wherein process1 and process2 are managed by a barrier statement, while process3 and process4 have no synchronizations directives:

```
import multiprocessing
from multiprocessing import Barrier, Lock, Process
from time import time
from datetime import datetime

def test_with_barrier(synchronizer, serializer):
    name = multiprocessing.current_process().name
    synchronizer.wait()
    now = time()
    with serializer:
        print("process %s ----> %s" \
                % (name,datetime.fromtimestamp(now)))

def test_without_barrier():
    name = multiprocessing.current_process().name
    now = time()
    print("process %s ----> %s" \
            % (name ,datetime.fromtimestamp(now)))

if __name__ == '__main__':
    synchronizer = Barrier(2)
    serializer = Lock()
    Process(name='p1 - test_with_barrier'\
            ,target=test_with_barrier,\
            args=(synchronizer,serializer)).start()
    Process(name='p2 - test_with_barrier'\
            ,target=test_with_barrier,\
            args=(synchronizer,serializer)).start()
    Process(name='p3 - test_without_barrier'\
```

```
                        ,target=test_without_barrier).start()
            Process(name='p4 - test_without_barrier'\
                        ,target=test_without_barrier).start()
```

By running the script, we can see that process1 and process2 print out the same timestamps:

```
C:\Python CookBook\Chapter 3 - Process Based Parallelism\Example Codes
Chapter 3>python process_barrier.py
process p1 - test_with_barrier ----> 2015-05-09 11:11:33.291229
process p2 - test_with_barrier ----> 2015-05-09 11:11:33.291229
process p3 - test_without_barrier ----> 2015-05-09 11:11:33.310230
process p4 - test_without_barrier ----> 2015-05-09 11:11:33.333231
```

How it works...

In the main program, we created four processes; however, we also need a barrier and lock primitive. The parameter 2 in the barrier statement stands for the total number of process that are to be managed:

```
    if __name__ == '__main__':
        synchronizer = Barrier(2)
        serializer = Lock()
        Process(name='p1 - test_with_barrier'\
                ,target=test_with_barrier,\
                args=(synchronizer,serializer)).start()
        Process(name='p2 - test_with_barrier'\
                ,target=test_with_barrier,\
                args=(synchronizer,serializer)).start()
```

The test_with_barrier_function executes the barrier's wait() method:

```
    def test_with_barrier(synchronizer, serializer):
        name = multiprocessing.current_process().name
        synchronizer.wait()
```

When the two processes have called the wait() method, they are released simultaneously:

```
        now = time()
        with serializer:
            print("process %s ----> %s" %(name \
                    ,datetime.fromtimestamp(now)))
```

The following figure shows you how a barrier works with the two processes:

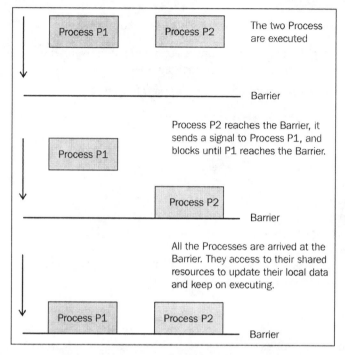

Process management with a barrier

How to manage a state between processes

Python multiprocessing provides a manager to coordinate shared information between all its users. A manager object controls a server process that holds Python objects and allows other processes to manipulate them.

A manager has the following properties:

- It controls the server process that manages a shared object
- It makes sure the shared object gets updated in all processes when anyone modifies it

How to do it...

Let's see an example of how to share a state between processes:

1. First, the program creates a manager list, shares it between *n* number of `taskWorkers`, and every worker updates an index.

2. After all workers finish, the new list is printed to `stdout`:

```python
import multiprocessing

def worker(dictionary, key, item):
    dictionary[key] = item

if __name__ == '__main__':
    mgr = multiprocessing.Manager()
    dictionary = mgr.dict()
    jobs = [ multiprocessing.Process\
                (target=worker, args=(dictionary, i, i*2))
                for i in range(10)
                ]
    for j in jobs:
        j.start()
    for j in jobs:
        j.join()
    print ('Results:', dictionary)
```

The output is as follows:

```
C:\Python CookBook\Chapter 3 - Process Based Parallelism\Example Codes
Chapter 3>python manager.py
key = 0 value = 0
key = 2 value = 4
key = 6 value = 12
key = 4 value = 8
key = 8 value = 16
key = 7 value = 14
key = 3 value = 6
key = 1 value = 2
key = 5 value = 10
key = 9 value = 18
Results: {0: 0, 1: 2, 2: 4, 3: 6, 4: 8, 5: 10, 6: 12, 7: 14, 8: 16, 9:
18}
```

How it works...

We declare the manager with the following statement:

```
mgr = multiprocessing.Manager()
```

In the next statement, a data structure of the type `dictionary` is created:

```
dictionary = mgr.dict()
```

Then, the multiprocess is launched:

```
jobs = [multiprocessing.Process \
        (target=taskWorker,args=(dictionary,i,i*2))
        for i in range(10)
        ]

for j in jobs:
        j.start()
```

Here, the target function `taskWorker` adds an item to the data structure dictionary:

```
def taskWorker(dictionary, key, item):
    dictionary[key] = value
```

Finally, we get the output and all the dictionaries are printed out:

```
for j in jobs:
        j.join()
    print ('Results:', d)
```

How to use a process pool

The multiprocessing library provides the `Pool` class for simple parallel processing tasks. The `Pool` class has the following methods:

- ▶ `apply()`: It blocks until the result is ready.
- ▶ `apply_async()`: This is a variant of the `apply()` method, which returns a result object. It is an asynchronous operation that will not lock the main thread until all the child classes are executed.
- ▶ `map()`: This is the parallel equivalent of the `map()` built-in function. It blocks until the result is ready, this method chops the iterable data in a number of chunks that submits to the process pool as separate tasks.

▶ map_async(): This is a variant of the map() method, which returns a result object. If a callback is specified, then it should be callable, which accepts a single argument. When the result becomes ready, a callback is applied to it (unless the call failed). A callback should be completed immediately; otherwise, the thread that handles the results will get blocked.

How to do it...

This example shows you how to implement a process pool to perform a parallel application. We create a pool of four processes and then we use the pool's map method to perform a simple calculation:

```
def function_square(data):
    result = data*data
    return result


if __name__ == '__main__':
    inputs = list(range(100))
    pool = multiprocessing.Pool(processes=4)
    pool_outputs = pool.map(function_square, inputs)
    pool.close()
    pool.join()
    print ('Pool    :', pool_outputs)
```

This is the result that we get after completing the calculation:

```
C:\Python CookBook\Chapter 3 - Process Based Parallelism\Example Codes
Chapter 3>\python process_pool.py
Pool    : [0, 1, 4, 9, 16, 25, 36, 49, 64, 81, 100, 121, 144, 169, 196,
225, 256, 289, 324, 361, 400, 441, 484, 529, 576, 625, 676, 729, 784,
841, 900, 961, 1024, 1089, 1156, 1225, 1296, 1369, 1444, 1521, 1600,
1681, 1764, 1849, 1936, 2025, 2116, 2209, 2304, 2401, 2500, 2601, 2704,
2809, 2916, 3025, 3136, 3249, 3364, 3481, 3600, 3721, 3844, 3969, 4096,
4225, 4356, 4489, 4624, 4761, 4900, 5041, 5184, 5329, 5476, 5625, 5776,
5929, 6084, 6241, 6400, 6561, 6724, 6889, 7056, 7225, 7396, 7569, 7744,
7921, 8100, 8281, 8464, 8649, 8836, 9025, 9216, 9409, 9604, 9801]
```

How it works...

The `multiprocessing.Pool` method applies `function_square` to the input element to perform a simple calculation. The total number of parallel processes is four:

```
pool = multiprocessing.Pool(processes=4)
```

The `pool.map` method submits to the process pool as separate tasks

```
pool_outputs = pool.map(function_square, inputs)
```

The parameter `inputs` is a list of integer from `0` to `100`:

```
inputs = list(range(100))
```

The result of the calculation is stored in `pool_outputs`. Then, the final result is printed:

```
print ('Pool    :', pool_outputs)
```

It is important to note that the result of the `pool.map()` method is equivalent to Python's built-in function `map()`, except that the processes run parallelly.

Using the mpi4py Python module

The Python programming language provides a number of MPI modules to write parallel programs. The most interesting of these is the `mpi4py` library. It is constructed on top of the MPI-1/2 specifications and provides an object-oriented interface, which closely follows MPI-2 C++ bindings. A C MPI user could use this module without learning a new interface. Therefore, it is widely used as an almost full package of an MPI library in Python.

The main applications of the module, which will be described in this chapter, are:

- ▸ Point-to-point communication
- ▸ Collective communication
- ▸ Topologies

Getting ready

The installation procedure of `mpi4py` using a Windows machine is, as follows (for other OS, refer to `http://mpi4py.scipy.org/docs/usrman/install.html#`):

1. Download the MPI software library `mpich` from `http://www.mpich.org/downloads/`.

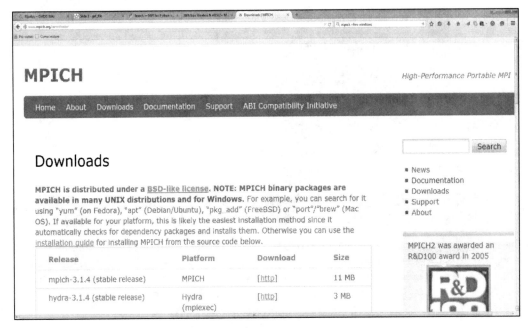

The MPICH download page

2. Open an admin Command Prompt by right-clicking on the command prompt icon and select **Run as administrator**.

3. Run `msiexec /i mpich_installation_file.msi` from the admin Command Prompt to install MPICH2.

4. During the installation, select the option that installs MPICH2 for all users.

5. Run `wmpiconfig` and store the username/password. Use your *real* Windows login name and password.

6. Add `C:\Program Files\MPICH2\bin` to the system path—no need to reboot the machine.

7. Check `smpd` using `smpd -status`. It should return `smpd running on $hostname$`.

8. To test the execution environment, go to the `$MPICHROOT\examples` directory and run `cpi.exe` using `mpiexec -n 4 cpi`.

9. Download the Python installer `pip` from `https://pip.pypa.io/en/stable/installing.html`.

   It will create a `pip.exe` file in the `Scripts` directory of your Python distribution.

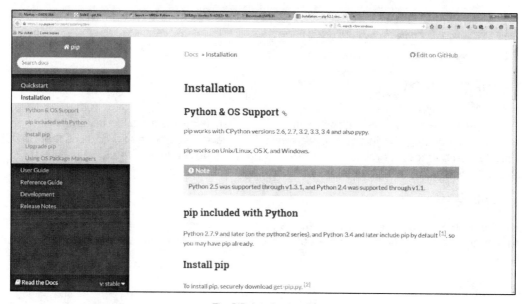

The PIP download page

10. Then, from the Command Prompt, type the following to install `mpi4py`:

    ```
    C:> pip install mpi4py
    ```

How to do it...

Let's start our journey to the MPI library by examining the classic code or a program that prints the phrase "Hello, world!" on each process that is instantiated:

```python
#hello.py
from mpi4py import MPI
comm = MPI.COMM_WORLD
rank = comm.Get_rank()
print ("hello world from process ", rank)
```

To execute the code, type the following command line:

```
C:> mpiexec  -n 5 python  helloWorld_MPI.py
```

This is the result that we would get after we execute this code:

```
('hello world from process ', 1)
('hello world from process ', 0)
('hello world from process ', 2)
('hello world from process ', 3)
('hello world from process ', 4)
```

How it works...

In MPI, the processes involved in the execution of a parallel program are identified by a sequence of non-negative integers called ranks. If we have a number *p* of processes that runs a program, the processes will then have a rank that goes from 0 to *p-1*. The function MPI that comes to us to solve this problem has the following function calls:

```
rank = comm.Get_rank()
```

This function returns the rank of the process that called it. The comm argument is called a communicator, as it defines its own set of all processes that can communicate together, namely:

```
comm = MPI.COMM_WORLD
```

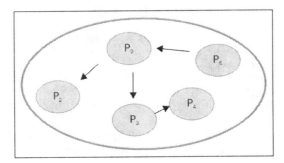

An example of communication between processes in MPI.COMM_WORLD

There's more...

It should be noted that, for illustration purposes only, the stdout output will not always be ordered, as multiple processes can apply at the same time by writing on the screen and the operating system arbitrarily chooses the order. So, we are ready for a fundamental observation: every process involved in the execution of MPI runs the same compiled binary, so each process receives the same instructions to be executed.

Point-to-point communication

One of the most important features among those provided by MPI is the point-to-point communication, which is a mechanism that enables data transmission between two processes: a process receiver, and process sender.

The Python module `mpi4py` enables point-to-point communication via two functions:

- ▸ `Comm.Send(data, process_destination)`: This sends data to the destination process identified by its rank in the communicator group
- ▸ `Comm.Recv(process_source)`: This receives data from the source process, which is also identified by its rank in the communicator group

The `Comm` parameter, which stands for communicator, defines the group of processes, that may communicate through message passing:

```
comm = MPI.COMM_WORLD
```

How to do it...

In the following example, we show you how to utilize the `comm.send` and `comm.recv` directives to exchange messages between different processes:

```
from mpi4py import MPI

comm=MPI.COMM_WORLD
rank = comm.rank
print("my rank is : " , rank)

if rank==0:
    data= 10000000
    destination_process = 4
    comm.send(data,dest=destination_process)
    print ("sending data %s " %data + \
            "to process %d" %destination_process)

if rank==1:
    destination_process = 8
    data= "hello"
    comm.send(data,dest=destination_process)
    print ("sending data %s :" %data + \
            "to process %d" %destination_process)
```

```
if rank==4:
    data=comm.recv(source=0)
    print ("data received is = %s" %data)


if rank==8:
    data1=comm.recv(source=1)
    print ("data1 received is = %s" %data1)
```

To run the script, type the following:

C:\>mpiexec -n 9 python pointToPointCommunication.py

This is the output that you'll get after you run the script:

```
('my rank is : ', 5)
('my rank is : ', 1)
sending data hello :to process 8
('my rank is : ', 3)
('my rank is : ', 0)
sending data 10000000 to process 4
('my rank is : ', 2)
('my rank is : ', 7)
('my rank is : ', 4)
data received is = 10000000
('my rank is : ', 8)
data1 received is = hello
('my rank is : ', 6)
```

How it works...

We ran the example with a total number of processes equal to nine. So in the communicator group, comm, we have nine tasks that can communicate with each other:

```
comm=MPI.COMM_WORLD
```

Also, to identify a task or processes inside the group, we use their rank value:

```
rank = comm.rank
```

We have two sender processes and two receiver processes.

The process of a rank equal to zero sends numerical data to the receiver process of a rank equal to four:

```
if rank==0:
    data= 10000000
    destination_process = 4
    comm.send(data,dest=destination_process)
```

Similarly, we must specify the receiver process of `rank` equal to four. Also, we note that the `comm.recv` statement must contain as an argument, the rank of the sender process:

```
...
if rank==4:
    data=comm.recv(source=0)
```

For the other sender and receiver processes, the process of a rank equal to one and the process of a rank equal to eight, respectively, the situation is the same but the only difference is the type of data. In this case, for the sender process, we have a string that is to be sent:

```
if rank==1:
    destination_process = 8
    data= "hello"
    comm.send(data,dest=destination_process)
```

For the receiver process of a rank equal to eight, the rank of the sender process is pointed out:

```
if rank==8:
    data1=comm.recv(source=1)
```

The following figure summarizes the point-to-point communication protocol in `mpi4py`:

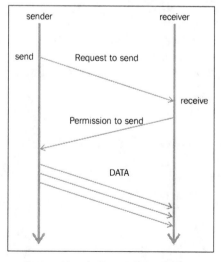

The send/receive transmission protocol

It is a two-step process, consisting of sending some data from one task (**sender**) and of receiving these data by another task (**receiver**). The sending task must specify the data to be sent and their destination (the receiver process), while the receiving task has to specify the source of the message to be received.

There's more...

The `comm.send()` and `comm.recv()` functions are *blocking* functions; they block the caller until the buffered data involved can safely be used. Also in MPI, there are two management methods of sending and receiving messages:

- ▶ The buffered mode
- ▶ The synchronous mode

In the buffered mode, the flow control returns to the program as soon as the data to be sent has been copied to a buffer. This does not mean that the message is sent or received. In the synchronous mode, however, the function only gets terminated when the corresponding receive function begins receiving the message.

Avoiding deadlock problems

A common problem we face is that of the deadlock. This is a situation where two (or more) processes block each other and wait for the other to perform a certain action that serves to another, and vice versa. The `mpi4py` module doesn't provide any specific functionality to resolve this but only some measures, which the developer must follow to avoid problems of deadlock.

How to do it...

Let's first analyze the following Python code, which will introduce a typical deadlock problem; we have two processes, `rank` equal to one and `rank` equal to five, that communicate which each other and both have the data sender and data receiver functionality:

```
from mpi4py import MPI

comm=MPI.COMM_WORLD
rank = comm.rank
print("my rank is : " , rank)
```

```
    if rank==1:
        data_send= "a"
        destination_process = 5
        source_process = 5

        data_received=comm.recv(source=source_process)
        comm.send(data_send,dest=destination_process)

        print ("sending data %s " %data_send + \
                "to process %d" %destination_process)
        print ("data received is = %s" %data_received)


    if rank==5:
        data_send= "b"
        destination_process = 1
        source_process = 1

        comm.send(data_send,dest=destination_process)
        data_received=comm.recv(source=source_process)


        print ("sending data %s :" %data_send + \
                "to process %d" %destination_process)
    print ("data received is = %s" %data_received)
```

How it works...

If we try to run this program (it makes sense to execute it with only two processes), we note
that none of the two processes are able to proceed:

```
C:\>mpiexec -n 9 python deadLockProblems.py
('my rank is : ', 8)
('my rank is : ', 3)
('my rank is : ', 2)
('my rank is : ', 7)
('my rank is : ', 0)
('my rank is : ', 4)
('my rank is : ', 6)
```

Both prepare to receive a message from the other and get stuck there. This happens because the function MPI `comm.recv()` as well as the `comm.send()` MPI blocks them. It means that the calling process waits for their completion. As for the `comm.send()` MPI, the completion occurs when the data has been sent and may be overwritten without modifying the message. The completion of the `comm.recv()` MPI, instead, is when the data has been received and can be used. To solve the problem, the first idea that occurs is to invert the `comm.recv()` MPI with the `comm.send()` MPI in this way:

```
if rank==1:
    data_send= "a"
    destination_process = 5
    source_process = 5
    comm.send(data_send,dest=destination_process)
    data_received=comm.recv(source=source_process)


if rank==5:
    data_send= "b"
    destination_process = 1
    source_process = 1
    data_received=comm.recv(source=source_process)
    comm.send(data_send,dest=destination_process)
```

This solution, however, even if correct from the logical point of view, not always ensures the avoidance of a deadlock. Since the communication is carried out through a buffer, where the `comm.send()` MPI copies the data to be sent, the program runs smoothly only if this buffer is able to hold them all. Otherwise, there is a deadlock: the sender cannot finish sending data because the buffer is committed and the receiver cannot receive data as it is blocked by a `comm.send()` MPI, which is not yet complete. At this point, the solution that allows us to avoid deadlocks is used to swap the sending and receiving functions so as to make them asymmetrical:

```
if rank==1:
    data_send= "a"
    destination_process = 5
    source_process = 5
    comm.send(data_send,dest=destination_process)
    data_received=comm.recv(source=source_process)


if rank==5:
    data_send= "b"
    destination_process = 1
    source_process = 1
    comm.send(data_send,dest=destination_process)
    data_received=comm.recv(source=source_process)
```

Finally, we get the correct output:

```
C:\>mpiexec -n 9 python deadLockProblems.py
```

```
('my rank is : ', 7)
('my rank is : ', 0)
('my rank is : ', 8)
('my rank is : ', 1)
sending data a to process 5
data received is = b
('my rank is : ', 5)
sending data b :to process 1
data received is = a
('my rank is : ', 2)
('my rank is : ', 3)
('my rank is : ', 4)
('my rank is : ', 6)
```

There's more...

The solution to the deadlock is not the only solution. There is, for example, a particular function that unifies the single call that sends a message to a given process and receives another message that comes from another process. This function is called Sendrecv:

```
Sendrecv(self, sendbuf, int dest=0, int sendtag=0, recvbuf=None, int
source=0, int recvtag=0, Status status=None)
```

As you can see, the required parameters are the same as the comm.send() MPI and the comm.recv() MPI. Also, in this case, the function blocks, but compared to the two already seen previously it offers the advantage of leaving the communication subsystem responsible for checking the dependencies between sending and receiving, thus avoiding the deadlock. In this way the code of the previous example becomes as shown:

```
if rank==1:
    data_send= "a"
    destination_process = 5
    source_process = 5
    data_received=comm.sendrecv(data_send,dest=destination_process,
                                source =source_process)
if rank==5:
    data_send= "b"
```

```
destination_process = 1
source_process = 1
data_received=comm.sendrecv(data_send,dest=destination_process,
                            source=source_process)
```

Collective communication using broadcast

During the development of a parallel code, we often find ourselves in the situation where we have to share between multiple processes the value of a certain variable at runtime or certain operations on variables that each process provides (presumably with different values).

To resolve this type of situations, the communication trees are used (for example the process 0 sends data to the processes 1 and 2, which respectively will take care of sending them to the processes 3, 4, 5, and 6, and so on).

Instead, MPI libraries provide functions ideal for the exchange of information or the use of multiple processes that are clearly optimized for the machine in which they are performed.

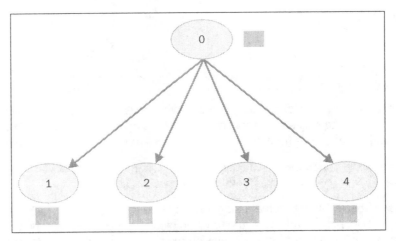

Broadcasting data from process 0 to processes 1, 2, 3, and 4

A communication method that involves all the processes belonging to a communicator is called a collective communication. Consequently, a collective communication generally involves more than two processes. However, instead of this, we will call the collective communication broadcast, wherein a single process sends the same data to any other process. The mpi4py functionalities in the broadcast are offered by the following method:

```
buf = comm.bcast(data_to_share, rank_of_root_process)
```

This function simply sends the information contained in the message process root to every other process that belongs to the comm communicator; each process must, however, call it by the same values of root and comm.

How to do it...

Let's now see an example wherein we've used the broadcast function. We have a root process of rank equal to zero that shares its own data, variable_to_share, with the other processes defined in the communicator group:

```
from mpi4py import MPI

comm = MPI.COMM_WORLD
rank = comm.Get_rank()

if rank == 0:
    variable_to_share = 100

else:
    variable_to_share = None

variable_to_share = comm.bcast(variable_to_share, root=0)
print("process = %d" %rank + " variable shared  = %d " \
                    %variable_to_share)
```

The output obtained with a communicator group of ten processes is:

```
C:\>mpiexec -n 10 python broadcast.py
process = 0 variable shared  = 100
process = 8 variable shared  = 100
process = 2 variable shared  = 100
process = 3 variable shared  = 100
process = 4 variable shared  = 100
process = 5 variable shared  = 100
process = 9 variable shared  = 100
process = 6 variable shared  = 100
process = 1 variable shared  = 100
process = 7 variable shared  = 100
```

How it works...

The process root of rank zero instantiates a variable, variabile_to_share, equal to 100. This variable will be shared with the other processes of the communication group:

```
if rank == 0:
    variable_to_share = 100
```

To perform this, we also introduce the broadcasting communication statement:

```
variable_to_share = comm.bcast(variable_to_share, root=0)
```

Here, the parameters in the function are the data to be shared and the root process or main sender process, as denoted in the previous figure. When we run the code, in our case, we have a communication group of ten processes, `variable_to_share` is shared between the others processes in the group. Finally, the `print` statement visualizes the rank of the running process and the value of its variable:

```
print("process = %d" %rank + " variable shared  = %d " \
                %variable_to_share)
```

There's more...

Collective communication allows simultaneous data transmission between multiple processes in a group. In `mpi4py` the collective communication are provided only in their blocking version (they block the caller method until the buffered data involved can safely be used.)

The most commonly collective operations are:

- Barrier synchronization across the group's processes
- Communication functions:
  - Broadcasting data from one process to all process in the group
  - Gathering data from all process to one process
  - Scattering data from one process to all process
- Reduction operation

Collective communication using scatter

The scatter functionality is very similar to a scatter broadcast but has one major difference, while `comm.bcast` sends the same data to all listening processes, `comm.scatter` can send the chunks of data in an array to different processes. The following figure illustrates the functionality of scatter:

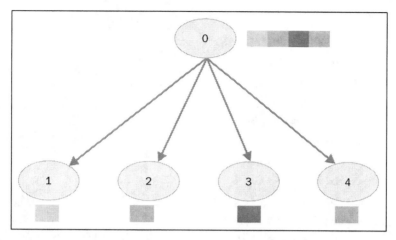

Scattering data from process 0 to processes 1, 2, 3, 4

The `comm.scatter` function takes the elements of the array and distributes them to the processes according to their rank, for which the first element will be sent to the process zero, the second element to the process 1, and so on. The function implemented in `mpi4py` is as follows:

```
recvbuf  = comm.scatter(sendbuf, rank_of_root_process)
```

How to do it...

In the next example, we see how to distribute data to different processes using the `scatter` functionality:

```
from mpi4py import MPI

comm = MPI.COMM_WORLD
rank = comm.Get_rank()

if rank == 0:
    array_to_share = [1, 2, 3, 4 ,5 ,6 ,7, 8 ,9 ,10]

else:
    array_to_share = None

recvbuf = comm.scatter(array_to_share, root=0)
print("process = %d" %rank + " recvbuf = %d " %array_to_share)
```

The output of the preceding code is, as follows:

```
C:\>mpiexec -n 10 python scatter.py
process = 0 variable shared  = 1
process = 4 variable shared  = 5
process = 6 variable shared  = 7
process = 2 variable shared  = 3
process = 5 variable shared  = 6
process = 3 variable shared  = 4
process = 7 variable shared  = 8
process = 1 variable shared  = 2
process = 8 variable shared  = 9
process = 9 variable shared  = 10
```

How it works...

The process of rank zero distributes the `array_to_share` data structure to other processes:

```
array_to_share = [1, 2, 3, 4 ,5 ,6 ,7, 8 ,9 ,10]
```

The `recvbuf` parameter indicates the value of the *i*th variable that will be sent to the *i*th process through the `comm.scatter` statement:

```
recvbuf = comm.scatter(array_to_share, root=0)
```

We also remark that one of the restrictions to `comm.scatter` is that you can scatter as many elements as the processors you specify in the execution statement. In fact attempting to scatter more elements than the processors specified (three in this example), you will get an error like this:

```
C:\> mpiexec -n 3 python scatter.py
Traceback (most recent call last):
  File "scatter.py", line 13, in <module>
    recvbuf = comm.scatter(array_to_share, root=0)
  File "Comm.pyx", line 874, in mpi4py.MPI.Comm.scatter (c:\users\utente\
appdata
```

```
\local\temp\pip-build-h14iaj\mpi4py\src\mpi4py.MPI.c:73400)
  File "pickled.pxi", line 658, in mpi4py.MPI.PyMPI_scatter (c:\users\
utente\app
data\local\temp\pip-build-h14iaj\mpi4py\src\mpi4py.MPI.c:34035)
  File "pickled.pxi", line 129, in mpi4py.MPI._p_Pickle.dumpv (c:\users\
utente\a
ppdata\local\temp\pip-build-h14iaj\mpi4py\src\mpi4py.MPI.c:28325)
ValueError: expecting 3 items, got 10
mpiexec aborting job...

job aborted:
rank: node: exit code[: error message]
0: Utente-PC: 123: mpiexec aborting job
1: Utente-PC: 123
2: Utente-PC: 123
```

There's more...

The `mpi4py` library provides two other functions that are used to scatter data:

- ▶ `comm.scatter(sendbuf, recvbuf, root=0)`: This sends data from one process to all other processes in a communicator.

- ▶ `comm.scatterv(sendbuf, recvbuf, root=0)`: This scatters data from one process to all other processes in a group that provides different amount of data and displacements at the sending side.

The `sendbuf` and `recvbuf` arguments must be given in terms of a list (as in, the point-to-point function `comm.send`):

```
buf = [data, data_size, data_type]
```

Here, `data` must be a buffer-like object of the size `data_size` and of the type `data_type`.

Collective communication using gather

The `gather` function performs the inverse of the `scatter` functionality. In this case, all processes send data to a root process that collects the data received. The `gather` function implemented in `mpi4py` is, as follows:

```
recvbuf = comm.gather(sendbuf, rank_of_root_process)
```

Here, `sendbuf` is the data that is sent and `rank_of_root_process` represents the process receiver of all the data:

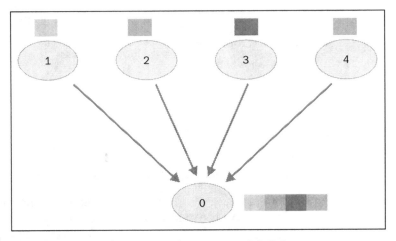

Gathering data from processes 1, 2, 3, 4

How to do it...

In the following example, we wanted to represent just the condition shown in the preceding figure. Each process builds its own data that is to be sent to the root processes that are identified with the rank zero:

```
from mpi4py import MPI

comm = MPI.COMM_WORLD
size = comm.Get_size()
rank = comm.Get_rank()
data = (rank+1)**2
```

```
data = comm.gather(data, root=0)
if rank == 0:
    print ("rank = %s " %rank +\
            "...receiving data to other process")
    for i in range(1,size):
        data[i] = (i+1)**2
        value = data[i]
        print(" process %s receiving %s from process %s"\
                %(rank , value , i))
```

Finally, we run the code with a group of processes equal to five:

```
C:\>mpiexec -n 5 python gather.py
rank = 0 ...receiving data to other process
 process 0 receiving 4 from process 1
 process 0 receiving 9 from process 2
 process 0 receiving 16 from process 3
 process 0 receiving 25 from process 4
```

The root process zero receives data from the other four processes, as we represented in the previous figure.

How it works...

We have *n* processes sending their data:

```
data = (rank+1)**2
```

If the rank of the process is zero, then the data is collected in an array:

```
if rank == 0:
    for i in range(1,size):
        data[i] = (i+1)**2
        value = data[i]
...
```

The gathering of data is given instead by the following function:

```
data = comm.gather(data, root=0)
```

There's more...

To collect data, `mpi4py` provides the following functions:

- ▸ **gathering to one task**: `comm.Gather`, `comm.Gatherv`, and `comm.gather`
- ▸ **gathering to all tasks**: `comm.Allgather`, `comm.Allgatherv`, and `comm.allgather`

Collective communication using Alltoall

The `Alltoall` collective communication combines the `scatter` and `gather` functionality. In `mpi4py`, there are three types of `Alltoall` collective communication:

- ▸ `comm .Alltoall(sendbuf, recvbuf)`: The all-to-all scatter/gather sends data from all-to-all processes in a group
- ▸ `comm.Alltoallv(sendbuf, recvbuf)`: The all-to-all scatter/gather vector sends data from all-to-all processes in a group, providing different amount of data and displacements
- ▸ `comm.Alltoallw(sendbuf, recvbuf)`: Generalized all-to-all communication allows different counts, displacements, and datatypes for each partner

How to do it...

In the following example, we'll see a `mpi4py` implementation of `comm.Alltoall`. We consider a communicator group of processes, where each process sends and receives an array of numerical data from the other processes defined in the group:

```python
from mpi4py import MPI
import numpy

comm = MPI.COMM_WORLD
size = comm.Get_size()
rank = comm.Get_rank()

a_size = 1
senddata = (rank+1)*numpy.arange(size,dtype=int)
recvdata = numpy.empty(size*a_size,dtype=int)
comm.Alltoall(senddata,recvdata)


print(" process %s sending %s receiving %s"\
      %(rank , senddata , recvdata))
```

We run the code with a communicator group of five processes and the output we get is as follows:

```
C:\>mpiexec -n 5 python alltoall.py
process 0 sending [0 1 2 3 4] receiving [0 0 0 0 0]
process 1 sending [0 2 4 6 8] receiving [1 2 3 4 5]
process 2 sending [ 0  3  6  9 12] receiving [ 2  4  6  8 10]
process 3 sending [ 0  4  8 12 16] receiving [ 3  6  9 12 15]
process 4 sending [ 0  5 10 15 20] receiving [ 4  8 12 16 20]
```

How it works...

The `comm.alltoall` method takes the *i*th object from `sendbuf` of the task *j* and copies it into the *j*th object of the `recvbuf` argument of the task *i*.

We could also figure out what happened using the following schema:

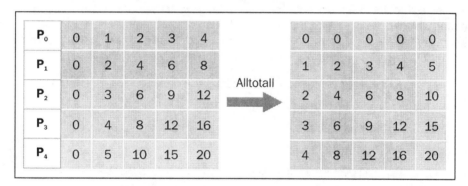

The Alltoall collective communication

The following are our observations regarding the schema:

- ▸ The process **P0** contains the data array [0 1 2 3 4], where it assigns **0** to itself, **1** to the process **P1**, **2** to the process **P2**, **3** to the process **P3**, and **4** to the process **P4**.

- ▸ The process **P1** contains the data array [0 2 4 6 8], where it assigns **0** to **P0**, **2** to itself, **4** to the process **P2**, **6** to the process **P3**, and **8** to the process **P4**.

- ▸ The process **P2** contains the data array [0 3 6 9 12], where it assigns **0** to **P0**, **3** to the process **P1**, **6** to itself, **9** to the process **P3**, and **12** to the process **P4**.

- ▸ The process **P3** contains the data array [0 4 8 12 16], where it assigns **0** to **P0**, **4** to the process **P1**, **8** to the process **P2**, **12** to itself, and **16** to the process **P4**.

- ▸ The process **P4** contains the data array [0 5 10 15 20], where it assigns **0** to **P0**, **5** to the process **P1**, **10** to the process **P2**, **15** to the process, and **P3** and **20** to itself.

There's more...

All-to-all personalized communication is also known as total exchange. This operation is used in a variety of parallel algorithms, such as the Fast Fourier transform, matrix transpose, sample sort, and some parallel database join operations.

The reduction operation

Similar to `comm.gather`, `comm.reduce` takes an array of input elements in each process and returns an array of output elements to the root process. The output elements contain the reduced result.

In `mpi4py`, we define the reduction operation through the following statement:

```
comm.Reduce(sendbuf, recvbuf, rank_of_root_process, op = type_of_
reduction_operation)
```

We must note that the difference with the `comm.gather` statement resides in the `op` parameter, which is the operation that you wish to apply to your data, and the `mpi4py` module contains a set of reduction operations that can be used. Some of the reduction operations defined by MPI are:

- ▶ `MPI.MAX`: This returns the maximum element
- ▶ `MPI.MIN`: This returns the minimum element
- ▶ `MPI.SUM`: This sums up the elements
- ▶ `MPI.PROD`: This multiplies all elements
- ▶ `MPI.LAND`: This performs a logical operation and across the elements
- ▶ `MPI.MAXLOC`: This returns the maximum value and the rank of the process that owns it
- ▶ `MPI.MINLOC`: This returns the minimum value and the rank of the process that owns it

How to do it...

Now, we'll see how to implement a sum of an array of elements with the reduction operation `MPI.SUM`, using the reduction functionality. Each process will manipulate an array of size three. For array manipulation, we used the functions provided by the `numpy` Python module:

```
import numpy
import numpy as np
from mpi4py import MPI
comm = MPI.COMM_WORLD
```

```
size = comm.size
rank = comm.rank

array_size = 3
recvdata = numpy.zeros(array_size,dtype=numpy.int)
senddata = (rank+1)*numpy.arange(a_size,dtype=numpy.int)
print(" process %s sending %s " %(rank , senddata))
comm.Reduce(senddata,recvdata,root=0,op=MPI.SUM)
print ('on task',rank,'after Reduce:    data = ',recvdata)
```

It makes sense to run the code with a communicator group of three processes, that is, the size of the manipulated array. Finally, we obtain the result as:

```
C:\>mpiexec -n 3 python reduction2.py
 process 2 sending [0 3 6]
on task 2 after Reduce:    data =  [0 0 0]
 process 1 sending [0 2 4]
on task 1 after Reduce:    data =  [0 0 0]
 process 0 sending [0 1 2]
on task 0 after Reduce:    data =  [ 0  6 12]
```

How it works...

To perform the reduction sum, we use the `comm.Reduce` statement and also identify with rank zero, the root process, which will contain `recvbuf`, that represents the final result of the computation:

```
comm.Reduce(senddata,recvdata,root=0,op=MPI.SUM)
```

Also, we must note that with the `op=MPI.SUM` option, we apply the sum operation to all of the elements of the column array. To better understand how the reduction operates, let's take a look at the following figure:

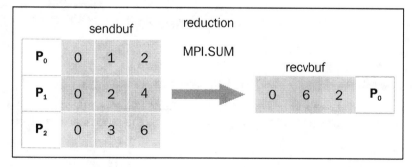

The reduction collective communication

The sending operation is as follows:

- ▸ The process **P0** sends the data array [0 1 2]
- ▸ The process **P1** sends the data array [0 2 4]
- ▸ The process **P2** sends the data array [0 3 6]

The reduction operation sums the *i*th elements of each task and then puts the result in the *i*th element of the array in the root process **P0**.

For the receiving operation, the process **P0** receives the data array [0 6 12].

How to optimize communication

An interesting feature that is provided by MPI concerns the virtual topologies. As already noted, all the communication functions (point-to-point or collective) refer to a group of processes. We have always used the `MPI_COMM_WORLD` group that includes all processes. It assigns a rank 0 to *n-1* for each process that belongs to a communicator of the size *n*. However, MPI allows us to assign a virtual topology to a communicator. It defines a particular assignment of labels to the different processes. A mechanism of this type permits you to increase the execution performance. In fact, if you build a virtual topology, then every node will communicate only with its virtual neighbor, optimizing the performance.

For example, if the rank was randomly assigned, a message could be forced to pass to many other nodes before it reaches the destination. Beyond the question of performance, a virtual topology makes sure that the code is more clear and readable. MPI provides two building topologies. The first construct creates Cartesian topologies, while the latter creates any kind of topologies. Specifically, in the second case, we must supply the adjacency matrix of the graph that you want to build. We will deal only with Cartesian topologies, through which it is possible to build several structures that are widely used: mesh, ring, toroid, and so on. The function used to create a Cartesian topology is, as follows:

```
comm.Create_cart((number_of_rows,number_of_columns))
```

Here, `number_of_rows` and `number_of_columns` specify the rows and columns of the grid that is to be made.

How to do it...

In the following example, we see how to implement a Cartesian topology of the size *M×N*. Also, we define a set of coordinates to better understand how all the processes are disposed:

```
from mpi4py import MPI
import numpy as np
```

```
UP = 0
DOWN = 1
LEFT = 2
RIGHT = 3
neighbour_processes = [0,0,0,0]
if __name__ == "__main__":
    comm = MPI.COMM_WORLD
    rank = comm.rank
    size = comm.size

    grid_rows = int(np.floor(np.sqrt(comm.size)))
    grid_column = comm.size // grid_rows


    if grid_rows*grid_column > size:
        grid_column -= 1
    if grid_rows*grid_column > size:
        grid_rows -= 1

    if (rank == 0) :
        print("Building a %d x %d grid topology:"\
            % (grid_rows, grid_column) )


    cartesian_communicator = \
                        comm.Create_cart( \
                            (grid_rows, grid_column), \
                            periods=(True, True), reorder=True)
    my_mpi_row, my_mpi_col = \
                cartesian_communicator.Get_coords\
                ( cartesian_communicator.rank )

    neighbour_processes[UP], neighbour_processes[DOWN]\
                        = cartesian_communicator.Shift(0, 1)
    neighbour_processes[LEFT],  \
                            neighbour_processes[RIGHT]  = \
                            cartesian_communicator.Shift(1, 1)
    print ("Process = %s \
row = %s \
column = %s ----> neighbour_processes[UP] = %s \
neighbour_processes[DOWN] = %s \
neighbour_processes[LEFT] =%s neighbour_processes[RIGHT]=%s" \
            %(rank, my_mpi_row, \
                my_mpi_col,neighbour_processes[UP], \
```

```
                     neighbour_processes[DOWN], \
                     neighbour_processes[LEFT] , \
                     neighbour_processes[RIGHT]))
```

By running the script, we obtain the following result:

```
C:\>mpiexec -n 4 python virtualTopology.py
Building a 2 x 2 grid topology:
Process = 0 row = 0 column = 0 ---->
neighbour_processes[UP] = -1
neighbour_processes[DOWN] = 2
neighbour_processes[LEFT] =-1
neighbour_processes[RIGHT] =1


Process = 1 row = 0 column = 1 ---->
neighbour_processes[UP] = -1
neighbour_processes[DOWN] = 3
neighbour_processes[LEFT] =0
neighbour_processes[RIGHT] =-1


Process = 2 row = 1 column = 0 ---->
neighbour_processes[UP] = 0
neighbour_processes[DOWN] = -1
neighbour_processes[LEFT] =-1
neighbour_processes[RIGHT] =3


Process = 3 row = 1 column = 1 ---->
neighbour_processes[UP] = 1
neighbour_processes[DOWN] = -1
neighbour_processes[LEFT] =2
neighbour_processes[RIGHT] =-1
```

For each process, the output should read as: if `neighbour_processes = -1`, then it has no topological proximity; otherwise, `neighbour_processes` shows the rank of the process closely.

How it works...

The resulting topology is a mesh of *2×2* (refer to the previous figure for a mesh representation), the size of which is equal to the number of processes in the input, that is, four:

```
grid_rows = int(np.floor(np.sqrt(comm.size)))
grid_column = comm.size // grid_rows
    if grid_rows*grid_column > size:
        grid_column -= 1
    if grid_rows*grid_column > size:
        grid_rows -= 1
```

Then, the Cartesian topology is built:

```
cartesian_communicator = comm.Create_cart( \
    (grid_rows, grid_column), periods=(False, False), reorder=True)
...
```

To find out the position of the *i*th process, we use the `Get_coords()` method in the following form:

```
my_mpi_row, my_mpi_col = cartesian_communicator.Get_coords( cartesian_
communicator.rank )
For each process, in addition to their coordinates, we calculated
and got to know which processes are topologically closer. For
this purpose, we used the comm.Shift function comm.Shift (rank_
source,rank_dest)
```

In this form we have:

```
neighbour_processes[UP], neighbour_processes[DOWN] = \ cartesian_
communicator.Shift(0, 1)

neighbour_processes[LEFT],  neighbour_processes[RIGHT] = \ cartesian_
communicator.Shift(1, 1)
```

The obtained topology is shown in the following figure:

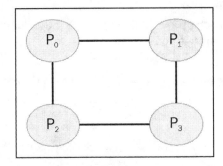

The virtual mesh 2x2 topology

There's more...

To obtain a toroidal topology of the size *M*×*N*, we need the following lines of code:

```
cartesian_communicator = comm.Create_cart( (grid_rows, grid_column),
periods=(True, True), reorder=True)
```

This corresponds to the following output:

```
C:\>mpiexec -n 4 python VirtualTopology.py
Building a 2 x 2 grid topology:
Process = 0 row = 0 column = 0 ---->
neighbour_processes[UP]  = 2
neighbour_processes[DOWN]  = 2
neighbour_processes[LEFT] =1
neighbour_processes[RIGHT]=1
Process = 1 row = 0 column = 1 ---->
neighbour_processes[UP]  = 3
neighbour_processes[DOWN]  = 3
neighbour_processes[LEFT] =0
neighbour_processes[RIGHT]=0
Process = 2 row = 1 column = 0 ---->
neighbour_processes[UP]  = 0
neighbour_processes[DOWN]  = 0
neighbour_processes[LEFT] =3 neighbour_processes[RIGHT]=3
Process = 3 row = 1 column = 1 ---->
neighbour_processes[UP]  = 1
neighbour_processes[DOWN]  = 1
neighbour_processes[LEFT] =2
neighbour_processes[RIGHT]=2
```

Also, it covers the topology represented here:

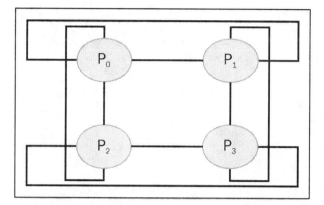

The virtual toroidal 2x2 topology

4

Asynchronous Programming

In this chapter, we will cover the following recipes:

- ▸ How to use the `concurrent.futures` Python module
- ▸ Event loop management with Asyncio
- ▸ Handling coroutines with Asyncio
- ▸ Task manipulation with Asyncio
- ▸ Dealing with Asyncio and Futures

Introduction

With the sequential and parallel execution model, there is a third model, called the asynchronous model, that is of fundamental importance to us along with the concept of event programming. The execution model of asynchronous activities can be implemented using a single stream of main control, both in uniprocessor systems and multiprocessor systems.

In the asynchronous model of a concurrent execution, various tasks intersect with the timeline, and all of this happens under the action of a single flow of control (single-threaded). The execution of a task can be suspended and then resumed, but this alternates the time of other tasks. The following figure expresses this concept in a clear manner:

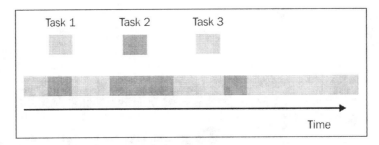

Asynchronous programming model

As you can see, the tasks (each with a different color) are interleaved with one another, but they are in a single thread of control; this implies that when one task is in execution, the other tasks are not. A key difference between the multithreaded programming model and the single-threaded asynchronous concurrent model is that in the first case, the operating system decides on the timeline, whether to suspend the activity of a thread and start another, while in the second case, the programmer must assume that a thread may be suspended and replaced with another at any time.

The programmer can program a task as a sequence of smaller steps that are executed intermittently; so if a task uses the output of another, the dependent task must be written to accept its input.

Using the concurrent.futures Python modules

With the release of Python 3.2, the `concurrent.future` module was introduced, which allows us to manage concurrent programming tasks, such as process and thread pooling, nondeterministic execution flows, and processes and thread synchronization.

This package is built by the following classes:

- `concurrent.futures.Executor`: This is an abstract class that provides methods to execute calls asynchronously.
- `submit (function ,argument)`: This schedules the execution of a function (called callable) on the arguments.

▸ `map (function,argument)`: This executes the function on arguments in an asynchronous mode.

▸ `shutdown (Wait = True)`: This signals the executor to free any resource.

▸ `concurrent.futures.Future`: This encapsulates the asynchronous execution of a callable function. Future objects are instantiated by submitting tasks (functions with optional parameters) to executors.

Executors are abstractions that are accessed through their subclasses: thread or process `ExecutorPools`. In fact, instantiation of threads and process is a resource-demanding task, so it is better to pool these resources and use them as repeatable launchers or executors (hence, the executors concept) for parallel or concurrent tasks.

Dealing with the process and thread pool

A thread or process pool (also called pooling) indicates a software manager that is used to optimize and simplify the use of threads and/or processes within a program. Through the pooling, you can submit the task (or tasks) that are to be executed to the pooler. The pool is equipped with an internal queue of tasks that are pending and a number of threads or processes that execute them. A recurring concept in pooling is reuse: a thread (or process) is used several times for different tasks during its lifecycle. It decreases the overhead of creating and increasing the performance of the program that takes advantage of the pooling. Reuse is not a rule, but it is one of the main reasons that lead a programmer to use pooling in his/her application.

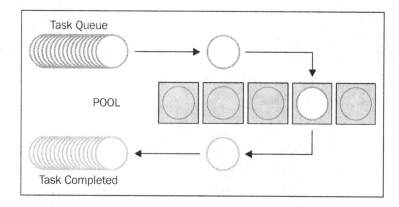

Pooling management

Getting ready

The `current.Futures` module provides two subclasses of the `Executor` class, respectively, which manipulates a pool of threads and a pool of processes asynchronously. The two subclasses are as follows:

- `concurrent.futures.ThreadPoolExecutor(max_workers)`
- `concurrent.futures.ProcessPoolExecutor(max_workers)`

The `max_workers` parameter identifies the max number of workers that execute the call asynchronously.

How to do it...

The following example shows you the functionality of process and thread pooling. The task to be performed is that we have a list of numbers from one to 10, `number_list`. For each element of the list, a count is made up to 10,000,000 (just to waste time) and then the latter number is multiplied with the *i*th element of the list.

By doing this, the following cases are evaluated:

- Sequential execution
- A thread pool with 5 workers

Consider the following code:

```
#
# Concurrent.Futures Pooling - Chapter 4 Asynchronous Programming
#

import concurrent.futures
import time

number_list = [1,2,3,4,5,6,7,8,9,10]

def evaluate_item(x):
    #count...just to make an operation
    result_item = count(x)
    #print the input item and the result
    print ("item " + str(x) + " result " + str(result_item))

def count(number) :
    for i in range(0,10000000):
        i=i+1
    return i*number
```

```
if __name__ == "__main__":

##Sequential Execution
    start_time = time.clock()
    for item in number_list:
        evaluate_item(item)
    print ("Sequential execution in " + \
           str(time.clock() - start_time), "seconds")

    ##Thread pool Execution
    start_time_1 = time.clock()
    with concurrent.futures.ThreadPoolExecutor(max_workers=5)\
        as executor:
        for item in number_list:
            executor.submit(evaluate_item, item)
    print ("Thread pool execution in " + \
           str(time.clock() - start_time_1), "seconds")

    ##Process pool Execution
    start_time_2 = time.clock()
    with concurrent.futures.ProcessPoolExecutor(max_workers=5)\
        as executor:
        for item in number_list:
            executor.submit(evaluate_item, item)
    print ("Process pool execution in " + \
           str(time.clock() - start_time_2), "seconds")
```

After running the code, we have the following results with the execution time:

```
C:\Python CookBook\Chapter 4- Asynchronous Programming\ >python
Process_pool_with_concurrent_futures.py
item 1 result 10000000
item 2 result 20000000
item 3 result 30000000
item 4 result 40000000
item 5 result 50000000
item 6 result 60000000
item 7 result 70000000
item 8 result 80000000
item 9 result 90000000
item 10 result 100000000
Sequential execution in 17.241238674183425 seconds
```

```
item 4 result 40000000
item 2 result 20000000
item 1 result 10000000
item 5 result 50000000
item 3 result 30000000
item 7 result 70000000
item 6 result 60000000
item 8 result 80000000
item 10 result 100000000
item 9 result 90000000
Thread pool execution in 17.14648646290675 seconds

item 3 result 30000000
item 1 result 10000000
item 2 result 20000000
item 4 result 40000000
item 5 result 50000000
item 6 result 60000000
item 7 result 70000000
item 9 result 90000000
item 8 result 80000000
item 10 result 100000000
Process pool execution in 9.913172716938618 seconds
```

How it works...

We build a list of numbers stored in `number_list` and for each element in the list, we operate the counting procedure until 100,000,000 iterations. Then, we multiply the resulting value for 100,000,000:

```
def evaluate_item(x):
    #count...just to make an operation
    result_item = count(x)

def count(number) :
    for i in range(0,10000000):
        i=i+1
    return i*number
```

In the main program, we execute the task that will be performed in a sequential mode:

```
if __name__ == "__main__":
    for item in number_list:
        evaluate_item(item)
```

Also, in a parallel mode, we will use the `concurrent.futures` module's pooling capability for a thread pool:

```
with concurrent.futures.ThreadPoolExecutor(max_workers=5)\
    as executor:
    for item in number_list:
        executor.submit(evaluate_item, item)
```

The `ThreadPoolExecutor` executes the given task using one of its internally pooled threads. It manages five threads working on its pool. Each thread takes a job out from the pool and executes it. When the job is executed, it takes the next job to be processed from the thread pool.

When all the jobs are processed, the execution time is printed:

```
print ("Thread pool execution in " + \
        str(time.clock() - start_time_1), "seconds")
```

For the process pooling implemented by the `ProcessPoolExecutor` class, we have:

```
with concurrent.futures.ProcessPoolExecutor(max_workers=5)\
    as executor:
    for item in number_list:
        executor.submit(evaluate_item, item)
```

Like `ThreadPoolExecutor`, the `ProcessPoolExecutor` class is an executor subclass that uses a pool of processes to execute calls asynchronously. However, unlike `ThreadPoolExecutor`, the `ProcessPoolExecutor` uses the multiprocessing module, which allows us to outflank the global interpreter lock and obtain a shorter execution time.

There's more...

The pooling is used in almost all server applications, where there is a need to handle more simultaneous requests from any number of clients. Many other applications, however, require that each task should be performed instantly or you have more control over the thread that executes it. In this case, pooling is not the best choice.

Event loop management with Asyncio

The Python module Asyncio provides facilities to manage events, coroutines, tasks and threads, and synchronization primitives to write concurrent code. The main components and concepts of this module are:

- ▶ **An event loop**: The Asyncio module allows a single event loop per process
- ▶ **Coroutines**: This is the generalization of the subroutine concept. Also, a coroutine can be suspended during the execution so that it waits for external processing (some routine in I/O) and returns from the point at which it had stopped when the external processing was done.
- ▶ **Futures**: This defines the `Future` object, such as the `concurrent.futures` module that represents a computation that has still not been accomplished.
- ▶ **Tasks**: This is a subclass of Asyncio that is used to encapsulate and manage coroutines in a parallel mode.

In this recipe, the focus is on handling events. In fact, in the context of asynchronous programming, events are very important since they are inherently asynchronous.

What is an event loop

Within a computational system, the entity that can generate events is called an event source, while the entity that negotiates to manage an event is called the event handler. Sometimes, there may be a third entity called an event loop. It realizes the functionality to manage all the events in a computational code. More precisely, the event loop acts cyclically during the whole execution of the program and keeps track of events that have occurred within a data structure to queue and then process them one at a time by invoking the event handler if the main thread is free. Finally, we report a pseudocode of an event loop manager:

```
while (1) {
events = getEvents();
for (e in events)
processEvent(e);
}
```

All the events in the `while` loop are caught and then processed by the event handler. The handler that processes an event is the only activity that takes place in the system. When the handler has ended, the control is passed on to the next event that is scheduled.

Getting ready

Asyncio provides the following methods that are used to manage an event loop:

- ▸ `loop = get_event_loop()`: Using this, you can get the event loop for the current context.

- ▸ `loop.call_later(time_delay,callback,argument)`: This arranges for the callback that is to be called after the given `time_delay` seconds.

- ▸ `loop.call_soon(callback,argument)`: This arranges for a callback that is to be called as soon as possible. The callback is called after `call_soon()` returns and when the control returns to the event loop.

- ▸ `loop.time()`: This returns the current time, as a float value, according to the event loop's internal clock.

- ▸ `asyncio.set_event_loop()`: This sets the event loop for the current context to loop.

- ▸ `asyncio.new_event_loop()`: This creates and returns a new event loop object according to this policy's rules.

- ▸ `loop.run_forever()`: This runs until `stop()` is called.

How to do it...

In this example, we show you how to use the loop event statements provided by the Asyncio library to build an application that works in an asynchronous mode. Let's consider the following code:

```
import asyncio
import datetime
import time

def function_1(end_time, loop):
    print ("function_1 called")
    if (loop.time() + 1.0) < end_time:
        loop.call_later(1, function_2, end_time, loop)
    else:
        loop.stop()
```

```python
def function_2(end_time, loop):
    print ("function_2 called ")
    if (loop.time() + 1.0) < end_time:
        loop.call_later(1, function_3, end_time, loop)
    else:
        loop.stop()


def function_3(end_time, loop):
    print ("function_3 called")
    if (loop.time() + 1.0) < end_time:
        loop.call_later(1, function_1, end_time, loop)
    else:
        loop.stop()


def function_4(end_time, loop):
    print ("function_5 called")
    if (loop.time() + 1.0) < end_time:
        loop.call_later(1, function_4, end_time, loop)
    else:
        loop.stop()

loop = asyncio.get_event_loop()

end_loop = loop.time() + 9.0
loop.call_soon(function_1, end_loop, loop)
#loop.call_soon(function_4, end_loop, loop)

loop.run_forever()
loop.close()
```

The output of the preceding code is as follows:

```
C:\Python Parallel Programming INDEX\Chapter 4- Asynchronous
Programming >python asyncio_loop.py
function_1 called
function_2 called
function_3 called
function_1 called
function_2 called
function_3 called
function_1 called
function_2 called
function_3 called
```

How it works...

In this example, we defined three asynchronous tasks, where each task calls the subsequent in the order, as shown in the following figure:

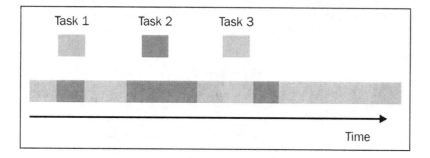

Task execution in the example

To accomplish this, we need to capture the event loop:

```
loop = asyncio.get_event_loop()
```

Then, we schedule the first call to `function_1()` by the `call_soon` construct:

```
end_loop = loop.time() + 9.0
loop.call_soon(function_1, end_loop, loop)
```

Let's note the definition of `function_1`:

```
def function_1(end_time, loop):
    print ("function_1 called")
    if (loop.time() + 1.0) < end_time:
        loop.call_later(1, function_2, end_time, loop)
    else:
        loop.stop()
```

This defines the asynchronous behavior of the application with the following arguments:

- ▸ `end_time`: This defines the upper time limit within `function_1` and makes the call to `function_2` through the `call_later` method
- ▸ `loop`: This is the loop event that was captured previously with the `get_event_loop()` method

The task of `function_1` is pretty simple, which is to print its name, but it could also be more computationally intensive:

```
print ("function_1 called")
```

After performing the task, it is compared to `loop.time ()` with the total length of the run; the total number of the cycles is `12` and if it is not passed this time, then it is executed with the `call_later` method with a delay of **1** second:

```
if (loop.time() + 1.0) < end_time:
        loop.call_later(1, function_2, end_time, loop)
    else:
        loop.stop()
```

For `funcion_2()` and `function_3()`, the operation is the same.

If the running time expires, then the loop event must end:

```
loop.run_forever()
loop.close()
```

Handling coroutines with Asyncio

We saw, in the course of the various examples presented, that when a program becomes very long and complex, it is convenient to divide it into subroutines, each of which realizes a specific task for which it implements a suitable algorithm. The subroutine cannot be executed independently, but only at the request of the main program, which is then responsible for coordinating the use of subroutines. Coroutines are a generalization of the subroutine. Like a subroutine, the coroutine computes a single computational step, but unlike subroutines, there is no main program that can be used to coordinate the results. This is because the coroutines link themselves together to form a pipeline without any supervising function responsible for calling them in a particular order. In a coroutine, the execution point can be suspended and resumed later after keeping track of its local state in the intervening time. Having a pool of coroutines, it is possible to interleave their computations: run the first one until it yields the control back, then run the second, and so on down the line.

The control component of the interleave is the even loop, which was explained in the previous recipe. It keeps track of all the coroutines and schedules when they will be executed.

The other important aspects of coroutines are, as follows:

- Coroutines allow multiple entry points that can be yielded multiple times
- Coroutines can transfer the execution to any other coroutines

The term "yield" is used to describe a coroutine that pauses and passes the control flow to another coroutine. Since coroutines can pass values along with the control flow to another coroutine, the phrase "yielding a value" is used to describe the yielding and passing of a value to the coroutine that receives the control.

Getting ready

To define a coroutine with the Asyncio module, we simply use an annotation:

```
import asyncio
@asyncio.coroutine
def coroutine_function( function_arguments ) :
    # DO_SOMETHING
```

How to do it...

In this example, we will see how to use the coroutine mechanism of Asyncio to simulate a finite state machine of five states. A **finite state machine or automaton (FSA)** is a mathematical model that is widely used not only in engineering disciplines, but also in sciences, such as mathematics and computer science. The automata through which we want to simulate the behavior is as follows:

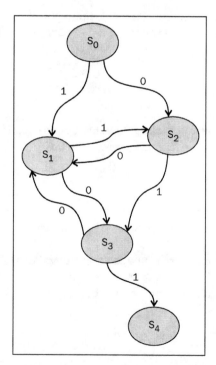

Finite state machine

In the preceding diagram, we have indicated with **S0, S1, S2, S3**, and **S4** the states of the system. Here, **0** and **1** are the values for which the automata can pass from one state to the next (this operation is called a transition). So for example, the state **S0** can be passed to the state **S1** only for the value **1** and **S0** can be passed to the state **S2** only for the value **0**. The Python code that follows, simulates a transition of the automaton from the state **S0**, the so-called **Start State**, up to the state **S4**, the **End State**:

```
#Asyncio Finite State Machine

import asyncio
import time
from random import randint


@asyncio.coroutine
def StartState():
    print ("Start State called \n")
    input_value = randint(0,1)
    time.sleep(1)
    if (input_value == 0):
        result = yield from State2(input_value)
    else :
        result = yield from State1(input_value)
    print("Resume of the Transition : \nStart State calling "\
            + result)


@asyncio.coroutine
def State1(transition_value):
    outputValue =  str(("State 1 with transition value = %s \n"\
                        %(transition_value)))
    input_value = randint(0,1)
    time.sleep(1)
    print("...Evaluating...")
    if (input_value == 0):
        result =  yield from State3(input_value)
    else :
        result = yield from State2(input_value)
    result = "State 1 calling " + result
    return (outputValue + str(result))


@asyncio.coroutine
def State2(transition_value):
```

```
            outputValue =  str(("State 2 with transition value = %s \n" \
                              %(transition_value)))
            input_value = randint(0,1)
            time.sleep(1)
            print("...Evaluating...")
            if (input_value == 0):
                result = yield from State1(input_value)
            else :
                result = yield from State3(input_value)
            result = "State 2 calling " + result
            return (outputValue + str(result))


@asyncio.coroutine
def State3(transition_value):
            outputValue =  str(("State 3 with transition value = %s \n" \
                              %(transition_value)))
            input_value = randint(0,1)
            time.sleep(1)
            print("...Evaluating...")
            if (input_value == 0):
                result = yield from State1(input_value)
            else :
                result = yield from EndState(input_value)
            result = "State 3 calling " + result
            return (outputValue + str(result))


@asyncio.coroutine
def EndState(transition_value):
            outputValue =  str(("End State with transition value = %s \n"\
                              %(transition_value)))
            print("...Stop Computation...")
            return (outputValue )

if __name__ == "__main__":
    print("Finite State Machine simulation with Asyncio Coroutine")
    loop = asyncio.get_event_loop()
    loop.run_until_complete(StartState())
```

After running the code, we have an output similar to this:

```
C:\Python CookBook\Chapter 4- Asynchronous Programming\codes - Chapter
4>python asyncio_state_machine.py
```

```
Finite State Machine simulation with Asyncio Coroutine
Start State called
...Evaluating...
...Evaluating...
...Evaluating...
...Evaluating...
...Evaluating...
...Evaluating...
...Evaluating...
...Evaluating...
...Evaluating...
...Evaluating...
...Evaluating...
...Evaluating...
...Stop Computation...
Resume of the Transition :
Start State calling State 1 with transition value = 1
State 1 calling State 3 with transition value = 0
State 3 calling State 1 with transition value = 0
State 1 calling State 2 with transition value = 1
State 2 calling State 3 with transition value = 1
State 3 calling State 1 with transition value = 0
State 1 calling State 2 with transition value = 1
State 2 calling State 1 with transition value = 0
State 1 calling State 3 with transition value = 0
State 3 calling State 1 with transition value = 0
State 1 calling State 2 with transition value = 1
State 2 calling State 3 with transition value = 1
State 3 calling End State with transition value = 1
```

How it works...

Each state of the automata has been defined with the following annotation:

```
@asyncio.coroutine
```

For example, the state S0 is defined as:

```
@asyncio.coroutine
def StartState():
    print ("Start State called \n")
    input_value = randint(0,1)
```

```
time.sleep(1)
if (input_value == 0):
    result = yield from State2(input_value)
else :
    result = yield from State1(input_value)
```

The transition to the next state is determined by `input_value`, which is defined by the `randint(0,1)` function of Python's module `random`. This function provides randomly the value 0 or 1. In this manner, it randomly determines to which state the finite state machine will be passed:

```
input_value = randint(0,1)
```

After determining the value at which state the finite state machine will be passed, the coroutine calls the next coroutine using the command `yield` from:

```
if (input_value == 0):
        result = yield from State2(input_value)
    else :
        result = yield from State1(input_value)
```

The variable result is the value that each coroutine returns. It is a string, and by the end of the computation, we can reconstruct the transition from the initial state of the automation, the Start State, up to the final state, the End State.

The main program starts the evaluation inside the event loop as:

```
if __name__ == "__main__":
    print("Finite State Machine simulation with Asyncio Coroutine")
    loop = asyncio.get_event_loop()
    loop.run_until_complete(StartState())
```

Task manipulation with Asyncio

Asyncio is designed to handle asynchronous processes and concurrent task executions on an event loop. It also provides us with the `asyncio.Task()` class for the purpose of wrapping coroutines in a task. Its use is to allow independently running tasks to run concurrently with other tasks on the same event loop. When a coroutine is wrapped in a task, it connects the task to the event loop and then runs automatically when the loop is started, thus providing a mechanism to automatically drive the coroutine.

Getting ready

The Asyncio module provides us with the `asyncio.Task(coroutine)` method to handle computations with tasks. It schedules the execution of a coroutine. A task is responsible for the execution of a coroutine object in an event loop. If the wrapped coroutine yields from a future, the task suspends the execution of the wrapped coroutine and waits for the completion of the future.

When the future is complete, the execution of the wrapped coroutine restarts with the result or the exception of the future. Also, we must note that an event loop only runs one task at a time. Other tasks may run parallelly if other event loops run in different threads. While a task waits for the completion of a future, the event loop executes a new task.

How to do it...

In the following sample code, we've shown you how three mathematical functions can be executed concurrently by the `Asyncio.Task()` statement:

```python
"""
Asyncio using Asyncio.Task to execute three math function in parallel
"""
import asyncio

@asyncio.coroutine
def factorial(number):
    f = 1
    for i in range(2, number+1):
        print("Asyncio.Task: Compute factorial(%s)" % (i))
        yield from asyncio.sleep(1)
        f *= i
    print("Asyncio.Task - factorial(%s) = %s" % (number, f))


@asyncio.coroutine
def fibonacci(number):
    a, b = 0, 1
    for i in range(number):
        print("Asyncio.Task: Compute fibonacci (%s)" % (i))
        yield from asyncio.sleep(1)
        a, b = b, a + b
    print("Asyncio.Task - fibonacci(%s) = %s" % (number, a))
```

```
@asyncio.coroutine
def binomialCoeff(n, k):
    result = 1
    for i in range(1, k+1):
        result = result * (n-i+1) / i
        print("Asyncio.Task: Compute binomialCoeff (%s)" % (i))
        yield from asyncio.sleep(1)
    print("Asyncio.Task - binomialCoeff(%s , %s) = \
                    %s" % (n,k,result))


if __name__ == "__main__":
    tasks = [asyncio.Task(factorial(10)),
             asyncio.Task(fibonacci(10)),
             asyncio.Task(binomialCoeff(20,10))]
    loop = asyncio.get_event_loop()
    loop.run_until_complete(asyncio.wait(tasks))
    loop.close()
```

The result of the preceding code is:

```
C:\ Python CookBook \Chapter 4- Asynchronous Programming\codes -
Chapter 4> python asyncio_Task.py
Asyncio.Task: Compute factorial(2)
Asyncio.Task: Compute fibonacci(0)
Asyncio.Task: Compute binomialCoeff (1)
Asyncio.Task: Compute factorial(3)
Asyncio.Task: Compute fibonacci (1)
Asyncio.Task: Compute binomialCoeff (2)
Asyncio.Task: Compute factorial(4)
Asyncio.Task: Compute fibonacci (2)
Asyncio.Task: Compute binomialCoeff (3)
Asyncio.Task: Compute factorial(5)
Asyncio.Task: Compute fibonacci (3)
Asyncio.Task: Compute binomialCoeff (4)
Asyncio.Task: Compute factorial(6)
Asyncio.Task: Compute fibonacci (4)
Asyncio.Task: Compute binomialCoeff (5)
Asyncio.Task: Compute factorial(7)
Asyncio.Task: Compute fibonacci (5)
Asyncio.Task: Compute binomialCoeff (6)
Asyncio.Task: Compute factorial(8)
Asyncio.Task: Compute fibonacci (6)
Asyncio.Task: Compute binomialCoeff (7)
Asyncio.Task: Compute factorial(9)
Asyncio.Task: Compute fibonacci (7)
```

```
Asyncio.Task: Compute binomialCoeff (8)
Asyncio.Task: Compute factorial(10)
Asyncio.Task: Compute fibonacci (8)
Asyncio.Task: Compute binomialCoeff (9)
Asyncio.Task - factorial(10) = 3628800
Asyncio.Task: Compute fibonacci (9)
Asyncio.Task: Compute binomialCoeff (10)
Asyncio.Task - fibonacci(10) = 55
Asyncio.Task - binomialCoeff(20 , 10) = 184756.0
```

How it works...

In this example, we defined three `coroutines`, `factorial`, `fibonacci`, and `binomialCoeff` each of which, as explained previously, is identified by the `@asyncio.coroutine` decorator:

```
@asyncio.coroutine
def factorial(number):
do Something

@asyncio.coroutine
def fibonacci(number):
do Something

@asyncio.coroutine
def binomialCoeff(n, k):
do Something
```

To perform these three tasks parallelly, we first put them in the list tasks, in the following manner:

```
if __name__ == "__main__":
    tasks = [asyncio.Task(factorial(10)),
             asyncio.Task(fibonacci(10)),
             asyncio.Task(binomialCoeff(20,10))]
```

Then, we get the `event_loop`:

```
loop = asyncio.get_event_loop()
```

Next, we run the tasks:

```
loop.run_until_complete(asyncio.wait(tasks))
```

Here, `asyncio.wait statement (tasks)` waits for the given coroutines to complete.

In the last statement, we close the event loop:

```
loop.close()
```

Dealing with Asyncio and Futures

Another key component of the Asyncio module is the `Future` class. This is very similar to `concurrent.futures.Futures`, but of course, it is adapted in the main mechanism of Asyncio's event loop. The `asyncio.Future` class represents a result (but can also be an exception) that is not yet available. It therefore represents an abstraction of something that is yet to be accomplished.

Callbacks that have to process any results are in fact added to the instances of this class.

Getting ready

To manage an object `Future` in Asyncio, we must declare the following:

```
import asyncio
future = asyncio.Future()
```

The basic methods of this class are:

- ▶ `cancel()`: This cancels the future and schedules callbacks
- ▶ `result()`: This returns the result that this future represents
- ▶ `exception()`: This returns the exception that was set on this future
- ▶ `add_done_callback(fn)`: This adds a callback that is to be run when `future` is executed
- ▶ `remove_done_callback(fn)`: This removes all instances of a callback from the "call when done" list
- ▶ `set_result(result)`: This marks the future as complete and sets its result
- ▶ `set_exception(exception)`: This marks the future as complete and sets an exception

How to do it...

The following example shows you how to use the `Futures` class for the management of two
coroutines `first_coroutine` and `second_coroutine` that perform the tasks, such as the
sum of the first *n* integers and second the factorial of *n*. The code is as follows:

```python
"""
Asyncio.Futures -   Chapter 4 Asynchronous Programming
"""
import asyncio
import sys

#SUM OF N INTEGERS
@asyncio.coroutine
def first_coroutine(future,N):
    count = 0
    for i in range(1,N+1):
        count=count + i
    yield from asyncio.sleep(4)
    future.set_result("first coroutine (sum of N integers) result = "\
                    + str(count))


#FACTORIAL(N)
@asyncio.coroutine
def second_coroutine(future,N):
    count = 1
    for i in range(2, N+1):
        count *= i
    yield from asyncio.sleep(3)
    future.set_result("second coroutine (factorial) result = "\
                    + str(count))

def got_result(future):
    print(future.result())
```

```
if __name__ == "__main__":
    N1 = int(sys.argv[1])
    N2 = int(sys.argv[2])

    loop = asyncio.get_event_loop()
    future1 = asyncio.Future()
    future2 = asyncio.Future()

    tasks = [
        first_coroutine(future1,N1),
        second_coroutine(future2,N2)]

    future1.add_done_callback(got_result)
    future2.add_done_callback(got_result)

    loop.run_until_complete(asyncio.wait(tasks))
    loop.close()
```

The following output is obtained after multiple runs:

```
C:\Python CookBook\Chapter 4- Asynchronous Programming\codes - Chapter
4>python Asyncio_future.py 1 1
first coroutine (sum of N integers) result = 1
second coroutine (factorial) result = 1

C:\Python CookBook\Chapter 4- Asynchronous Programming\codes - Chapter
4>python Asyncio_future.py 2 2
first coroutine (sum of N integers) result = 3
second coroutine (factorial) result = 2

C:\ Python CookBook\Chapter 4- Asynchronous Programming\codes -
Chapter 4>python Asyncio_future.py 3 3
first coroutine (sum of N integers) result = 6
second coroutine (factorial) result = 6

C:\ Python CookBook\Chapter 4- Asynchronous Programming\codes -
Chapter 4>python Asyncio_future.py 5 5
first coroutine (sum of N integers) result = 15
second coroutine (factorial) result = 120
```

How it works...

In the main program, we define the objects' future to associate the coroutines:

```
if __name__ == "__main__":

future1 = asyncio.Future()
future2 = asyncio.Future()
```

While defining the tasks, we pass the object future as an argument of coroutines:

```
tasks = [first_coroutine(future1,N1),
          second_coroutine(future2,N2)]
```

Finally, we add a callback that is to be run when the `future` gets executed:

```
future1.add_done_callback(got_result)
future2.add_done_callback(got_result)
```

Here, `got_result` is a function that prints the final result of the future:

```
def got_result(future):
    print(future.result())
```

In the coroutine wherein we pass the object future as an argument, after the computation, we set a sleep time of 3 seconds for the first coroutine and 4 seconds for the second coroutine:

```
yield from asyncio.sleep(sleep_time)
```

Then, we mark the future as complete and set its result with the help of `future.set_result()`.

There's more...

Swapping the sleep time between the coroutines, we invert the output results (we first do that for the second coroutine output):

```
C:\Python CookBook\Chapter 4- Asynchronous Programming\codes - Chapter
4>python Asyncio_future.py 1 10
second coroutine (factorial) result = 3628800
first coroutine (sum of N integers) result = 1
```

5
Distributed Python

In this chapter, we will cover the following recipes:

- ▸ Using Celery to distribute tasks
- ▸ How to create a task with Celery
- ▸ Scientific computing with SCOOP
- ▸ Handling map functions with SCOOP
- ▸ Remote method invocation with Pyro4
- ▸ Chaining objects with Pyro4
- ▸ Developing a client-server application with Pyro4
- ▸ Communicating sequential processes with PyCSP
- ▸ Using MapReduce with Disco
- ▸ A remote procedure call with RPyC

Introduction

The basic idea of distributed computing is to break each workload into an arbitrary number of tasks, usually indicated with the name, into reasonable pieces for which a computer in a distributed network will be able to finish and return the results flawlessly. In distributed computing, there is the absolute certainty that the machines on your network are always available (latency difference, unpredictable crash or network computers, and so on). So, you need a continuous monitoring architecture.

The fundamental problem that arises from the use of this kind of technology is mainly focused on the proper management of traffic (that is devoid of errors both in transmission and reception) of any kind (data, jobs, commands, and so on). Further, a problem stems from a fundamental characteristic of distributed computing: the coexistence in the network of machines that support different operating systems which are often incompatible with others. In fact, the need to actually use the multiplicity of resources in a distributed environment has, over time, led to the identification of different calculation models. Their goal is essentially to provide a framework for the description of the cooperation between the processes of a distributed application. We can say that, basically, the different models are distinguished according to a greater or lesser capacity to use the opportunities provided by the distribution. The most widely used model is the client-server model. It allows processes located on different computers to cooperate in real time through the exchange of messages, thereby achieving a significant improvement over the previous model, which requires the transfer of all the files, in which computations are performed on the data offline. The client-server model is typically implemented through remote procedure calls, which extend the scope of a local call, or through the paradigm of distributed objects (Object-Oriented Middleware).This chapter will then present some of the solutions proposed by Python for the implementation of these computing architectures. We will then describe the libraries that implement distributed architectures using the OO approach and remote calls, such as Celery, SCOOP, Pyro4, and RPyC, but also using different approaches, such as PyCSP and Disco, which are the Python equivalent of the MapReduce algorithm.

Using Celery to distribute tasks

Celery is a Python framework used to manage a distributed task, following the Object-Oriented Middleware approach. Its main feature consists of handling many small tasks and distributing them on a large number of computational nodes. Finally, the result of each task will then be reworked in order to compose the overall solution.

To work with Celery, we need the following components:

- The Celery module (of course!!)
- A message broker. This is a Celery-independent software component, the middleware, used to send and receive messages to distributed task workers. A message broker is also known as a message middleware. It deals with the exchange of messages in a communication network. The addressing scheme of this type of middleware is no longer of the point-to-point type but is a message-oriented addressing scheme. The best known is the Publish/Subscribe paradigm.

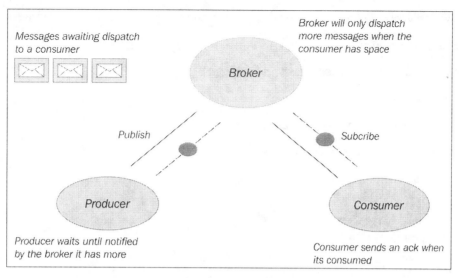

The message broker architecture

Celery supports many types of message brokers—the most complete of which are RabbitMQ and Redis.

How to do it...

To install Celery, we use the `pip` installer. In Command Prompt, just type the following:

```
pip install celery
```

After this, we must install the message broker. There are several choices available for us to do this, but in our examples, we use RabbitMQ, which is a message-oriented middleware (also called broker messaging), that implements the **Advanced Message Queuing Protocol** (**AMQP**). The RabbitMQ server is written in Erlang, and it is based on the **Open Telecom Platform** (**OTP**) framework for the management of clustering and failover. To install RabbitMQ, download and run Erlang (`http://www.erlang.org/download.html`), and then just download and run the RabbitMQ installer (`http://www.rabbitmq.com/download.html`). It takes a few minutes to download and will set up RabbitMQ and run it as a service with a default configuration.

Finally, we install Flower (`http://flower.readthedocs.org`), which is a web-based tool used to monitor tasks (running progress, task details, and graphs and stats).

To install it, just type the following from Command Prompt:

```
pip install -U flower
```

Then, we can verify the Celery installation. In Command Prompt, just type the following:

```
C:\celery --version
```

After this, the text shown as follows should appear:

```
3.1.18 (Cipater)
```

The usage of Celery is pretty simple, as shown:

```
Usage: celery <command> [options]
```

Here, the options are as shown:

```
Options:
  -A APP, --app=APP       app instance to use (e.g. module.attr_name)
  -b BROKER, --broker=BROKER
                          url to broker.  default is 'amqp://guest@
localhost//'
  --loader=LOADER         name of custom loader class to use.
  --config=CONFIG         Name of the configuration module
  --workdir=WORKING_DIRECTORY
                          Optional directory to change to after
detaching.
  -C, --no-color
  -q, --quiet
  --version               show program's version number and exit
  -h, --help              show this help message and exit
```

See also

▸ For more complete details about the Celery installation procedure, you can visit `www.celeryproject.com`

How to create a task with Celery

In this recipe, we'll show you how to create and call a task using the Celery module. Celery provides the following methods that make a call to a task:

▸ `apply_async(args[, kwargs[, …]])`: This task sends a task message

▸ `delay(*args, **kwargs)`: This is a shortcut to send a task message, but does not support execution options

The `delay` method is better to use because it can be called as a regular function:

```
task.delay(arg1, arg2, kwarg1='x', kwarg2='y')
```

While using `apply_async` you should write:

```
task.apply_async (args=[arg1, arg2] kwargs={'kwarg1': 'x','kwarg2':
'y'})
```

How to do it...

To perform this simple task, we implement the following two simple scripts:

```
###
## addTask.py :Executing a simple task
###

from celery import Celery

app = Celery('addTask',broker='amqp://guest@localhost//')

@app.task
def add(x, y):
    return x + y
while the second script is :

###
#addTask.py : RUN the AddTask example with
###

import addTask

if __name__ == '__main__':
    result = addTask.add.delay(5,5)
```

We must note again that the RabbitMQ service starts automatically on our server upon installation. So, to execute the Celery worker server, we simply type the following command from Command Prompt:

```
celery -A addTask worker --loglevel=info
```

The output is shown in the first Command Prompt:

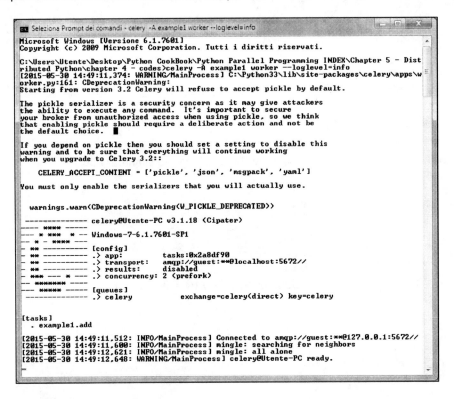

Let's note the warnings in the output to disable pickle as a serializer for security concerns. The default serialization format is pickle simply because it is convenient (it supports the task of sending complex Python objects as task arguments). Whether you use pickle or not, you may want to turn off this warning by setting the CELERY_ACCEPT_CONTENT configuration variable; for reference, take a look at http://celery.readthedocs.org/en/latest/configuration.html.

Now, we launch the addTask_main script from a second Command Prompt:

Finally, the result from the first Command Prompt should be like this:

```
[2015-05-30 15:19:37,123: INFO/MainProcess] Connected to amqp://guest:**@127.0.0.1:5672//
[2015-05-30 15:19:37,231: INFO/MainProcess] mingle: searching for neighbors
[2015-05-30 15:19:38,248: INFO/MainProcess] mingle: all alone
[2015-05-30 15:19:38,296: WARNING/MainProcess] celery@Utente-PC ready.
[2015-05-30 15:19:43,466: INFO/MainProcess] Received task: addTask.add[2c8af4c3-929a-4a38-9582-8d53b062eb0f]
[2015-05-30 15:19:43,468: INFO/MainProcess] Task addTask.add[2c8af4c3-929a-4a38-9582-8d53b062eb0f] succeeded in 0s: 10
[2015-05-30 15:31:29,545: INFO/MainProcess] Received task: addTask.add[4b076fa4-18c9-4d9e-9a6d-b0bd6f378e0a]
[2015-05-30 15:31:29,548: INFO/MainProcess] Task addTask.add[4b076fa4-18c9-4d9e-9a6d-b0bd6f378e0a] succeeded in 0s: 10
[2015-05-30 15:31:42,140: INFO/MainProcess] Received task: addTask.add[fe391d19-a89f-400a-af21-d7ff79cdd775]
[2015-05-30 15:31:42,144: INFO/MainProcess] Task addTask.add[fe391d19-a89f-400a-af21-d7ff79cdd775] succeeded in 0s: 10
```

The result is `10` (you can read it in the last line), as we expected.

How it works...

Let's focus on the first script, `addTask.py`. In the first two lines of code, we create a Celery application instance that uses the RabbitMQ service ad broker:

```
from celery import Celery
app = Celery('addTask', broker='amqp://guest@localhost//')
```

The first argument in the Celery function is the name of the current module (`addTask.py`) and the second argument is the broker keyboard argument, which indicates the URL used to connect the broker (RabbitMQ). Then, we introduce the task. Each task must be added with the annotation (decorator) `@app.task`.

The decorator helps Celery to identify which functions can be scheduled in the task queue. After the decorator, we create the task that the workers can execute. Our first task will be a simple function that performs the sum of two numbers:

```
@app.task
def add(x, y):
    return x + y
```

In the second script, `AddTask_main.py`, we call our task by using the `delay()` method:

```
if __name__ == '__main__':
    result = addTask.add.delay(5,5)
```

Let's remember that this method is a shortcut to the `apply_async()` method, which gives us greater control of the task execution.

There's more...

If RabbitMQ operates under its default configuration, Celery can connect with no other information other than `amqp://scheme`.

Scientific computing with SCOOP

Scalable Concurrent Operations in Python (**SCOOP**) is a Python module to distribute concurrent tasks (called **Futures**) on heterogeneous computational nodes. Its architecture is based on the **ØMQ** package, which provides a way to manage Futures between the distributed systems. The main application of SCOOP resides in scientific computing that requires the execution of many distributed tasks using all the computational resources available.

To distribute its futures, SCOOP uses a variation of the broker patterns:

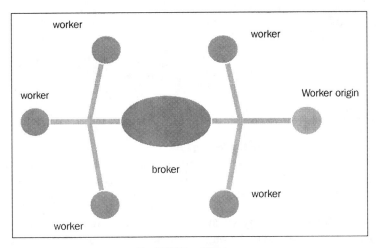

The SCOOP architecture

The central element of the communication system is the broker that interacts with all the independent workers to dispatch messages between them. The Futures are created in the worker elements instead of the central node (the broker) with a centralized serialization procedure. This makes the topology architecture more reliable and makes performance better. In fact, the broker's main workload consists of networking and interprocess I/O between workers with relatively low CPU processing time.

Getting ready

The SCOOP module is available at `https://github.com/soravux/scoop/` and its software dependencies are as follows:

- ▸ Python >= 2.6 or >= 3.2
- ▸ Distribute >= 0.6.2 or setuptools >= 0.7
- ▸ Greenlet >= 0.3.4
- ▸ pyzmq >= 13.1.0 and libzmq >= 3.2.0
- ▸ SSH for remote execution

SCOOP can be installed on Linux, Mac, and Windows machines. Like Disco, its remote usage requires an SSH software, and it must be enabled as a password-less authentication between every computing node. For a complete reference about the SCOOP installation procedure, you can read the information guide at `http://scoop.readthedocs.org/en/0.7/install.html`.

On a Windows machine, you can install SCOOP simply by typing the following command:

```
pip install SCOOP
```

Otherwise, you can type the following command from SCOOP's distribution directory:

```
Python setup.py install
```

How to do it...

SCOOP is a library full of functionality that is primarily used in scientific computing problems. Among the methods used to find a solution to these problems that are computationally expensive, there is the Monte Carlo algorithm. A complete discussion of this method would take up many pages of a book, but in this example, we want to show you how to parallelize a Monte Carlo method for the solution of the following problem, the calculation of the number π, using the features of SCOOP. So, let's consider the following code:

```
import math
from random import random
from scoop import futures
from time import time
```

```
def evaluate_number_of_points_in_unit_circle(attempts):
    points_fallen_in_unit_disk = 0
    for i in range (0,attempts) :
        x = random()
        y = random()
        radius = math.sqrt(x*x + y*y)
        #the test is ok if the point fall in the unit circle
        if radius < 1 :
            #if ok the number of points in a disk is increased
            points_fallen_in_unit_disk = \
                    points_fallen_in_unit_disk + 1
    return points_fallen_in_unit_disk


def pi_calculus_with_Montecarlo_Method(workers, attempts):
    print("number of workers %i - number of attempts %i"
%(workers,attempts))
    bt = time()
    #in this point we call scoop.futures.map function
    #the evaluate_number_of_points_in_unit_circle \
    #function is executed in an asynchronously way
    #and several call this function can be made concurrently
    evaluate_task = \
                futures.map(evaluate_points_in_circle,
                        [attempts] * workers)
    taskresult= sum(evaluate_task)
    print ("%i points fallen in a unit disk after " \
            %(Taskresult/attempts))
    piValue = (4. * Taskresult/ float(workers * attempts))

    computationalTime = time() - bt
    print("value of pi = " + str(piValue))
    print ("error percentage = " + \
            str((((abs(piValue - math.pi)) * 100) / math.pi)))
    print("total time: " + str(computationalTime))

if __name__ == "__main__":
    for i in range (1,4):
        #let's fix the numbers of workers...only two,
        #but it could be much greater
        pi_calculus_with_Montecarlo_Method(i*1000, i*1000)
        print(" ")
```

To run a SCOOP program, you must open Command Prompt and type the following instructions:

```
python -m scoop name_file.py
```

For our script, we'll expect output like this:

```
C:\Python CookBook\Chapter 5 - Distributed Python\chapter 5 -
codes>python -m scoop pi_calculus_with_montecarlo_method.py
[2015-06-01 15:16:32,685] launcher  INFO    SCOOP 0.7.2 dev on win32
using Python 3.3.0 (v3.3.0:bd8afb90e
bf2, Sep 29 2012, 10:55:48) [MSC v.1600 32 bit (Intel)], API: 1013
[2015-06-01 15:16:32,685] launcher  INFO    Deploying 2 worker(s) over 1
host(s).
[2015-06-01 15:16:32,685] launcher  INFO    Worker d--istribution:
[2015-06-01 15:16:32,686] launcher  INFO       127.0.0.1:      1 +
origin
Launching 2 worker(s) using an unknown shell.
number of workers 1000 - number of attempts 1000
785 points fallen in a unit disk after
value of pi = 3.140636
error percentage = 0.03045122952842962
total time: 10.258585929870605


number of workers 2000 - number of attempts 2000
1570 points fallen in a unit disk after
value of pi = 3.141976
error percentage = 0.012202295220195048
total time: 20.451170206069946


number of workers 3000 - number of attempts 3000
2356 points fallen in a unit disk after
value of pi = 3.1413777777777776
error percentage = 0.006839709526630775
total time: 32.3558509349823


[2015-06-01 15:17:36,894] launcher  (127.0.0.1:59239) INFO    Root
process is done.
[2015-06-01 15:17:36,896] launcher  (127.0.0.1:59239) INFO    Finished
cleaning spawned subprocesses.
```

The correct value of pi becomes more precise as we increase the number of attempts and workers.

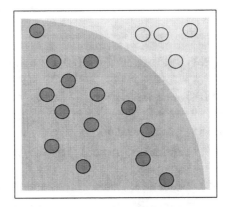

Monte Carlo evaluation of π: counting points inside the circle

How it works...

The code presented in the preceding section is just one of the many implementations of the Monte Carlo method for the calculation of π. The evaluate_ points_in_circle () function is taken randomly and then given a point of coordinates (x, y), and then it is determined whether or not this point falls within the circle of the unit area.

Whenever the points_fallen_in_unit_disk condition is verified, the variable is incremented. When the inner loop of the function ends, it will represent the total number of points falling within the circle. This number is sufficient to calculate the value of pi. In fact, the probability that the point falls within the circumference is π / 4, that is the ratio between the area of the unit circle, equal to π and the area of the circumscribed square equal to 4.

So, by calculating the ratio between the number of points fallen inside the disc, taskresult, and the number of shots made, *workers * attempts*, you obtain an approximation of π/4 and of course, also of the number π:

```
piValue = ( 4. * taskresult / float (workers attempts *))
```

The SCOOP function is as shown:

```
futures.map (evaluate_points_in_circle, [attempts] * workers)
```

This takes care of distributing the computational load between the available workers and at the same time, collects all the results. It executes evaluate_points_in_circle in an asynchronous way and makes several calls to evaluate_points_in_circle concurrently.

Handling map functions with SCOOP

A common task that is very useful when dealing with lists or other sequences of data is to apply the same operation to each element of the list and then collect the result. For example, a list update may be done in the following way from the Python IDLE:

```
>>>items = [1,2,3,4,5,6,7,8,9,10]
>>>updated_items = []
>>>for x in items:
>>>    updated_items.append(x*2)


>>> updated_items
>>>  [2, 4, 6, 8, 10, 12, 14, 16, 18, 20]
```

This is a common operation. However, Python has a built-in feature that does most of the work.

The Python function map (aFunction, aSequence) applies a passed-in function to each item in an iterable object and returns a list containing all the function call results. Now, the same example would be:

```
>>>items = [1,2,3,4,5,6,7,8,9,10]
>>>def multiplyFor2(x):return x*2
>>>print(list(map(multiplyFor2,items)))
>>>[2, 4, 6, 8, 10, 12, 14, 16, 18, 20]
```

Here, we passed in the map function the user-defined function multiplyFor2. It is applied to each item in the items list, and finally, we collect the result in a new list that is printed.

Also, we can pass in a lambda function (a function defined and called without being bound to an identifier) as an argument instead of a function. The same example now becomes:

```
>>>items = [1,2,3,4,5,6,7,8,9,10]
>>>print(list(map(lambda x:x*2,items)))
>>>[2, 4, 6, 8, 10, 12, 14, 16, 18, 20]
```

The map built-in function has performance benefits because it is faster than a manually coded for loop.

Getting ready

The SCOOP Python modules define more than one map function that allow asynchronous computation that could be propagated to its workers. These functions are:

- ▶ `futures.map((func, iterables, kargs)`: This returns a generator that iterates the results in the same order as its inputs. It can thus act as a parallel substitute for the standard Python `map()` function.

- ▶ `futures.map_as_completed(func, iterables, kargs)`: This will yield results as soon as they are made available.

- ▶ `futures. scoop.futures.mapReduce(mapFunc, reductionOp, iterables, kargs)`: This allows us to parallelize a reduction function after we apply the `map()` function. It returns a single element.

How to do it...

In this example, we'll compare the `MapReduce` version of SCOOP with its serial implementation:

```
"""
Compare SCOOP MapReduce with a serial implementation
"""
import operator
import time

from scoop import futures


def simulateWorkload(inputData):
    time.sleep(0.01)
    return sum(inputData)

def CompareMapReduce():
    mapScoopTime = time.time()
    res = futures.mapReduce(
        simulateWorkload,
        operator.add,
        list([a] * a for a in range(1000)),
    )
    mapScoopTime = time.time() - mapScoopTime
    print("futures.map in SCOOP executed in {0:.3f}s \
            with result:{1}".format(
```

```
                mapScoopTime,
                res
                )
            )


        mapPythonTime = time.time()
        res = sum(
            map(
                simulateWorkload,
                list([a] * a for a in range(1000))
            )
        )
        mapPythonTime = time.time() - mapPythonTime
        print("map Python executed in: {0:.3f}s \
                with result: {1}".format(
            mapPythonTime,
            res
            )
        )


    if __name__ == '__main__':
        CompareMapReduce()
```

To evaluate the script, you must type the following command:

```
python -m scoop map_reduce.py
```

```
> [2015-06-12 20:13:25,602] launcher  INFO    SCOOP 0.7.2 dev on win32
using Python 3.4.3 (v3.4.3:9b73f1c3e601, Feb 24 2015, 22:43:06) [MSC
v.1600 32 bit (Intel)], API: 1013
[2015-06-12 20:13:25,602] launcher  INFO Deploying 2 worker(s) over 1
host(s).
[2015-06-12 20:13:25,602] launcher  INFO Worker d--istribution:
[2015-06-12 20:13:25,602] launcher  INFO 127.0.0.1:       1 + origin
Launching 2 worker(s) using an unknown shell.
futures.map in SCOOP executed in 8.459s with result: 332833500
map Python executed in: 10.034s with result: 332833500
[2015-06-12 20:13:45,344] launcher  (127.0.0.1:2559) INFO    Root process
is done.
[2015-06-12 20:13:45,368] launcher  (127.0.0.1:2559) INFO    Finished
cleaning spawned subprocesses.
```

How it works...

In this example, we compare the SCOOP implementation of the `MapReduce` function with the serial implementation. The core of the script is the `CompareMapReduce()` function that contains the two implementations. Also in this function, we evaluate the execution time according to the following schema:

```
mapScoopTime = tme.time()
        #Run SCOOP MapReduce
mapScoopTime = time.time() - mapScoopTime

mapPythonTime = time.time()
        #Run serial MapReduce
mapPythonTime = time.time() - mapPythonTime
```

Then in the output, we report the resulting time:

```
futures.map in SCOOP executed in 8.459s with result: 332833500
map Python executed in: 10.034s with result: 332833500
```

To obtain the comparable execution time, we simulate a computational workload that introduces a `time.sleep` statement in the `simulatedWordload` function:

```
def simulateWorkload(inputData, chose=None):
    time.sleep(0.01)
    return sum(inputData)
```

The SCOOP implementation of `mapReduce` is as follows:

```
res = futures.mapReduce(
        simulateWorkload,
        operator.add,
        list([a] * a for a in range(1000)),
    )
```

The `futures-mapReduce` function has the following arguments:

- ▶ `simulateWork`: This will be called to execute the Futures. We also need to remember that a callable must return a value.

- ▶ `operator.add`: This will be called to reduce the Futures results. However, it also must support two parameters and return a single value.

- ▶ `list(......)`: This is the iterable object that will be passed to the callable object as a separate Future.

The serial implementation of `mapReduce` is, as follows:

```
res = sum(
    map(
        simulateWorkload,
        list([a] * a for a in range(1000))
    )
)
```

The Python standard `map()` function has two arguments: the `simulateWorkload` function and the `list()` iterable object. However, to reduce the result, we used the Python function `sum`.

Remote Method Invocation with Pyro4

Python Remote Objects (**Pyro4**) is a library that resembles Java's **Remote Method Invocation** (**RMI**), which allows you to invoke a method of a remote object (that belongs to a different process and is potentially on a different machine) almost as if the object were local (that is, it belonged to the same process in which it runs the invocation). In this sense, the Remote Method Invocation technology can be traced from a conceptual point of view. The idea of a **remote procedure call** (**RPC**) is reformulated for the object-oriented paradigm (in which, of course, the procedures are replaced by methods). The use of a mechanism for remote method invocation in an object-oriented system entails the significant advantages of uniformity and symmetry in the project, since it allows us to model the interactions between distributed processes using the same conceptual tool that is used to represent the interactions between the different objects of an application or the method call.

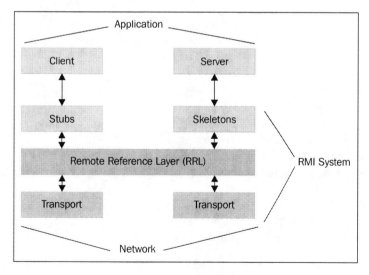

Remote Method Invocation

As you can see from the preceding figure, Pyro4 allows us to manage and distribute objects in the client-server style. This means that the main parts of a Pyro4 system may switch from a client called to a remote object to an object called to serve a function. It is important to note that during the remote calling, there are always two distinct parts that a client and server accepts and executes the client call. Finally, the entire management of this mechanism is provided by Pyro4 in a distributed way.

Getting ready

The installation procedure is quite simple with the pip installer; from your command shell, type: `pip install pyro`.

Otherwise, you can download the complete package from `https://github.com/irmen/Pyro4` and install the package with the Python `setup.py` install command from the package directory.

For our examples, we'll use a Python3.3 distro on a Windows machine.

How to do it...

In this example, we'll see how to build and use a simple client-server communication using the Pyro4 middleware. So, we must have two Python scripts.

The code for the server (`server.py`) is:

```
import Pyro4

class Server(object):
    def welcomeMessage(self, name):
        return ("Hi welcome " + str (name))

def startServer():
    server = Server()
    daemon = Pyro4.Daemon()
    ns = Pyro4.locateNS()
    uri = daemon.register(server)
    ns.register("server", uri)
    print("Ready. Object uri =", uri)
    daemon.requestLoop()

    if __name__ == "__main__":
        startServer()
```

The code for the client (`client.py`) is as follows:

```python
import Pyro4

uri = input("What is the Pyro uri of the greeting object? ").strip()
name = input("What is your name? ").strip()
server = Pyro4.Proxy("PYRONAME:server")
print(server.welcomeMessage(name))
```

To run the example, we need a Pyro name server running. To do this, you can type the following command from Command Prompt:

```
python  -m Pyro4.naming
```

After this, you'll see the following message:

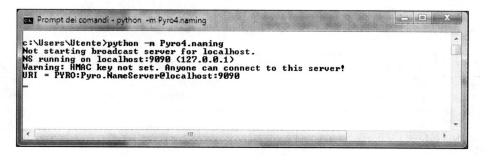

This means that the name server is running in your network. Then, you can start the server and the client scripts in two separate console windows. To run the server, just type the following:

python server.py

Now, you'll see something similar to what is shown in the following screenshot:

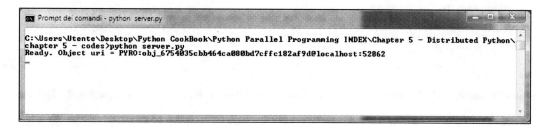

To run the client, just type:

python client.py

After this, a message like this will appear:

insert the PYRO4 server URI (help : PYRONAME:server)

After the correct insertion, you must insert the name of the Pyro4 server, that is, PYRONAME:server:

insert the PYRO4 server URI (help : PYRONAME:server) PYRONAME:server

You'll see the following message asking you to type your name:

What is your name? Rashmi

Finally, you'll see a welcome message, Hi welcome Rashmi, as shown in the following screenshot:

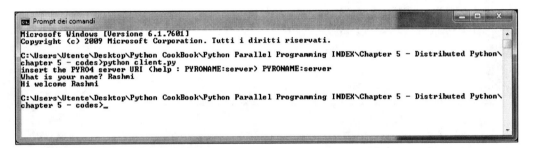

How it works...

The server contains the object (the Server class) that can be accessed remotely. In our example, this object only has the welcomeMessage() method that returns a string with the name inserted in the client session:

```
class Server(object):
    def welcomeMessage(self, name):
        return ("Hi welcome " + str (name))
```

To start the server (the startServer() function), we must follow some simple steps:

1. Build the instance (named server) of the Server class: server = Server().

2. Make a Pyro daemon: `daemon = Pyro4.Daemon()`. Pyro4 uses daemon objects to dispatch incoming calls to appropriate objects. A server must create one daemon that manages everything from its instance. Each server has a daemon that knows about all the Pyro objects that the server provides.

3. To execute this script, we have to run a Pyro name server. So, we have to locate this name server that runs: `ns = Pyro4.locateNS()`.

4. Then, we need to register the server as Pyro Object `object`. It will be known only inside the Pyro daemon: `uri = daemon.register(server)`. It returns the URI for the registered object.

5. Finally, we can register the object server with a name in the name server:

   `ns.register("server", uri)`.

6. The function ends with a call to daemon's `eventloop` method. It starts the event loop of the server and waits for calls.

The Pyro4 API enables the developer to distribute objects in a transparent way. Our client scripts send the requests to the server program to execute the `welcomeMessage()` method. The remote call is performed first by creating a Proxy object. In fact, Pyro4 clients use proxy objects to forward method calls to the remote objects and pass results back to the calling code:

```
server = Pyro4.Proxy("PYRONAME:server")
```

Now, we'll call the server's method that prints a welcome message:

```
print(server.welcomeMessage(name))
```

Chaining objects with Pyro4

In this recipe, we'll show you how to create a chain of objects, which call each other, with Pyro4. Let's suppose that we want to build a distributed architecture like this:

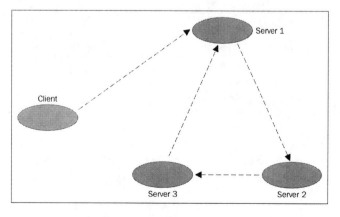

Chaining an object with Pyro4

We have four objects: a client and three servers disposed in a chain topology, as shown in the preceding figure. The client forwards a request to **Server1** and starts the chain call, forwarding the request to **Server2**. Then, it calls the next object in the chain and **Server3**. The chain call ends when **Server3** calls **Server1** again.

The example we're going to show highlights the aspects of the management of remote objects, which can be easily extended to handle more complex distributed architectures.

How to do it...

To implement a chain of objects with Pyro4, we need five Python scripts. The first one is the client (`client.py`). Here is the code for it:

```python
from __future__ import print_function
import Pyro4

obj = Pyro4.core.Proxy("PYRONAME:example.chain.A")
print("Result=%s" % obj.process(["hello"]))
```

Each server will be characterized by the parameter `this`, which identifies it in the chain, and the parameter `next`, which defines the next server (that is, subsequent to `this`) in the chain.

For a visualization of the implemented chain you can see the figure associated with this recipe.

- `server_1.py`:

```python
from __future__ import print_function
import Pyro4
import chainTopology

this = "1"
next = "2"

servername = "example.chainTopology." + this

daemon = Pyro4.core.Daemon()
obj = chainTopology.Chain(this, next)
uri = daemon.register(obj)
ns = Pyro4.naming.locateNS()
ns.register(servername, uri)

# enter the service loop.
print("server_%s started " % this)
daemon.requestLoop()
```

- server_2.py:

```python
from __future__ import print_function
import Pyro4
import chainTopology

this = "2"
next = "3"

servername = "example.chainTopology." + this

daemon = Pyro4.core.Daemon()
obj = chain.chainTopology(this, next)
uri = daemon.register(obj)
ns = Pyro4.naming.locateNS()
ns.register(servername, uri)

# enter the service loop.
print("server_%s started " % this)
daemon.requestLoop()
```

- server_3.py:

```python
from __future__ import print_function
import Pyro4
import chainTopology

this = "3"
next = "1"

servername = "example.chainTopology." + this

daemon = Pyro4.core.Daemon()
obj = chain.chainTopology(this, next)
uri = daemon.register(obj)
ns = Pyro4.naming.locateNS()
ns.register(servername, uri)

# enter the service loop.
print("server_%s started " % this)
daemon.requestLoop()
```

The last script is the `chain` object, as shown in the following code:

▸ `chainTopology.py`:

```python
from __future__ import print_function
import Pyro4

class Chain(object):
    def __init__(self, name, next):
        self.name = name
        self.nextName = next
        self.next = None

    def process(self, message):
        if self.next is None:
            self.next = Pyro4.core.Proxy("PYRONAME:example.chain." \
                                        + self.nextName)
        if self.name in message:
            print("Back at %s; the chain is closed!" % self.name)
            return ["complete at " + self.name]
        else:
            print("%s forwarding the message to the object %s" \
                    % (self.name, self.nextName))
            message.append(self.name)
            result = self.next.process(message)
            result.insert(0, "passed on from " + self.name)
            return result
```

To execute this example, start by running the Pyro4 name server:

```
C:>python -m Pyro4.naming
Not starting broadcast server for localhost.
NS running on localhost:9090 (127.0.0.1)
Warning: HMAC key not set. Anyone can connect to this server!
URI = PYRO:Pyro.NameServer@localhost:9090
```

Then, run the three servers. In three separate Command Prompts, type the `python server_name.py` command.

A message like this should appear after this for `server_1`:

```
Prompt dei comandi - python server_1.py
Microsoft Windows [Versione 6.1.7601]
Copyright (c) 2009 Microsoft Corporation. Tutti i diritti riservati.

C:\Users\Utente\Desktop\Python CookBook\Python Parallel Programming INDEX\Chapter 5 - Distributed Python\
chapter 5 - codes\chain>python server_1.py
server_1 started
```

For `server_2`, something similar to what is shown in the following screenshot will appear:

```
Prompt dei comandi - python server_2.py
C:\Users\Utente\Desktop\Python CookBook\Python Parallel Programming INDEX\Chapter 5 - Distributed Python\
chapter 5 - codes\chain>python server_2.py
server_2 started
```

A message similar to what is shown in the following screenshot should appear for `server_3`:

```
Prompt dei comandi - python server_3.py
Microsoft Windows [Versione 6.1.7601]
Copyright (c) 2009 Microsoft Corporation. Tutti i diritti riservati.

C:\Users\Utente\Desktop\Python CookBook\Python Parallel Programming INDEX\Chapter 5 - Distributed Python\
chapter 5 - codes\chain>python server_3.py
server_3 started
```

Finally, you must run the `client.py` script from another command shell:

```
Prompt dei comandi
Microsoft Windows [Versione 6.1.7601]
Copyright (c) 2009 Microsoft Corporation. Tutti i diritti riservati.

C:\Users\Utente\Desktop\Python CookBook\Python Parallel Programming INDEX\Chapter 5 - Distributed Python\
chapter 5 - codes\chain>python client.py
Result=['passed on from 1', 'passed on from 2', 'passed on from 3', 'complete at 1']
```

The preceding message shows as a result the forwarding request passed across the three servers, when it comes back to `server_1` the task is completed. Also, here, we can focus on the behavior of the object servers when the request is forwarded to the next object in the chain. To see what happens next, refer to the message below the start message in the following screenshot for `server_1`:

```
Prompt dei comandi - python server_1.py
Microsoft Windows [Versione 6.1.7601]
Copyright (c) 2009 Microsoft Corporation. Tutti i diritti riservati.

C:\Users\Utente\Desktop\Python CookBook\Python Parallel Programming INDEX\Chapter 5 - Distributed Python\
chapter 5 - codes\chain>python server_1.py
server_1 started
1 forwarding the message to the object 2
1 forwarding the message to the object 2
Back at 1; the chain is closed!
```

The result of `server_2` is as follows:

```
Prompt dei comandi - python server_2.py

C:\Users\Utente\Desktop\Python CookBook\Python Parallel Programming INDEX\Chapter 5 - Distributed Python\
chapter 5 - codes\chain>python server_2.py
server_2 started
2 forwarding the message to the object 3
```

The result of `server_3` is as follows:

```
Prompt dei comandi - python server_3.py

C:\Users\Utente\Desktop\Python CookBook\Python Parallel Programming INDEX\Chapter 5 - Distributed Python\
chapter 5 - codes\chain>python server_3.py
server_3 started
3 forwarding the message to the object 1
```

How it works...

The core of this example is the `Chain` class that we defined in the `chainTopology.py` script. It allows communication between the three servers. In fact, each server calls the class to find out which is the next element in the chain (refer to the method process in `chainTopology.py`). Also, it executes the call with the `Pyro4.core.proxy` statement:

```
if self.next is None:
            self.next = Pyro4.core.Proxy("PYRONAME:example.
chainTopology." + self.nextName)
```

If the chain is closed (the last call is done from `server_3` to `server_1`), a closing message is printed out:

```
if self.name in message:
            print("Back at %s; the chain is closed!" % self.name)
            return ["complete at " + self.name]
```

A forwarding message is printed out if there is a next element in the chain:

```
print("%s forwarding the message to the object %s" % (self.name, self.
nextName))
            message.append(self.name)
            result = self.next.process(message)
            result.insert(0, "passed on from " + self.name)
            return result
```

The code for the server is the same and only differs on the definition of the current element and the next element of the chain, for example, this is the definition for the first server (`server_1`):

```
this = "1"
next = "2"
```

The remaining lines of the following code define, in the same manner as the previous example, the communication with the next element in the chain:

```
servername = "example.chainTopology." + this
daemon = Pyro4.core.Daemon()
obj = chainTopology.Chain(this, next)
uri = daemon.register(obj)
ns = Pyro4.naming.locateNS()
ns.register(servername, uri)
daemon.requestLoop()
```

Finally, in the client script, we start the process by calling the first element (`server 1`) in the chain:

```
obj = Pyro4.core.Proxy("PYRONAME:example.chainTopology.1")
```

Developing a client-server application with Pyro4

In this recipe, we'll show you how to build a simple client-server application with Pyro4. The application that we'll show here is not complete, but is equipped with all the methods that will successfully complete and improve it.

A client-server application indicates a network architecture in which, generally, a client computer or terminal connects to a server for the use of a certain service, such as the sharing of a certain resource hardware/software with other clients and relying on the underlying protocol architecture. In our system, the server manages an online shopping site, while the clients manage the customers that are registered on this site and connect to it for shopping.

How to do it...

For the sake of simplicity, we have three scripts. The first one represents the object `client` in which we have customer management, the second script is the object `shop`, and the third script is the object `server`.

For the server (`server.py`), the code is as follows:

```
#
#    The Shops server
#

from __future__ import print_function
import Pyro4
import shop

ns = Pyro4.naming.locateNS()
daemon = Pyro4.core.Daemon()
uri = daemon.register(shop.Shop())
ns.register("example.shop.Shop", uri)
print(list(ns.list(prefix="example.shop.").keys()))
daemon.requestLoop()
```

The code for the client (`client.py`) is as follows:

```
from __future__ import print_function
import sys
import Pyro4

# A Shop client.
class client(object):
    def __init__(self, name , cash):
        self.name = name
        self.cash = cash
    def doShopping_deposit_cash(self, Shop):
        print("\n*** %s is doing shopping with %s:"\
                % (self.name, Shop.name()))
        print("Log on")
        Shop.logOn(self.name)
        print("Deposit money %s" %self.cash)
        Shop.deposit(self.name, self.cash)
        print("balance=%.2f" % Shop.balance(self.name))
        print("Deposit money %s" %self.cash)
        Shop.deposit(self.name, 50)
        print("balance=%.2f" % Shop.balance(self.name))
        print("Log out")
        Shop.logOut(self.name)

    def doShopping_buying_a_book(self, Shop):
        print("\n*** %s is doing shopping with %s:"\
```

```
                    % (self.name, Shop.name()))
            print("Log on")
            Shop.logOn(self.name)
            print("Deposit money %s" %self.cash)
            Shop.deposit(self.name, self.cash)
            print("balance=%.2f" % Shop.balance(self.name))
            print ("%s is buying a book for %s$"\
                    %(self.name,37))
            Shop.buy(self.name,37)
            print("Log out")
            Shop.logOut(self.name)

    if __name__ == '__main__':
        ns = Pyro4.naming.locateNS()
        uri = ns.lookup("example.shop.Shop")
        print(uri)
        Shop = Pyro4.core.Proxy(uri)
        meeta = client('Meeta',50)
        rashmi = client('Rashmi',100)
        rashmi.doShopping_buying_a_book(Shop)
        meeta.doShopping_deposit_cash(Shop)
        print("")
        print("")
        print("")
        print("")

        print("The accounts in the %s:" % Shop.name())
        accounts = Shop.allAccounts()
        for name in accounts.keys():
                print("   %s : %.2f"\
                        % (name, accounts[name]))
```

This is the code for the object `shop` (`shop.py`):

```
    class Account(object):
        def __init__(self):
            self._balance = 0.0

        def pay(self, price):
            self._balance -= price

        def deposit(self, cash):
            self._balance += cash
```

```
        def balance(self):
            return self._balance


class Shop(object):
    def __init__(self):
        self.accounts = {}
        self.clients = ['Meeta','Rashmi','John','Ken']

    def name(self):
        return 'BuyAnythingOnline'

    def logOn(self, name):
        if name in self.clients :
            self.accounts[name] = Account()
        else :
            self.clients.append(name)
            self.accounts[name] = Account()

    def logOut(self, name):
        print('logout %s' %name)

    def deposit(self, name, amount):
        try:
            return self.accounts[name].deposit(amount)
        except KeyError:
            raise KeyError('unknown account')

    def balance(self, name):
        try:
            return self.accounts[name].balance()
        except KeyError:
            raise KeyError('unknown account')

    def allAccounts(self):
        accs = {}
        for name in self.accounts.keys():
            accs[name] = self.accounts[name].balance()
        return accs

    def buy(self,name,price):
        balance = self.accounts[name].balance()
        self.accounts[name].pay(price)
```

To execute the code, you must first enable the Pyro4 name sever:

```
C:>python -m Pyro4.naming
Not starting broadcast server for localhost.
NS running on localhost:9090 (127.0.0.1)
Warning: HMAC key not set. Anyone can connect to this server!
URI = PYRO:Pyro.NameServer@localhost:9090
```

Then, start the server by using the `python server.py` command. A shell like the one shown in the following screenshot will appear when you do this:

Finally, you should start the customer simulation with the following command:

```
python client.py
```

The following text will be printed out with the use of the following command:

```
C:\Users\Utente\Desktop\Python CookBook\Python Parallel Programming
INDEX\Chapter 5 - Distributed Python\
chapter 5 - codes\banks>python client.py
PYRO:obj_8c4a5b4ae7554c2c9feee5b0113902e0@localhost:59225


*** Rashmi is doing shopping with BuyAnythingOnline:
Log on
Deposit money 100
balance=100.00
Rashmi is buying a book for 37$
Log out


*** Meeta is doing shopping with BuyAnythingOnline:
Log on
Deposit money 50
balance=50.00
```

```
Deposit money 50
balance=100.00
Log out


The accounts in the BuyAnythingOnline:
  Meeta : 100.00
  Rashmi : 63.00
```

This output shows a simple session for two customers, `Meeta` and `Rashmi`.

How it works...

The server side of the application must locate the `Shop()` object, calling the statement:

```
ns = Pyro4.naming.locateNS()
```

Then, it must enable a communication channel:

```
daemon = Pyro4.core.Daemon()
uri = daemon.register(shop.Shop())
ns.register("example.shop.Shop", uri)
daemon.requestLoop()
```

The `shop.py` script contains classes for account and shop management. The `shop` class manages each account. It provides methods to log in and log out, manage customer's money, and to buy items:

```
class Shop(object):

    def logOn(self, name):
        if name in self.clients :
            self.accounts[name] = Account()
        else :
            self.clients.append(name)
            self.accounts[name] = Account()

    def logOut(self, name):
        print('logout %s' %name)

    def deposit(self, name, amount):
        try:
            return self.accounts[name].deposit(amount)
        except KeyError:
            raise KeyError('unknown account')
```

```
def balance(self, name):
    try:
        return self.accounts[name].balance()
    except KeyError:
        raise KeyError('unknown account')

def buy(self,name,price):
    balance = self.accounts[name].balance()
    self.accounts[name].pay(price)
```

Each customer has their own `Account` object that provides methods for customer deposit management:

```
class Account(object):
    def __init__(self):
        self._balance = 0.0

    def pay(self, price):
        self._balance -= price

    def deposit(self, cash):
        self._balance += cash

    def balance(self):
        return self._balance
```

Finally, the `client.py` script contains the class that is used to start the simulation. In the main program, we instantiate two customers, `Rashmi` and `Meeta`:

```
meeta = client('Meeta',50)
rashmi = client('Rashmi',100)
rashmi.doShopping_buying_a_book(Shop)
meeta.doShopping_deposit_cash(Shop)
```

They deposit some cash end on the site and then start with their shopping as shown:

- ▶ Rashmi buys a book:

```
def doShopping_buying_a_book(self, Shop):
        Shop.logOn(self.name)
        Shop.deposit(self.name, self.cash)
        Shop.buy(self.name,37)
        Shop.logOut(self.name)
```

▶ Meeta twice deposits $100 in her account:

```
def doShopping_deposit_cash(self, Shop):
    Shop.logOn(self.name)
    Shop.deposit(self.name, self.cash)
    Shop.deposit(self.name, 50)
    Shop.logOut(self.name)
```

▶ At the end of the simulation, the main program reports the count's deposit of Meeta and Rashmi:

```
print("The accounts in the %s:" % Shop.name())
    accounts = Shop.allAccounts()
    for name in accounts.keys():
            print(" %s : %.2f"\
                    % (name, accounts[name]))
```

Communicating sequential processes with PyCSP

PyCSP is a Python module based on communicating sequential processes, which is a programming paradigm developed to build concurrent programs via message passing. The PyCSP module is characterized by:

▶ The exchange of messages between processes

▶ The possibility of using a thread to use shared memory

▶ The exchange of messages is done through channels

The channels allow:

▶ An exchange of values between processes

▶ The synchronization of processes

PyCSP allows the use of different channel types: One2One, One2Any, Any2One, and Any2One. These names indicate the number of writers and readers that can communicate over the channel.

Getting ready

PyCSP can be installed using the `pip` installer via the following command:

pip install python-csp

Also, it is possible to download the entire distribution from GitHub (https://github.com/futurecore/python-csp).

Download it and then type the following from the installation directory:

```
python setup.py install
```

For our examples, we will use the Python Version 2.7

How to do it...

In this first example, we want to introduce the basic concepts of PyCSP, the processes, and channels. So, we have defined two processes named counter and printer. We now want to see how to define the communication between these processes:

Let's consider the following code:

```
from pycsp.parallel import *

@process
def processCounter(cout, limit):
  for i in xrange(limit):
    cout(i)
  poison(cout)

@process
def processPrinter(cin):
  while True:
    print cin(),

A = Channel('A')
Parallel(
  processCounter(A.writer(), limit=5),
  processPrinter(A.reader())
)

shutdown()
```

To execute this code, simply press the run button on the Python2.7 IDLE. An output like this will be shown after this:

```
Python 2.7.9 (default, Dec 10 2014, 12:28:03) [MSC v.1500 64 bit (AMD64)]
on win32
Type "copyright", "credits" or "license()" for more information.
>>> =======================RESTART ==========================
>>>
0 1 2 3 4
>>>
```

How it works...

In this example, we used the functions defined in the `pycsp.parallel` module:

```
from pycsp.parallel import *
```

This module has the Any2Any channel type, which allows multiple processes, which are attached to the ends of the channels, to communicate through it. To create the channel A, we use the following statement:

```
A = Channel('A')
```

This new channel is automatically hosted in the current Python interpreter. For each Python interpreter that imports the `pycsp.parallel` module, only a port that handles all the channels started in the Python interpreter will be listed. However, this module does not provide a name server available for the channels. So to connect to a hosted channel, you must know the right location.

For example, to connect the channel B to the localhost port `8888`, we input the following code:

```
A = pycsp.Channel('B', connect=('localhost, 8888))
```

In PyCSP, we have three basic ways to manage a channel:

- ▶ `channel.Disconnect()`: This allows the Python interpreter to quit. It is used in a client-server setting, where a client wants to be Disconnected after it receives a reply from a server.
- ▶ `channel.reader()`: This creates and returns the reader end of the channel.
- ▶ `channel.writer()`: This creates and returns the writer end of the channel.

To indicate a process, we use the `@process` decorator. In PyCSP, each generated CSP process is implemented as a single OS thread. In this example, we have two processes: a counter and a printer. The process counter has two arguments: `cout` to redirect its output and `limit`, which defines the total number of items to be printed:

```
@process
def counter(cout, limit):
  for i in xrange(limit):
    cout(i)
  poison(cout)
```

The poison statement, `poison(cout)`, means that the channel end is poisoned. This means that all subsequent reads and writes on this channel will throw an exception that can be used to end the current procedure or Disconnect the channel. We also note that the poisoning may cause a race condition if there are multiple concurrent procedures.

The process printer only has one argument, which is the item to print, defined in the `cin` variable:

```
@process
def printer(cin):
  while True:
    print cin(),
```

The core of the script is in the following line of code:

```
A = Channel('A')
```

This defines the `A` channel, which permits communication between the two processes.

Finally, the `Parallel` statement is as follows:

```
Parallel(
  counter(A.writer(), limit=10),
  printer(A.reader())
)
```

This starts all the processes and blocks them only if the counter and process have terminated communication with each other. This statement represents the basic idea of CSP: concurrent processes synchronize with each other by synchronizing their I/O through the channel A. The way to do this is to allow I/O to occur only when a process counter states that it is ready to output to a process printer specifically and the process printer states that it is ready to input from a process counter. If one of these happens without the other being true, the process is put in a wait queue until the other process is ready.

Each PyCSP application creates a server thread to manage the incoming communication over the channels. So, it is always necessary to terminate each PyCSP application with a call to the `shutdown()` method:

```
shutdown()
```

PyCSP provides two methods to trace its execution:

- ▶ `TraceInit(<filename>, stdout=<True | False>)`: This is used to start the trace
- ▶ `TraceQuit()`: This is used to stop the trace

These must be placed in the following schema:

```
from pycsp.common.trace import *

TraceInit("trace.log")

"""
 PROCESSES TO BE TRACED

"""

TraceQuit()
shutdown()
```

For our example, we have built the log trace (with a limit count equal to three):

```
{'chan_name': 'A', 'type': 'Channel'}

{'chan_name': 'A', 'type': 'ChannelEndWrite'}

{'chan_name': 'A', 'type': 'ChannelEndRead'}

{'processes': [{'func_name': 'processCounter', 'process_id':
'9cb4b3720ed111e5bb4c0024813d643d.processCounter'}, {'func_name':
'processPrinter', 'process_id': '9cb63a0f0ed111e5993a0024813d643d.
processPrinter'}], 'process_id': '9c42428f0ed111e59ba10024813d643d.__
INIT__', 'type': 'BlockOnParallel'}

{'func_name': 'processCounter', 'process_id':
'9cb4b3720ed111e5bb4c0024813d643d.processCounter', 'type':
'StartProcess'}

{'func_name': 'processPrinter', 'process_id':
'9cb63a0f0ed111e5993a0024813d643d.processPrinter', 'type':
'StartProcess'}

{'process_id': '9cb4b3720ed111e5bb4c0024813d643d.processCounter', 'chan_
name': 'A', 'type': 'BlockOnWrite', 'id': 0}

{'process_id': '9cb63a0f0ed111e5993a0024813d643d.processPrinter', 'chan_
name': 'A', 'type': 'BlockOnRead', 'id': 0}

{'process_id': '9cb63a0f0ed111e5993a0024813d643d.processPrinter', 'chan_
name': 'A', 'type': 'DoneRead', 'id': 0}

{'process_id': '9cb4b3720ed111e5bb4c0024813d643d.processCounter', 'chan_
name': 'A', 'type': 'DoneWrite', 'id': 0}

{'process_id': '9cb4b3720ed111e5bb4c0024813d643d.processCounter', 'chan_
name': 'A', 'type': 'BlockOnWrite', 'id': 1}

{'process_id': '9cb63a0f0ed111e5993a0024813d643d.processPrinter', 'chan_
name': 'A', 'type': 'BlockOnRead', 'id': 1}
```

```
{'process_id': '9cb63a0f0ed111e5993a0024813d643d.processPrinter', 'chan_
name': 'A', 'type': 'DoneRead', 'id': 1}

{'process_id': '9cb4b3720ed111e5bb4c0024813d643d.processCounter', 'chan_
name': 'A', 'type': 'DoneWrite', 'id': 1}

{'process_id': '9cb4b3720ed111e5bb4c0024813d643d.processCounter', 'chan_
name': 'A', 'type': 'BlockOnWrite', 'id': 2}

{'process_id': '9cb63a0f0ed111e5993a0024813d643d.processPrinter', 'chan_
name': 'A', 'type': 'BlockOnRead', 'id': 2}

{'process_id': '9cb63a0f0ed111e5993a0024813d643d.processPrinter', 'chan_
name': 'A', 'type': 'DoneRead', 'id': 2}

{'process_id': '9cb4b3720ed111e5bb4c0024813d643d.processCounter', 'chan_
name': 'A', 'type': 'DoneWrite', 'id': 2}

{'process_id': '9cb4b3720ed111e5bb4c0024813d643d.processCounter', 'chan_
name': 'A', 'type': 'Poison', 'id': 3}

{'func_name': 'processCounter', 'process_id':
'9cb4b3720ed111e5bb4c0024813d643d.processCounter', 'type': 'QuitProcess'}

{'process_id': '9cb63a0f0ed111e5993a0024813d643d.processPrinter', 'chan_
name': 'A', 'type': 'BlockOnRead', 'id': 3}

{'func_name': 'processPrinter', 'process_id':
'9cb63a0f0ed111e5993a0024813d643d.processPrinter', 'type': 'QuitProcess'}

{'process_id': '9cb63a0f0ed111e5993a0024813d643d.processPrinter', 'chan_
name': 'A', 'type': 'Poison', 'id': 3}

{'processes': [{'func_name': 'processCounter', 'process_id':
'9cb4b3720ed111e5bb4c0024813d643d.processCounter'}, {'func_name':
'processPrinter', 'process_id': '9cb63a0f0ed111e5993a0024813d643d.
processPrinter'}], 'process_id': '9c42428f0ed111e59ba10024813d643d.__
INIT__', 'type': 'DoneParallel'}

{'type': 'TraceQuit'}
```

There's more...

CSP is a formal language used to describe the interactions of concurrent processes. It falls under the mathematical theory of competition, which is known as algebra processes. It has been used in practice as a tool for the specification and verification of the competition aspects of a wide variety of systems. The rules of the CSP-inspired programming language Occam are now widely used as a parallel programming language.

 For those of you who are interested in CSP's theory, we suggest you go through Hoare's original book, which is available online at http://www.usingcsp.com/cspbook.pdf.

Using MapReduce with Disco

Disco is a Python module based on the MapReduce framework introduced by Google, which allows the management of large distributed data in computer clusters. The applications written using Disco can be performed in the economic cluster of machines with a very short learning curve. In fact, the technical difficulties related to the processes that are distributed as load balancing, job scheduling, and the communications protocol are completely managed by Disco and hidden from the developer.

The typical applications of this module are essentially as follows:

▸ Web indexing

▸ URL access counter

▸ Distributed sort

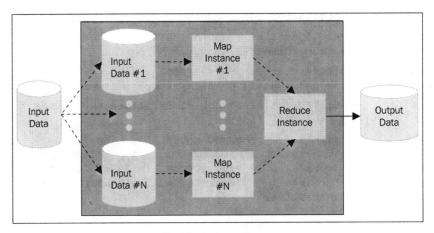

The MapReduce schema

The MapReduce algorithm implemented in Disco is as follows:

▸ **Map**: The master node takes the input data, breaks it into smaller subtasks, and distributes the work to the slave nodes. The single map node produces the intermediate result of the map() function in the form of pairs [key, value] stored on a distributed file whose location is given to the master at the end of this step.

▸ **Reduce**: The master node collects the results. It combines the pairs [key, value] in the lists of values that share the same key and sorts them for the key (lexicographical and increasing or user-defined). The pairs of the form [key, IteratorList (value, value, ...)] are passed to the nodes that run the reducer function reduce().

Moreover, the output data that is stored on files, can be the input for a new map and reduce procedure, allowing, in this way, to concatenate more MapReduce jobs.

Getting ready

 The Disco module is available at `https://github.com/Discoproject/Disco`.

You need a Linux/Unix distribution to install it.

The following are the prerequisites (on each server):

- The SSH daemon and client
- Erlang/OTP R14A or newer version
- Python 2.6.6 or newer version, Python 3.2 or newer version

Finally, to install Disco, type the following lines:

```
git clone git://github.com/Discoproject/Disco.git $Disco_HOME
cd $Disco_HOME
make
cd lib && python setup.py install --user && cd ..
bin/Disco nodaemon
```

The next step is to enable a password-less login for all servers in the Disco clusters. For a single machine installation, you must run the following command:

```
ssh-keygen -N '' -f ~/.ssh/id_dsa
```

Then, type the following:

```
cat ~/.ssh/id_dsa.pub >> ~/.ssh/authorized_keys
```

Now if you try to log in to all servers in the cluster or localhost, you will not need to give a password nor answer any questions after the first log in attempt.

 For any questions about Disco's installation, refer to `http://Disco.readthedocs.org/en/latest/intro.html`.

In the next example, we have used a Python 2.7 distro on a Linux machine.

How to do it...

In the following example, we examine a typical MapReduce problem using the Disco module. Given a text, we must count all the occurrences of some words in the text:

```python
from Disco.core import Job, result_iterator

def map(line, params):
    import string
    for word in line.split():
        strippedWord = word.translate\
                    (string.maketrans("",""), string.punctuation)
        yield strippedWord, 1

def reduce(iter, params):
    from Disco.util import kvgroup
    for word, counts in kvgroup(sorted(iter)):
        yield word, sum(counts)

if __name__ == '__main__':
    job = Job().run(input="There are known knowns.\
                    These are things we know that we know.\
                    There are known unknowns. \
                    That is to say,\
                    there are things that \
                    we know we do not know.\
                    But there are also unknown unknowns.\
                    There are things \
                    we do not know we do not know",
                map=map,
                reduce=reduce)


    sort_in_numerical_order =\
                    open('SortNumerical.txt', 'w')
    sort_in_alpbabetically_order = \
                    open('SortAlphabetical.txt', 'w')

    wordCount = []
    for word, count in \
        result_iterator(job.wait(show=True)):
        sort_in_alpbabetically_order.write('%s \t %d\n' %
                    (str(word), int(count)) )
```

```
        wordCount.append((word,count))

    sortedWordCount =sorted(wordCount, \
                        key=lambda count: count[1],\
                        reverse=True)

    for word, count in sortedWordCount:
        sort_in_numerical_order.write('%s \t %d\n'\
                                    % (str(word), int(count)) )

    sort_in_alpbabetically_order.close()
    sort_in_numerical_order.close()
```

After running the script, we have the two resulting files that we've reported in the following table:

Sortnumerical.txt		SortAlphabetical.txt	
6	are	also	1
6	know	are	6
6	we	but	1
5	there	do	3
3	do	is	1
3	not	know	6
3	that	known	2
3	things	knowns	1
2	known	not	3
2	unknowns	say	1
1	also	to	1
1	but	that	3
1	is	there	5
1	knowns	these	1
1	say	things	3
1	to	unknown	1
1	these	unknowns	2
1	unknown	we	6

How it works...

The core of this example are the `map` and `reduce` functions. The `map` function Disco has two arguments line that represent the sentence to be analyzed. However, `params` will be ignored in this example.

Here, the sentence is split in to one or more words, the punctuation symbols are ignored, and all words are converted to lowercase:

```
def map(line, params):
    import string
    for word in line.split():
        strippedWord = word.translate\
                    (string.maketrans("",""), string.punctuation)
        yield strippedWord, 1
```

The result of a `map` function on a line of text is a series of tuples in the form of a key and a value. For example, the sentence "There are known knowns" takes on this form:

```
[("There", 1), ("are", 1), ("known", 1), ("knowns",1)]
```

Let's remember that the MapReduce framework manipulates enormous datasets that are larger than the common memory space in a single machine, so the keyword yield at the end of the map function allows Disco to manage datasets in a smarter way. The `reduce` function operates on two arguments, `iter`, that are iterable objects (it acts like a list data structure), while the `params` argument linked in the map function is ignored in this example.

Each iterable object is sorted into alphabetical order using the Python function sorted:

```
def reduce(iter, params):
    from Disco.util import kvgroup
    for word, counts in kvgroup(sorted(iter)):
        yield word, sum(counts)
```

On the sorted list, we apply Disco's function `kvgroup`. It groups values of consecutive keys, which are compared to be equal. Finally, the occurrence of each word in the text is obtained through the Python function `sum`.

In the main part, we use Disco's job function to execute the `mapReduce` function:

```
job = Job().run(input="There are known knowns.\
                    These are things we know that we know.\
                    There are known unknowns. \
                    That is to say,\
                    there are things that \
                    we know we do not know.\
                    But there are also unknown unknowns.\
```

```
                              There are things \
                              we do not know we do not know",
                    map=map,
                    reduce=reduce)
```

Finally, the results are ordered into numerical and alphabetical order and they are printed in two output files:

```
sort_in_numerical_order = open('SortNumerical.txt', 'w')

sort_in_alpbabetically_order = open('SortAlphabetical.txt', 'w')
```

There's more...

Disco is a very powerful framework that is rich with different functionalities. A full discussion of this module is beyond the scope of this book.

 To get a complete introduction, refer to `http://Discoproject.org/`.

A remote procedure call with RPyC

Remote Python Call (**RPyC**) is a Python module that is used for remote procedure calls as well as for distributed computing. The idea at the base of RPC is to provide a mechanism to transfer control from a program (client) to another (server), similar to what happens with the invocation of a subroutine in a centralized program. The advantages of this approach are that it has very simple semantics and knowledge and familiarity of the centralized mechanism of a function call. In a procedure invocation, the client process is suspended until the process server has performed the necessary computations and has given the results of computations. The effectiveness of this method is due to the fact that the client-server communication takes the form of a procedure call instead of invocations to the transport layer so that all the details of the operation of the network are hidden from the application program by placing them in local procedures called stubs. The main features of RPyC are:

▶ In syntactic transparency a remote procedure call can have the same syntax as a local call

▶ In semantic transparency a remote procedure call is semantically equivalent to the local one

▶ Handling synchronous and asynchronous communication

▶ Symmetric communication protocol means that both the client and server can serve a request

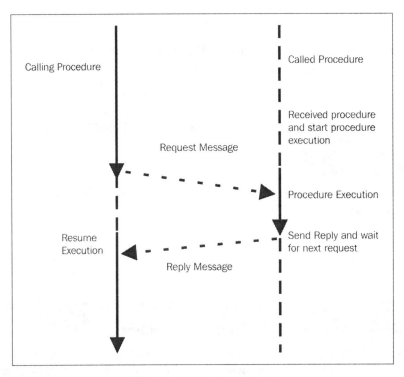

The remote procedure call model

Getting ready

The installation procedure is quite simple with the `pip` installer. From your command shell, type the following:

pip install rpyc

Otherwise, you can go to `https://github.com/tomerfiliba/rpyc` and download the complete package (it is a `.zip` file). Finally, to install rypc, you must type the command: `Python setup.py` install from the package directory.

After the installation, you can just explore this library. In our examples, we will run a client and server on the same machine, localhost. Running a server with rypc is very simple: go to the directory `../rpyc-master/bin` of the `rpyc` package directory and then execute the file `rpyc_classic.py`:

C:\ Python CookBook\ Chapter 5- Distributed Python\rpyc-master\bin>python rpyc_classic.py

After running this script, you'll read on Command Prompt the following output message:

```
INFO:SLAVE/18812:server started on [0.0.0.0]:18812
```

How to do it...

We are now ready for the first example that shows you how to redirect stdout of a remote process:

```
import rpyc
import sys
c = rpyc.classic.connect("localhost")
c.execute("print ('hi python cookbook')")
c.modules.sys.stdout = sys.stdout
c.execute("print ('hi here')")
```

By running this script, you'll see the redirected output in the server side:

```
C:\Python CookBook\Chapter 5- Distributed Python\rpyc-master\bin>python
rpyc_classic.py
INFO:SLAVE/18812:server started on [0.0.0.0]:18812
INFO:SLAVE/18812:accepted 127.0.0.1:6279
INFO:SLAVE/18812:welcome [127.0.0.1]:6279
hi python cookbook
```

How it works...

The first step is to run a client that connects to the server:

```
import rpyc

c = rpyc.classic.connect("localhost")
```

Here, the client-side statement rpyc.classic.connect (host, port) creates a socket connection to the given host and port. Sockets define the endpoint of a connection. rpyc uses sockets to communicate with other programs, which may be distributed on different computers.

Next, we have the following statement:

```
c.execute("print ('hi python cookbook')")
```

This executes the print statement on the server (a remote exec statement).

6
GPU Programming with Python

In this chapter, we will cover the following recipes:

- ▶ Using the PyCUDA module
- ▶ How to build a PyCUDA application
- ▶ Understanding the PyCUDA Memory Model with matrix manipulation
- ▶ Kernel invocations with GPUArray
- ▶ Evaluating element-wise expressions with PyCUDA
- ▶ The MapReduce operation with PyCUDA
- ▶ GPU programming with NumbaPro
- ▶ Using GPU-accelerated libraries with NumbaPro
- ▶ Using the PyOpenCL module
- ▶ How to build a PyOpenCL application
- ▶ Evaluating element-wise expressions with PyOpenCL
- ▶ Testing your GPU application with PyOpenCL

Introduction

The **graphics processing unit** (**GPU**) is an electronic circuit that specializes in processing data to render images from polygonal primitives. Although they were designed to carry out rendering images, the GPU has continued to evolve, becoming more complex and efficient in serving both the real-time and offline rendering community and in performing any scientific computations. GPUs are characterized by a highly parallel structure, which allows it to manipulate large datasets in an efficient manner. This feature combined with the rapid improvement in graphics hardware performance and the extent of programmability caught the attention of the scientific world with the possibility of using GPU for purposes other than just rendering images. Traditional GPUs are fixed function devices where the whole rendering pipeline is built on hardware. This restricts graphics programmers, leading them to use different, efficient and high-quality rendering algorithms. Hence, a new GPU was built with millions of lightweight parallel cores, which were programmable to render graphics using **shaders**. This is one of the biggest advancements in the field of computer graphics and the gaming industry. With lots of programmable cores available, the GPU vendors started developing models for parallel programming. Each GPU is indeed composed of several processing units called **Streaming Multiprocessor** (**SM**) that represent the first logic level of parallelism; and each SM infact works simultaneously and independently from the others.

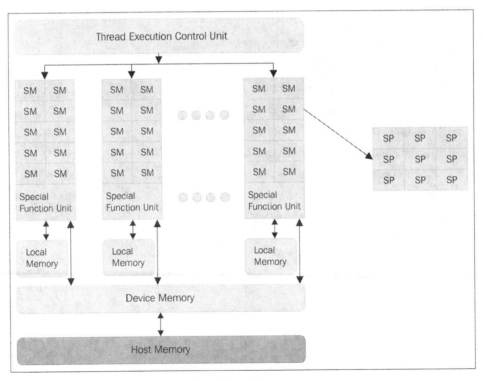

The GPU architecture

Each SM is in turn divided into a group of **Stream Processors** (**SP**), each of which has a core of real execution and can sequentially run a thread. An SP represents the smallest unit of an execution logic and represents the level of finer parallelism. The division in SM and SP is structural in nature, but it is possible to outline a further logical organization of the SP of a GPU, which are grouped together in logical blocks characterized by a particular mode of execution. All cores that make up a group run the same instruction at the same time. This is just the **Single instruction, multiple data** (**SIMD**) model, which we described in the first chapter of this book.

Each SM also has a number of registers, which represent an area of memory for quick access that is temporary, local (not shared between the cores), and limited in size. This allows storage of frequently used values from a single core. The **general-purpose computing on graphics processing units** (**GP-GPU**) is the field devoted to the study of the techniques needed to exploit the computing power of the GPU to perform calculations quickly, thanks to the high level of parallelism inside. As seen before, GPUs are structured quite differently from conventional processors; for this, they have problems of a different nature and require specific programming techniques. The most outstanding feature that distinguishes a graphics processor is the high number of cores available, which allow us to carry out many threads of execution competitors, which are partially synchronized for the execution of the same operation. This feature is very useful and efficient in situations where you want to split your work in many parts to perform the same operations on different data. On the contrary, it is hard to make the best use of this architecture when there is a strong sequential and logical order to be respected in the operations to be carried out; otherwise, the work cannot be evenly divided into many small subparts. The programming paradigm that characterizes the GPU computing is called Stream Processing because the data can be viewed as a homogeneous flow of values to which the same operations are applied synchronously.

Currently, the most efficient solutions to exploit the computing power provided by GPU cards are the software libraries CUDA and OpenCL. In the following recipes, we will present the realization of these software libraries in the Python programming language.

Using the PyCUDA module

PyCUDA is a Python wrap for **Compute Unified Device Architecture** (**CUDA**), the software library developed by NVIDIA for GPU programming. The CUDA programming model is the starting point of understanding how to program the GPU properly with PyCUDA. There are concepts that must be understood and assimilated to be able to approach this tool correctly and to understand the more specific topics that are covered in the following recipes.

A hybrid programming model

The programming model "hybrid" of CUDA (and consequently of PyCUDA, which is a Python wrapper) is implemented through specific extensions to the standard library of the C language. These extensions have been created, whenever possible, syntactically like the function calls in the standard C library. This allows a relatively simple approach to a hybrid programming model that includes the host and device code. The management of the two logical parts is done by the NVCC compiler. Here is a brief description of how this compiler works:

1. It separates a device code from a host-code device.
2. It invokes a default compiler (for example, GCC) to compile the host code.
3. It builds the device code in the binary form (Cubin objects) or in the form assembly (code PTX).
4. It generates a host key "global" that also includes code PTX.

The compiled CUDA code is converted to a device-specific binary by the driver, during runtime. All the previously mentioned steps are executed by PyCUDA at runtime, which makes it a **Just-in-time** (**JIT**) compiler. The drawback of this approach is the increased load time of the application, which is the only way to maintain compatibility "forward", that is, you can perform operations on a device that does not exist at the time of the actual compilation. A JIT compilation therefore makes an application compatible with future devices that are built on architectures with higher computing power, so it is not yet possible to generate any binary code.

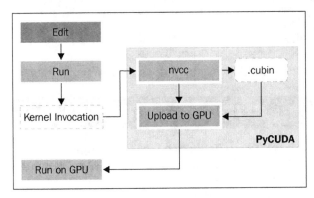

The PyCUDA execution model

The kernel and thread hierarchy

An important element of a CUDA program is a **kernel**. It represents the code that is executed parallelly on the basis of specifications that will be clarified later with the examples described here. Each kernel's execution is done by computing units that are called **threads**. Unlike threads in CPU, GPU threads are lighter in such a way that the change of context is not one of the factors to be taken into account in a code performance evaluation because it can be considered as instantaneous. To determine the number of threads that must perform a single kernel and their logical organization, CUDA defines a two-level hierarchy. In the highest level, it defines a so-called grid of blocks. This grid represents a bidimensional structure where the thread blocks are distributed, which are three-dimensional.

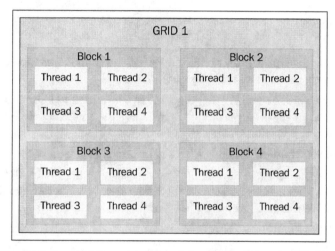

The distribution of (3-dimensional) threads in a two-level hierarchy of PyCUDA

Based on this structure, a kernel function must be launched with additional parameters that specify precisely the size of the grid and block.

Getting ready

On the Wiki page `http://wiki.tiker.net/PyCuda/Installation`, the basic instructions to install PyCuda on the main operative systems (Linux, Mac, and Windows) are explained.

With these instructions, you will build a 32-bit PyCUDA library for a Python 2.7 distro:

1. The first step is to download and install all the components provided by NVDIA to develop with CUDA (refer to `https://developer.nvidia.com/cuda-toolkit-archive`) for all the available versions. These components are:

   ❏ The CUDA toolkit is available at `http://developer.download.nvidia.com/compute/cuda/4_2/rel/toolkit/cudatoolkit_4.2.9_win_32.msi`.

   ❏ The NVIDIA GPU Computing SDK is available at `http://developer.download.nvidia.com/compute/cuda/4_2/rel/sdk/gpucomputingsdk_4.2.9_win_32.exe`.

   ❏ The NVIDIA CUDA Development Driver is available at `http://developer.download.nvidia.com/compute/cuda/4_2/rel/drivers/devdriver_4.2_winvista-win7_32_301.32_general.exe`.

2. Download and install NumPy (for 32-bit Python 2.7) and Visual Studio C++ 2008 Express (be sure to set all the system variables).

3. Open the file `msvc9compiler.py` located at `/Python27/lib/distutils/`. After the line 641: `ld_args.append ('/IMPLIB:' + implib_file)`, add the new line `ld_args.append('/MANIFEST')`.

4. Download PyCUDA from `https://pypi.python.org/pypi/pycuda`.

5. Open Visual Studio 2008 Command Prompt, click on Start, go to **All Programs | Microsoft Visual Studio 2008 | Visual Studio Tools | Visual Studio Command Prompt (2008)**, and follow the given steps:

   1. Go in the `PyCuda` directory.

   2. Execute `python configure.py`.

   3. Edit the created file `siteconf.py`:

   ```
   BOOST_INC_DIR = []
   BOOST_LIB_DIR = []
   BOOST_COMPILER = 'gcc43'
   USE_SHIPPED_BOOST = True
   BOOST_PYTHON_LIBNAME = ['boost_python']
   BOOST_THREAD_LIBNAME = ['boost_thread']
   CUDA_TRACE = False
   CUDA_ROOT = 'C:\\Program Files\\NVIDIA GPU Computing
   Toolkit\\CUDA\\v4.2'
   CUDA_ENABLE_GL = False
   CUDA_ENABLE_CURAND = True
   CUDADRV_LIB_DIR = ['${CUDA_ROOT}/lib/Win32']
   CUDADRV_LIBNAME = ['cuda']
   ```

```
CUDART_LIB_DIR = ['${CUDA_ROOT}/lib/Win32']
CUDART_LIBNAME = ['cudart']
CURAND_LIB_DIR = ['${CUDA_ROOT}/lib/Win32']
CURAND_LIBNAME = ['curand']
CXXFLAGS = ['/EHsc']
LDFLAGS = ['/FORCE']
```

6. Finally, install PyCUDA with the following commands in VS2008 Command Prompt:

```
python setup.py build
python setup.py install
```

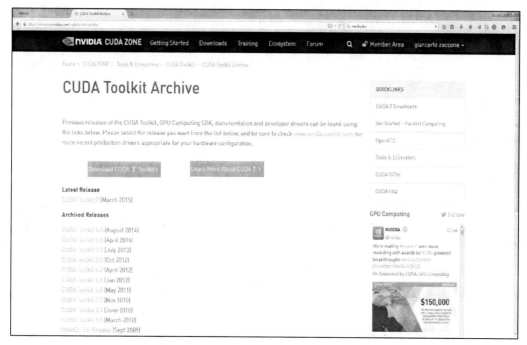

The CUDA toolkit download page

How to do it...

The present example has a dual function. The first is to verify that PyCUDA is properly installed and the second is to read and print the characteristics of the GPU cards:

```
import pycuda.driver as drv
drv.init()
print "%d device(s) found." % drv.Device.count()
for ordinal in range(drv.Device.count()):
```

```
dev = drv.Device(ordinal)
print "Device #%d: %s" % (ordinal, dev.name())
print " Compute Capability: %d.%d" % dev.compute_capability()
print " Total Memory: %s KB" % (dev.total_memory()//(1024))
```

After running the code, we should have an output like this:

```
C:\ Python CookBook\ Chapter 6 - GPU Programming with Python\Chapter 6 -
codes>python PyCudaInstallation.py


1 device(s) found.
Device #0: GeForce GT 240
 Compute Capability: 1.2
 Total Memory: 1048576 KB
```

How it works...

The execution is pretty simple. In the first line of code, `pycuda.driver` is imported and then initialized:

```
import pycuda.driver as drv
drv.init()
```

The `pycuda.driver` module exposes the driver level to the programming interface of CUDA, which is more flexible than the CUDA C "runtime-level" programming interface, and it has a few features that are not present at runtime.

Then, it cycles into `drv.Device.count()`, and for each GPU card found, the name of the cards and main characteristics (computing capability and total memory) are printed:

```
print "Device #%d: %s" % (ordinal, dev.name())
print " Compute Capability: %d.%d" % dev.compute_capability()
print " Total Memory: %s KB" % (dev.total_memory()//(1024))
```

See also

▸ PyCUDA is developed by Andreas Klöckner (http://mathema.tician.de/aboutme/). For any other information concerning PyCUDA, you can refer to http://documen.tician.de/pycuda/.

How to build a PyCUDA application

The PyCUDA programming model is designed for the common execution of a program on a CPU and GPU, so as to allow you to perform the sequential parts on the CPU and the numeric parts, which are more intensive on the GPU. The phases to be performed in the sequential mode are implemented and executed on the CPU (host), while the steps to be performed in parallel are implemented and executed on the GPU (device). The functions to be performed in parallel on the device are called kernels. The steps to execute a generic function kernel on the device are as follows:

1. The first step is to allocate the memory on the device.
2. Then we need to transfer data from the host memory to that allocated on the device.
3. Next, we need to run the device:
    1. Run the configuration.
    2. Invoke the kernel function.
4. Then, we need to transfer the results from the memory on the device to the host memory.
5. Finally, release the memory allocated on the device.

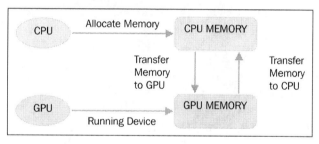

The PyCUDA programming model

How to do it...

To show the PyCUDA workflow, let's consider a 5×5 random array and the following procedure:

1. Create the 5×5 array on the CPU.
2. Transfer the array to the GPU.
3. Perform a task on the array in the GPU (double all the items in the array).
4. Transfer the array from the GPU to the CPU.
5. Print the results.

The code for this is as follows:

```
import pycuda.driver as cuda
import pycuda.autoinit
from pycuda.compiler import SourceModule

import numpy

a = numpy.random.randn(5,5)
a = a.astype(numpy.float32)

a_gpu = cuda.mem_alloc(a.nbytes)
cuda.memcpy_htod(a_gpu, a)

mod = SourceModule("""
  __global__ void doubleMatrix(float *a)
  {
    int idx = threadIdx.x + threadIdx.y*4;
    a[idx] *= 2;
  }
  """)

func = mod.get_function("doubleMatrix")
func(a_gpu, block=(5,5,1))

a_doubled = numpy.empty_like(a)
cuda.memcpy_dtoh(a_doubled, a_gpu)
print ("ORIGINAL MATRIX")
print a
print ("DOUBLED MATRIX AFTER PyCUDA EXECUTION")
print a_doubled
```

The example output should be like this:

```
C:\Python CookBook\Chapter 6 - GPU Programming with Python\ >python
PyCudaWorkflow.py
ORIGINAL MATRIX
[[-0.59975582  1.93627465  0.65337795  0.13205571 -0.46468592]
 [ 0.01441949  1.40946579  0.5343408  -0.46614054 -0.31727529]
 [-0.06868593  1.21149373 -0.6035406  -1.29117763  0.47762445]
 [ 0.36176383 -1.443097    1.21592784 -1.04906416 -1.18935871]
 [-0.06960868 -1.44647694 -1.22041082  1.17092752  0.3686313 ]]
```

```
DOUBLED MATRIX AFTER PyCUDA EXECUTION
[[-1.19951165   3.8725493    1.3067559    0.26411143 -0.92937183]
 [ 0.02883899   2.81893158   1.0686816   -0.93228108 -0.63455057]
 [-0.13737187   2.42298746  -1.2070812   -2.58235526  0.95524889]
 [ 0.72352767  -1.443097     1.21592784  -1.04906416 -1.18935871]
 [-0.06960868  -1.44647694  -1.22041082   1.17092752  0.3686313 ]]
```

How it works...

The preceding code starts with the following imports:

```
import pycuda.driver as cuda
import pycuda.autoinit
from pycuda.compiler import SourceModule
```

The import pycuda.autoinit statement automatically picks a GPU to run based on its availability and number. It also creates a GPU context for the subsequent code to run. If needed, both the chosen device and the created context are available from pycuda. autoinit as importable symbols, whereas the SourceModule component is the object where a C-like code for the GPU must be written.

The first step is to generate the input 5×5 matrix. Since most GPU computations involve large arrays of data, the numpy module must be imported:

```
import numpy
a = numpy.random.randn(5,5)
```

Then, the items in the matrix are converted into a single precision mode, many NVIDIA cards support only a single precision:

```
a = a.astype(numpy.float32)
```

The first operation that needs to be done in order to implement a GPU is to load the input array from the host memory (CPU) to the device (GPU). This is done at the beginning of the operation and consists of two steps that are performed by invoking the following two functions provided PyCUDA:

▸ The memory allocation on the device is performed via the function cuda.mem_ alloc. The device and host memory may *not ever* communicate while performing a function kernel. This means that, to run a function parallelly on the device, the data related to it *must* be present in the memory of the device itself. Before you copy data from the host memory to the device memory, you must allocate the memory required on the device: a_gpu = cuda.mem_alloc(a.nbytes).

▶ Copy the matrix from the host memory to that of the device with the following function:

```
call cuda.memcpy_htod : cuda.memcpy_htod(a_gpu, a).
```

Also note that a_gpu is one-dimensional and on the device, we need to handle it as such. All these operations do not require the invocation of a kernel and are made directly by the main processor. The SourceModule entity serves to define the (C-like) kernel function doubleMatrix that multiplies each array entry by 2:

```
mod = SourceModule("""
    __global__ void doubleMatrix(float *a)
    {
        int idx = threadIdx.x + threadIdx.y*4;
        a[idx] *= 2;
    }
    """)
```

The __global__ qualifier directive indicates that the function doubleMatrix will be processed on the device. Only the CUDA nvcc compiler will perform this task.

Let's take a look at the function's body:

```
int idx = threadIdx.x + threadIdx.y*4;
```

The idx parameter is the matrix index identified by the thread coordinates threadIdx.x and threadIdx.y. Then, the element matrix with the index idx is multiplied by 2:

```
a[idx] *= 2;
```

Note that this kernel function will be executed once in 16 different threads. Both the variables threadIdx.x and threadIdx.y contain indices between 0 and 3 and the pair is different for each thread. Threads scheduling is directly linked to the GPU architecture and its intrinsic parallelism. A block of threads is assigned to a single **Streaming Multiprocessor (SM)**, and the threads are further divided into groups called **warps**. The size of a warp depends on the architecture under consideration. The threads of the same warp are managed by the control unit called the **warp scheduler**. To take full advantage of the inherent parallelism of SM, the threads of the same warp must execute the same instruction. If this condition does not occur, we speak of the divergence of threads. If the same warp threads execute different instructions, the control unit cannot handle all the warps. It must follow the sequences of instructions for every single thread (or for homogeneous subsets of threads) in a serial mode. Let's observe how the thread block is divided into various warps, threads are divided by the value of threadIdx.

The threadIdx structure consists of three fields: threadIdx.x, threadIdx.y, and threadIdx.z.

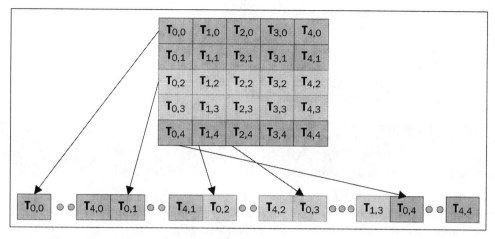

Thread blocks subdivision: T(x,y) where x = threadIdx.x and y = threadIdx.y

We can see that the code in the kernel function will be automatically compiled by the nvcc CUDA compiler. If there are no errors, the pointer of this compiled function will be created. In fact, `mod.get_function("doubleMatrix")` returns an identifier to the `func` function that we created:

```
func = mod.get_function("doubleMatrix ")
```

To perform a function on the device, you must first configure the execution appropriately. This means that you need to determine the size of the coordinates to identify and distinguish the thread belonging to different blocks. This will be done using the block parameter inside the `func` call:

```
func(a_gpu, block = (5, 5, 1))
```

The `block = (5, 5, 1)` function tells us that we are calling a kernel function with the a_gpu linearized input matrix and a single thread block of the size 5 threads in the x direction, 5 threads in the y direction, and 1 thread in the z direction, 16 threads in total. This structure is designed with the parallel implementation of the algorithm in mind. The division of the workload results in an early form of parallelism that is sufficient and necessary to make use of the computing resources provided by the GPU. Once you've configured the kernel's invocation, you can invoke the kernel function that executes instructions parallelly on the device. Each thread executes the same code kernel.

After the computation in the GPU device, we use an array to store the results:

```
a_doubled = numpy.empty_like(a)
cuda.memcpy_dtoh(a_doubled, a_gpu)
```

This will be printed as follows:

```
print a
print a_doubled
```

There's more...

A warp executes one common instruction at a time. So, to maximize the efficiency of the structure all must agree with the same thread's path of execution. When more than one thread block is assigned to a multiprocessor to run, they are partitioned into warps that are scheduled by a component called the warp scheduler.

Understanding the PyCUDA memory model with matrix manipulation

A PyCUDA program, to make the most of available resources, should respect the rules dictated by the structure and the internal organization of the SM that imposes constraints on the performance of the thread. In particular, the knowledge and correct use of the various types of memory that the GPU makes available is fundamental in order to achieve maximum efficiency in the programs. In the CUDA-capable GPU card, there are four types of memories, which are defined, as follows:

- **Registers**: In this, a register is allocated for each thread. This can only access its register but not the registers of other threads, even if they belong to the same block.

- **The shared memory**: Here, each block has its own shared memory between the threads that belong to it. Even this memory is extremely fast.

- **The constant memory**: All threads in a grid have constant access to the memory, but can be accessed only while reading. The data present in it persists for the entire duration of the application.

- **The global memory**: All threads of all the grids (so all kernels) have access to the global memory. The constant memory data present in it persists for the entire duration of the application.

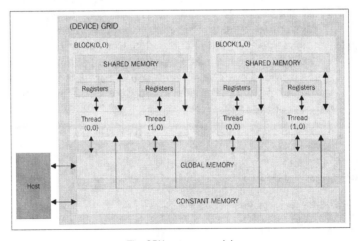

The GPU memory model

One of the key points to understand how to make the PyCUDA programs with satisfactory performance is that not all memory is the same, but you have to try to make the best of each type of memory. The basic idea is to minimize the global memory access via the use of the shared memory. The technique is usually used to divide the domain/codomain of the problem in such a way so that we enable a block of threads to perform its elaborations in a closed subset of data. In this way, the threads adhering to the concerned block will work together to load the shared global memory area that is to be processed in the memory, to then proceed to exploiting the higher speed of this memory zone.

The basic steps to be performed for each thread will then be as follows:

1. Load data from the global memory to the shared memory.
2. Synchronize all the threads of the block so that everyone can read safety positions shared memory filled by other threads.
3. Process the data of the shared memory.
4. Make a new synchronization as necessary to ensure that the shared memory has been updated with the results.
5. Write the results in the global memory.

How to do it...

To better understand this technique, we'll present an example which will clarify this approach. This example is based on the product of two matrices. The previous figure shows the product of matrices in the standard way and the correspondent sequential code to calculate where each element must be loaded from a row and a column of the matrix input:

```
void SequentialMatrixMultiplication(float*M,float *N,float *P, int
width)
{
   for (int i=0; i< width; ++i)
       for(int j=0;j < width; ++j) {
           float sum = 0;
           for (int k = 0 ; k < width; ++k) {
               float a = M[I * width + k];
               float b = N[k * width + j];
               sum += a * b;
                   }
           P[I * width + j] = sum;
       }
}
```

If each thread was entrusted with the task of calculating an element of the matrix, the memory accesses would dominate the execution time of the algorithm. What we can do is rely on a block of threads for the task of calculating a submatrix of output so that it is possible to reuse the data loaded from the global memory and to collaborate threads in order to minimize the memory accesses for each of them.

The following example shows this technique:

```
import numpy as np
from pycuda import driver, compiler, gpuarray, tools

# -- initialize the device
import pycuda.autoinit

kernel_code_template = """
__global__ void MatrixMulKernel(float *a, float *b, float *c)
{
    int tx = threadIdx.x;
    int ty = threadIdx.y;
    float Pvalue = 0;
    for (int k = 0; k < %(MATRIX_SIZE)s; ++k) {
        float Aelement = a[ty * %(MATRIX_SIZE)s + k];
        float Belement = b[k * %(MATRIX_SIZE)s + tx];
        Pvalue += Aelement * Belement;
    }

    c[ty * %(MATRIX_SIZE)s + tx] = Pvalue;
}
"""
MATRIX_SIZE = 5

a_cpu = np.random.randn(MATRIX_SIZE, MATRIX_SIZE).astype(np.float32)
b_cpu = np.random.randn(MATRIX_SIZE, MATRIX_SIZE).astype(np.float32)
c_cpu = np.dot(a_cpu, b_cpu)
a_gpu = gpuarray.to_gpu(a_cpu)
b_gpu = gpuarray.to_gpu(b_cpu)

c_gpu = gpuarray.empty((MATRIX_SIZE, MATRIX_SIZE), np.float32)

kernel_code = kernel_code_template % {
    'MATRIX_SIZE': MATRIX_SIZE
    }
```

```
mod = compiler.SourceModule(kernel_code)

matrixmul = mod.get_function("MatrixMulKernel")

matrixmul(
    a_gpu, b_gpu,
    c_gpu,
    block = (MATRIX_SIZE, MATRIX_SIZE, 1),
    )

# print the results
print "-" * 80
print "Matrix A (GPU):"
print a_gpu.get()

print "-" * 80
print "Matrix B (GPU):"
print b_gpu.get()

print "-" * 80
print "Matrix C (GPU):"
print c_gpu.get()

print "-" * 80
print "CPU-GPU difference:"
print c_cpu - c_gpu.get()

np.allclose(c_cpu, c_gpu.get())
```

The example output will be as follows:

C:\Python CookBook\Chapter 6 - GPU Programming with Python\python PyCudaMatrixManipulation.py

```
--------------------------------------------------------------------------
Matrix A (GPU):
[[ 0.90780383 -0.4782407   0.23222363 -0.63184392  1.05509627]
 [-1.27266967 -1.02834761 -0.15528528 -0.09468858  1.037099  ]
 [-0.18135822 -0.69884419  0.29881889 -1.15969539  1.21021318]
 [ 0.20939326 -0.27155793 -0.57454145  0.1466181   1.84723163]
 [ 1.33780348 -0.42343542 -0.50257754 -0.73388749 -1.883829  ]]
--------------------------------------------------------------------------
```

Matrix B (GPU):
```
[[ 0.04523897  0.99969769 -1.04473436  1.28909719  1.10332143]
 [-0.08900332 -1.3893919   0.06948703 -0.25977209 -0.49602833]
 [-0.6463753  -1.4424541  -0.81715286  0.67685211 -0.94934392]
 [ 0.4485206  -0.77086055 -0.16582981  0.08478995  1.26223004]
 [-0.79841441 -0.16199949 -0.35969591 -0.46809086  0.20455229]]
```

Matrix C (GPU):
```
[[-1.19226956  1.55315971 -1.44614291  0.90420711  0.43665022]
 [-0.73617989  0.28546685  1.02769876 -1.97204924 -0.65403283]
 [-1.62555301  1.05654192 -0.34626681 -0.51481217 -1.35338223]
 [-1.0040834   1.00310731 -0.4568972  -0.90064859  1.47408712]
 [ 1.59797418  3.52156591 -0.21708387  2.31396151  0.85150564]]
```

CPU-GPU difference:
```
[[  0.00000000e+00   0.00000000e+00   0.00000000e+00  -5.96046448e-08
    0.00000000e+00]
 [  0.00000000e+00   5.96046448e-08   0.00000000e+00   0.00000000e+00
    5.96046448e-08]
 [ -1.19209290e-07   2.38418579e-07   0.00000000e+00  -5.96046448e-08
    0.00000000e+00]
 [  0.00000000e+00   0.00000000e+00  -2.98023224e-08  -5.96046448e-08
    0.00000000e+00]
 [  1.19209290e-07   0.00000000e+00   0.00000000e+00   0.00000000e+00
    0.00000000e+00]]
```

How it works...

Let's consider the PyCUDA programming workflow. First of all, we must prepare the input matrix and the output matrix to store the results:

```python
MATRIX_SIZE = 2
a_cpu = np.random.randn(MATRIX_SIZE, MATRIX_SIZE).astype(np.float32)
b_cpu = np.random.randn(MATRIX_SIZE, MATRIX_SIZE).astype(np.float32)
c_cpu = np.dot(a_cpu, b_cpu)
```

Then, we transfer these matrixes in the GPU device with the PyCUDA function `gpuarray.to_gpu()`:

```
a_gpu = gpuarray.to_gpu(a_cpu)
b_gpu = gpuarray.to_gpu(b_cpu)
c_gpu = gpuarray.empty((MATRIX_SIZE, MATRIX_SIZE), np.float32)
```

The core of the algorithm is the kernel function:

```
__global__ void MatrixMulKernel(float *a, float *b, float *c)
{
    int tx = threadIdx.x;
    int ty = threadIdx.y;
    float Pvalue = 0;

    for (int k = 0; k < %(MATRIX_SIZE)s; ++k) {
        float Aelement = a[ty * %(MATRIX_SIZE)s + k];
        float Belement = b[k * %(MATRIX_SIZE)s + tx];
        Pvalue += Aelement * Belement;
    }

    c[ty * %(MATRIX_SIZE)s + tx] = Pvalue;
}
```

Note that the `__global__` keyword specifies that this function is a kernel function, and it must be called from a host to generate the thread hierarchy on the device.

The `threadIdx.x` and `threadIdy.y` are the threads indexes in the grid. We also note again that all these threads execute the same kernel code, so different threads will have different values with different thread coordinates. In this parallel version, the loop variables *i* and *j* of the sequential version (refer to the code in the *How to do it* section) are now replaced with `threadIdx.x` and `threadIdx.y`. The loop iteration through these indexes is simply replaced by these thread indexes, so in the parallel version, we have only one loop iteration. When the kernel `MatrixMulKernel` is invoked, it is executed as a grid of the size 2×2 of parallel threads:

```
mod = compiler.SourceModule(kernel_code)
matrixmul = mod.get_function("MatrixMulKernel")
matrixmul(
    a_gpu, b_gpu,
    c_gpu,
    block = (MATRIX_SIZE, MATRIX_SIZE, 1),
    )
```

Each CUDA thread grid typically comprises of thousands to millions of lightweight GPU threads per kernel invocation. Creating enough threads to fully utilize the hardware often requires a large amount of data parallelism; for example, each element of a large array might be computed in a separate thread.

Finally, we print out the results to verify that the computation is ok and report the differences between the `c_cpu` and `c_gpu` matrix products:

```
print "-" * 80
print "CPU-GPU difference:"
print c_cpu - c_gpu.get()


np.allclose(c_cpu, c_gpu.get())
```

Kernel invocations with GPUArray

In the previous recipe, we saw how to invoke a kernel function using the class:

```
pycuda.compiler.SourceModule(kernel_source, nvcc="nvcc", options=None,
other_options)
```

It creates a module from the CUDA source code called `kernel_source`. Then, the NVIDIA nvcc compiler is invoked with options to compile the code.

However, PyCUDA introduces the class `pycuda.gpuarray.GPUArray` that provides a high-level interface to perform calculations with CUDA:

```
class pycuda.gpuarray.GPUArray(shape, dtype, *, allocator=None,
order="C")
```

This works in a similar way to `numpy.ndarray`, which stores its data and performs its computations on the compute device. The `shape` and `dtype` arguments work exactly as in NumPy.

All the arithmetic methods in GPUArray support the broadcasting of scalars. The creation of `gpuarray` is quite easy. One way is to create a NumPy array and convert it, as shown in the following code:

```
>>> import pycuda.gpuarray as gpuarray
>>> from numpy.random import randn
>>> from numpy import float32, int32, array
>>> x = randn(5).astype(float32)
>>> x_gpu = gpuarray.to_gpu(x)
```

You can print `gpuarray` as you do normally:

```
>>> xarray([-0.24655211,   0.00344609,   1.45805557,   0.22002029,
1.28438667])
>>> x_gpuarray([-0.24655211,   0.00344609,   1.45805557,   0.22002029,
1.28438667])
```

How to do it...

The following example represents not only an easy introduction, but also a common use case of GPU computations, perhaps in the form of an auxiliary step between other calculations. The script for this is as follows:

```python
import pycuda.gpuarray as gpuarray
import pycuda.driver as cuda
import pycuda.autoinit
import numpy

a_gpu = gpuarray.to_gpu(numpy.random.randn(4,4).astype(numpy.float32))
a_doubled = (2*a_gpu).get()
print a_doubled
print a_gpu
```

The output is (running the function from Python IDLE) as follows:

```
C \Python Parallel Programming INDEX\Chapter 6 - GPU Programming wit
h Python\python PyCudaGPUArray.py
ORIGINAL MATRIX
[[-0.60254627  1.16694951   1.48510635  -1.46718287   2.11878467]
 [ 2.63159704 -3.6541729    2.44197178  -1.12101364   0.22178674]
 [-0.87713826 -1.9803952    0.98741448  -2.83859134  -1.55612338]
 [ 0.79552311 -0.25934356  -1.12207913  -0.21778747  -4.0459609 ]
 [-1.74858582  1.34928024  -2.55908132   2.22259712   0.82242775]]

DOUBLED MATRIX AFTER PyCUDA EXECUTION USING GPUARRAY CALL
[[-0.30127314   0.58347476   0.74255317  -0.73359144   1.05939233]
 [ 1.31579852 -1.82708645   1.22098589  -0.56050682   0.11089337]
 [-0.43856913 -0.9901976    0.49370724  -1.41929567  -0.77806169]
 [ 0.39776155 -0.12967178  -0.56103957  -0.10889374  -2.02298045]
 [-0.87429291  0.67464012  -1.27954066   1.11129856   0.41121387]]
```

How it works...

Of course, we have to import all the required modules:

```
import pycuda.gpuarray as gpuarray
import pycuda.driver as cuda
import pycuda.autoinit
import numpy
```

The `a_gpu` input matrix contains all the items that are generated randomly. To perform the computation in the GPU, (double all the items in the matrix) we have only one statement:

```
a_doubled = (2*a_gpu).get()
```

The result is put in the `a_doubled` matrix (using the `get()` method). Finally, the result is printed as follows:

```
print a_doubled
```

There's more...

The `pycuda.gpuarray.GPUArray` supports all arithmetic operators and a number of methods and functions, all patterned after the corresponding functionality in NumPy. In addition to this, many special functions are available in `pycuda.cumath`. The arrays of approximately uniformly distributed random numbers may be generated using the functionality in `pycuda.curandom`.

Evaluating element-wise expressions with PyCUDA

The `PyCuda.elementwise.ElementwiseKernel` function allows us to execute the kernel on complex expressions that are made of one or more operands into a single computational step, which is as follows:

```
ElementwiseKernel(arguments,operation,name,optional_parameters)
```

Here, we note that:

▶ `arguments`: This is a C argument list of all the parameters that are involved in the kernel's execution.

▶ `operation`: This is the operation that is to be executed on the specified arguments. If the argument is a vector, each operation will be performed for each entry.

▶ `name`: This is the kernel's name.

▶ `optional_parameters`: These are the compilation directives that are not used in the following example.

How to do it...

In this example, we'll show you the typical use of the ElementwiseKernel call. We have two vectors of 50 elements, input_vector_a and input_vector_b, that are built in a random way. The task here is to evaluate their linear combination.

The code for this is as follows:

```
import pycuda.autoinit
import numpy
from pycuda.curandom import rand as curand
from pycuda.elementwise import ElementwiseKernel
import numpy.linalg as la


input_vector_a = curand((50,))
input_vector_b = curand((50,))
mult_coefficient_a = 2
mult_coefficient_b = 5


linear_combination = ElementwiseKernel(
        "float a, float *x, float b, float *y, float *c",
        "c[i] = a*x[i] + b*y[i]",
        "linear_combination")

linear_combination_result = gpuarray.empty_like(input_vector_a)
linear_combination(mult_coefficient_a, input_vector_a,\
                   mult_coefficient_b, input_vector_b,\
                   linear_combination_result)


print ("INPUT VECTOR A =")
print (input_vector_a)

print ("INPUT VECTOR B = ")
print (input_vector_b)

print ("RESULTING VECTOR C = ")
print linear_combination_result

print ("CHECKING THE RESULT EVALUATING THE DIFFERENCE VECTOR BETWEEN C
AND THE LINEAR COMBINATION OF A AND B")
print ("C - (%sA + %sB) = "%(mult_coefficient_a,mult_coefficient_b))
```

```
print (linear_combination_result - (mult_coefficient_a*input_vector_a\
                                + mult_coefficient_b*input_
vector_b))
assert la.norm((linear_combination_result - \
            (mult_coefficient_a*input_vector_a +\
            mult_coefficient_b*input_vector_b)).get()) < 1e-5
```

The output for this from Command Prompt is as follows:

```
C:\Python CookBook\Chapter 6 - GPU Programming with Python\ >python
PyCudaElementWise.py
INPUT VECTOR A =
[ 0.73191601  0.7004351   0.87159222  0.49621502  0.19640177
0.75579387
   0.35208538  0.97497243  0.36948711  0.34328628  0.06811771
0.04270195
   0.15690483  0.39899695  0.2927697   0.36201504  0.09503061
0.45646626
   0.35608584  0.01598917  0.75943208  0.49343511  0.79146844
0.33111155
   0.18454118  0.83971804  0.01466237  0.77959627  0.54659295
0.4575595
   0.55539894  0.23285247  0.14676388  0.72028935  0.87861985
0.13928016
   0.18071586  0.8029055   0.05551658  0.49400434  0.40941685
0.55373788
   0.07541087  0.55443048  0.19723719  0.72457349  0.46491891
0.65380263
   0.93845034  0.27472526]
INPUT VECTOR B =
[ 0.29464501  0.21645674  0.93407696  0.48678038  0.71135205
0.0588627
   0.99216938  0.879906    0.07517455  0.84360296  0.57358545
0.73907417
   0.06841258  0.1816148   0.53327322  0.30980903  0.96774238
0.90884209
   0.39139062  0.97678316  0.41284555  0.17893282  0.47421032
0.13706622
   0.62038481  0.22524452  0.67131585  0.06617502  0.02492006
0.99894243
   0.28288943  0.55505407  0.14323047  0.54854101  0.2742492
0.01146096
   0.45902726  0.03561942  0.78358203  0.32014725  0.13187674
0.42909116
   0.2633251   0.07679776  0.80823648  0.57373965  0.40740359
0.26024994
   0.61452144  0.46388686]
```

```
RESULTING VECTOR C =
[ 2.93705702   2.48315382   6.41356945   3.42633176   3.94956398
1.80590129
   5.6650176    6.34947491   1.11484694   4.90458727   3.00416279
3.78077483
   0.65587258   1.70606792   3.25190544   2.2730751    5.02877283
5.45714283
   2.6691246    4.91589403   3.58309197   1.88153434   3.95398855
1.34755421
   3.47100639   2.80565882   3.38590407   1.89006758   1.21778619
5.90983152
   2.52524495   3.24097538   1.00968003   4.18328381   3.12848568
0.33586511
   2.65656805   1.78390813   4.02894306   2.58874488   1.47821736
3.25293159
   1.46744728   1.49284983   4.43565702   4.31784534   2.96685553
2.60885501
   4.94950771   2.86888456]
```

CHECKING THE RESULT EVALUATING THE DIFFERENCE VECTOR BETWEEN C AND THE LINEAR COMBINATION OF A AND B

```
C - (2A + 5B) =
[ 0.  0.  0.  0.  0.  0.  0.  0.  0.  0.  0.  0.  0.  0.  0.  0.  0.
0.
  0.  0.  0.  0.  0.  0.  0.  0.  0.  0.  0.  0.  0.  0.  0.  0.  0.
0.
  0.  0.  0.  0.  0.  0.  0.  0.  0.  0.  0.  0.  0.  0.]
```

How it works...

After the usual import, we note:

```
from pycuda.elementwise import ElementwiseKernel
```

We must build all the elements that are to be manipulated. Let's remember that the task to be done is to evaluate a linear combination of two vectors `input_vector_a` and `input_vector_b`. These two vectors are initialized using the PyCUDA `curandom` library, which is used for the generation of pseudorandom numbers:

To import the library, use the following code:

```
from pycuda.curandom import rand as curand
```

To define the random vector (50 elements), use:

```
input_vector_a = curand((50,))
input_vector_b = curand((50,))
```

We defined the two coefficients of multiplication that are to be used in the calculation of the linear combination of these two vectors:

```
mult_coefficient_a = 2
mult_coefficient_b = 5
```

The core example is the kernel invocation for which we use the PyCUDA `ElementwiseKernel` construct, shown as follows:

```
linear_combination = ElementwiseKernel(
        "float a, float *x, float b, float *y, float *c",
        "c[i] = a*x[i] + b*y[i]",
        "linear_combination")
```

The first line of the argument list (in a C-style definition) defines all the parameters to be inserted for the calculation:

```
        "float a, float *x, float b, float *y, float *c",
```

The second line defines how to manipulate the arguments list. For each value of the index i, a sum of these components must be evaluated:

```
    "c[i] = a*x[i] + b*y[i]",
```

The last line gives the `linear_combination` name to `ElementwiseKernel`.

After the kernel, the resulting vector is defined. It is an empty vector of the same dimension as of the input vector:

```
linear_combination_result = gpuarray.empty_like(input_vector_a)
Finally evaluate the kernel:
linear_combination(mult_coefficient_a, input_vector_a,\
                   mult_coefficient_b, input_vector_b,\
                   linear_combination_result)
```

You can check the results using the following code:

```
assert la.norm((linear_combination_result - \
               (mult_coefficient_a*input_vector_a +\
               mult_coefficient_b*input_vector_b)).get()) < 1e-5
```

The `assert` function tests the result and triggers an error if the condition is `false`.

There's more...

In addition to the `curand` library, derived from the CUDA library, PyCUDA provides other math libraries, so you can take a look at the libraries listed at `http://documen.tician.de/pycuda`.

The MapReduce operation with PyCUDA

PyCUDA provides a functionality to perform reduction operations on the GPU. This is possible with the `pycuda.reduction.ReductionKernel` method:

```
ReductionKernel(dtype_out, arguments, map_expr ,reduce_expr,
                name,optional_parameters)
```

Here, we note that:

 ▸ `dtype_out`: This is the output's data type. It must be specified by the `numpy.dtype` data type.

 ▸ `arguments`: This is a C argument list of all the parameters involved in the reduction's operation.

 ▸ `map_expr`: This is a string that represents the mapping operation. Each vector in this expression must be referenced with the variable `i`.

 ▸ `reduce_expr`: This is a string that represents the reduction operation. The operands in this expression are indicated by lowercase letters, such as `a, b, c, ..., z`.

 ▸ `name`: This is the name associated with `ReductionKernel`, with which the kernel is compiled.

 ▸ `optional_parameters`: These are not important in this recipe as they are the compiler's directives.

The method executes a kernel on vector arguments (at least one), performs `map_expr` on each entry of the vector argument, and then performs `reduce_expr` on its outcome.

How to do it...

This example shows the implementation of a dot product of two vectors (500 elements) through an instantiation of the `ReductionKernel` class. The dot product, or scalar product, is an algebraic operation that takes two equal length sequences of numbers (usually coordinate vectors) and returns a single number that is the sum of the products of the corresponding entries of the two sequences of numbers. This is a typical MapReduce operation, where the Map operation is an index-by-index product and the reduction operation is the sum of all the products.

The PyCUDA code for this task is very short:

```
import pycuda.gpuarray as gpuarray
import pycuda.autoinit
import numpy
from pycuda.reduction import ReductionKernel

vector_length = 400
```

```
input_vector_a = gpuarray.arange(vector_length, dtype=numpy.int)
input_vector_b = gpuarray.arange(vector_length, dtype=numpy.int)
dot_product = ReductionKernel(numpy.int,
                    arguments="int *x, int *y",
                    map_expr="x[i]*y[i]",
                    reduce_expr="a+b", neutral="0")

dot_product = dot_product (input_vector_a, input_vector_b).get()

print("INPUT VECTOR A")
print input_vector_a

print("INPUT VECTOR B")
print input_vector_b

print("RESULT DOT PRODUCT OF A * B")
print dot_product
```

Running the code from Command Prompt, you will have an output like this:

```
C:\Python CookBook\Chapter 6 - GPU Programming with Python\>python
PyCudaReductionKernel.py
```

```
INPUT VECTOR A
[  0   1   2   3   4   5   6   7   8   9  10  11  12  13  14  15  16  17
  18  19  20  21  22  23  24  25  26  27  28  29  30  31  32  33  34  35
  36  37  38  39  40  41  42  43  44  45  46  47  48  49  50  51  52  53
  54  55  56  57  58  59  60  61  62  63  64  65  66  67  68  69  70  71
  72  73  74  75  76  77  78  79  80  81  82  83  84  85  86  87  88  89
  90  91  92  93  94  95  96  97  98  99 100 101 102 103 104 105 106 107
 108 109 110 111 112 113 114 115 116 117 118 119 120 121 122 123 124 125
 126 127 128 129 130 131 132 133 134 135 136 137 138 139 140 141 142 143
 144 145 146 147 148 149 150 151 152 153 154 155 156 157 158 159 160 161
 162 163 164 165 166 167 168 169 170 171 172 173 174 175 176 177 178 179
 180 181 182 183 184 185 186 187 188 189 190 191 192 193 194 195 196 197
 198 199 200 201 202 203 204 205 206 207 208 209 210 211 212 213 214 215
 216 217 218 219 220 221 222 223 224 225 226 227 228 229 230 231 232 233
 234 235 236 237 238 239 240 241 242 243 244 245 246 247 248 249 250 251
 252 253 254 255 256 257 258 259 260 261 262 263 264 265 266 267 268 269
```

270 271 272 273 274 275 276 277 278 279 280 281 282 283 284 285 286 287
288 289 290 291 292 293 294 295 296 297 298 299 300 301 302 303 304 305
306 307 308 309 310 311 312 313 314 315 316 317 318 319 320 321 322 323
324 325 326 327 328 329 330 331 332 333 334 335 336 337 338 339 340 341
342 343 344 345 346 347 348 349 350 351 352 353 354 355 356 357 358 359
360 361 362 363 364 365 366 367 368 369 370 371 372 373 374 375 376 377
378 379 380 381 382 383 384 385 386 387 388 389 390 391 392 393 394 395
396 397 398 399]

INPUT VECTOR B

[0   1   2   3   4   5   6   7   8   9 10 11 12 13 14 15 16 17
 18 19 20 21 22 23 24 25 26 27 28 29 30 31 32 33 34 35
 36 37 38 39 40 41 42 43 44 45 46 47 48 49 50 51 52 53
 54 55 56 57 58 59 60 61 62 63 64 65 66 67 68 69 70 71
 72 73 74 75 76 77 78 79 80 81 82 83 84 85 86 87 88 89
 90 91 92 93 94 95 96 97 98 99 100 101 102 103 104 105 106 107
108 109 110 111 112 113 114 115 116 117 118 119 120 121 122 123 124 125
126 127 128 129 130 131 132 133 134 135 136 137 138 139 140 141 142 143
144 145 146 147 148 149 150 151 152 153 154 155 156 157 158 159 160 161
162 163 164 165 166 167 168 169 170 171 172 173 174 175 176 177 178 179
180 181 182 183 184 185 186 187 188 189 190 191 192 193 194 195 196 197
198 199 200 201 202 203 204 205 206 207 208 209 210 211 212 213 214 215
216 217 218 219 220 221 222 223 224 225 226 227 228 229 230 231 232 233
234 235 236 237 238 239 240 241 242 243 244 245 246 247 248 249 250 251
252 253 254 255 256 257 258 259 260 261 262 263 264 265 266 267 268 269
270 271 272 273 274 275 276 277 278 279 280 281 282 283 284 285 286 287
288 289 290 291 292 293 294 295 296 297 298 299 300 301 302 303 304 305
306 307 308 309 310 311 312 313 314 315 316 317 318 319 320 321 322 323
324 325 326 327 328 329 330 331 332 333 334 335 336 337 338 339 340 341
342 343 344 345 346 347 348 349 350 351 352 353 354 355 356 357 358 359
360 361 362 363 364 365 366 367 368 369 370 371 372 373 374 375 376 377
378 379 380 381 382 383 384 385 386 387 388 389 390 391 392 393 394 395
396 397 398 399]

RESULT DOT PRODUCT OF A * B
21253400

How it works...

In this script, the input vectors `input_vector_a` and `input_vector_b` are integer vectors. Each of them, as you can see from the preceding output result, ranges from 0 to 399 elements (400 elements in total):

```
vector_length = 400

input_vector_a = gpuarray.arange(vector_length, dtype=numpy.int)
input_vector_b = gpuarray.arange(vector_length, dtype=numpy.int)
```

After the definition of the inputs, we can define the MapReduce operation by calling the `ReductionKernel` PyCUDA function:

```
dot_product = ReductionKernel(numpy.int,
                    arguments="int *x, int *y",
                    map_expr="x[i]*y[i]",
                    reduce_expr="a+b", neutral="0")
```

This kernel operation is defined as follows:

▶ The first entry in the argument list tells us that the output will be an integer

▶ The second entry defines the data types for the inputs (array of integers) in a C-like notation

▶ The third entry is the map operation, which is the product of the *i*th element of the two vectors

▶ The fourth operation is the reduction operation, which is the sum of all the products

Observe that the end result of calling the `ReductionKernel` instance is a `GPUArray` scalar that still resides in the GPU. It can be brought to the CPU by a call to its `get` method or can be used in place of the GPU.

Then, the kernel function is invoked, as shown:

```
dot_product = dot_product(input_vector_a, input_vector_b).get()
```

The input vectors and the resulting dot product are printed out:

```
print input_vector_a
print input_vector_b
print dot_product
```

GPU programming with NumbaPro

NumbaPro is a Python compiler that provides a CUDA-based API to write CUDA programs. It is designed for array-oriented computing tasks, much like the widely used NumPy library. The data parallelism in array-oriented computing tasks is a natural fit for accelerators such as GPUs. NumbaPro understands NumPy array types and uses them to generate efficient compiled code for execution on GPUs or multicore CPUs.

The compiler works by allowing you to specify type signatures for Python functions, which enable compilation at runtime (called the JIT compilation).

The most important decorators are:

> ▸ numbapro.jit: This allows a developer to write CUDA-like functions. When encountered, the compiler translates the code under the decorator into the pseudo assembly PTX language to be executed in the GPU.

> ▸ numbapro.autojit: This annotates a function for a deferred compilation procedure. This means that each function with this signature is compiled exactly once.

> ▸ numbapro.vectorize: This creates a so-called ufunc object (the Numpy universal function) that takes a function and executes it parallelly in vector arguments.

> ▸ guvectorize: This creates a so-called gufunc object (the NumPy generalized universal function). A gufunc object may operate on entire subarrays (refer to http://docs.continuum.io/numbapro/generalizedufuncs.html for more references.)

All these decorators have a compiler directive called a target that selects the code generation target. The NumbaPro compiler supports the parallel and GPU targets. The parallel target is available to vectorize the operations, while the GPU directive offloads the computation to a NVIDIA CUDA GPU.

Getting ready

NumbaPro is part of Anaconda Accelerate, which is a commercially licensed product (NumbaPro is also available under a free license for academic users) from Continuum Analytics. It is built on top of the BSD-licensed, open source Numba project, which itself relies heavily on the capabilities of the LLVM compiler. The GPU backend of NumbaPro utilizes the LLVM-based NVIDIA Compiler SDK.

To get started with NumbaPro, the first step is to download and install the Anaconda Python distribution (`http://continuum.io/downloads`), which is a completely free, enterprise-ready Python distribution for large-scale data processing, predictive analytics, and scientific computing. It includes many popular packages (Numpy, Scipy, Matplotlib, iPython, and so on) and `conda`, which is a powerful package manager.

Once you have Anaconda installed, you must type the following instructions from Anaconda's Command Prompt:

```
> conda update conda
```

```
> conda install accelerate
```

```
> conda install numbapro
```

NumbaPro does not ship the CUDA driver. It is the user's responsibility to ensure that their systems are using the latest drivers. After the installation, it's possible to perform the detection of the CUDA library and GPU, so let's open Python from the Anaconda console and type:

```
import numbapro
numbapro.check_cuda()
```

The output of these two lines of code should be as follows (we used a 64-bit Anaconda distro):

```
C:\Users\Giancarlo\Anaconda>python
Python 2.7.10 |Anaconda 2.3.0 (64-bit)| (default, May 28 2015, 16:44:52)
[MSC v.1500 64 bit (AMD64)] on win32
Type "help", "copyright", "credits" or "license" for more information.
Anaconda is brought to you by Continuum Analytics.
Please check out: http://continuum.io/thanks and https://binstar.org
>>> import numbapro
Vendor:  Continuum Analytics, Inc.
Package: mkl
Message: trial mode expires in 30 days
Vendor:  Continuum Analytics, Inc.
Package: mkl
Message: trial mode expires in 30 days
Vendor:  Continuum Analytics, Inc.
Package: numbapro
Message: trial mode expires in 30 days
>>> numbapro.check_cuda()
------------------------------libraries detection-----------------------
```

```
Finding cublas
        located at C:\Users\Giancarlo\Anaconda\DLLs\cublas64_60.dll
        trying to open library...        ok
Finding cusparse
        located at C:\Users\Giancarlo\Anaconda\DLLs\cusparse64_60.dll
        trying to open library...        ok
Finding cufft
        located at C:\Users\Giancarlo\Anaconda\DLLs\cufft64_60.dll
        trying to open library...        ok
Finding curand
        located at C:\Users\Giancarlo\Anaconda\DLLs\curand64_60.dll
        trying to open library...        ok
Finding nvvm
        located at C:\Users\Giancarlo\Anaconda\DLLs\nvvm64_20_0.dll
        trying to open library...        ok
        finding libdevice for compute_20...        ok
        finding libdevice for compute_30...        ok
        finding libdevice for compute_35...        ok
----------------------------hardware detection------------------------
Found 1 CUDA devices
id 0            GeForce 840M                                [SUPPORTED]
                    compute capability: 5.0
                        pci device id: 0
                            pci bus id: 8
Summary:
        1/1 devices are supported
PASSED
True
>>>
```

How to do it...

In this example, we give a demonstration of the NumbaPro compiler using the annotation @guvectorize. In the following task, we try to execute a matrix multiplication using the Numbapro module:

```python
from numbapro import guvectorize
import numpy as np

@guvectorize(['void(int64[:,:], int64[:,:], int64[:,:])'],
             '(m,n),(n,p)->(m,p)')
def matmul(A, B, C):
    m, n = A.shape
    n, p = B.shape
    for i in range(m):
        for j in range(p):
            C[i, j] = 0
            for k in range(n):
                C[i, j] += A[i, k] * B[k, j]


dim = 10
A = np.random.randint(dim, size=(dim, dim))
B = np.random.randint(dim, size=(dim, dim))


C = matmul(A, B)
print("INPUT MATRIX A")
print(":\n%s" % A)
print("INPUT MATRIX B")
print(":\n%s" % B)
print("RESULT MATRIX C = A*B")
print(":\n%s" % C)
```

After running the code (using the Anaconda console), we should have an output like this:

```
INPUT MATRIX A
:
[[7 7 8 5 8 5 1 9 5 9]
 [3 5 5 4 6 7 6 5 3 1]
 [7 1 6 8 7 9 0 3 3 3]
 [7 4 4 3 7 8 1 2 1 2]
 [4 7 7 1 3 5 5 6 7 6]
 [5 0 1 5 8 4 4 4 4 9]
```

```
     [1 3 2 0 7 3 7 2 3 4]
     [0 2 9 0 7 5 9 7 4 7]
     [7 3 7 6 5 6 4 2 2 7]
     [2 1 9 7 1 0 3 5 7 3]]
INPUT MATRIX B
:
[[2 9 8 4 2 3 9 7 3 1]
 [9 1 3 3 8 0 7 6 3 5]
 [7 4 9 6 6 5 9 7 6 6]
 [6 8 3 1 5 4 4 7 7 5]
 [6 2 5 1 2 8 6 0 5 8]
 [4 4 5 7 6 0 1 1 3 8]
 [2 7 8 6 1 9 8 4 1 6]
 [2 2 9 8 3 6 1 4 7 4]
 [9 9 6 9 3 3 3 2 4 9]
 [8 4 6 7 8 8 8 6 7 8]]

RESULT MATRIX C = A*B
:
[[368 284 402 331 304 295 361 291 327 378]
 [231 207 278 226 188 199 236 177 193 273]
 [248 247 280 217 208 190 243 198 232 279]
 [201 181 232 175 173 149 218 156 170 225]
 [297 239 331 301 239 225 290 225 229 315]
 [235 229 270 222 181 248 246 175 219 280]
 [174 142 201 166 124 185 192 108 129 217]
 [267 213 348 297 212 292 289 194 233 334]
 [266 254 305 239 228 230 303 234 232 288]
 [227 219 255 215 166 189 214 196 204 229]]
```

How it works...

The `@guvectorize` annotation works on array arguments. This decorator takes an extra argument to specify the `gufunc` signature. The arguments are explained, as follows:

▸ The first three arguments specify the types of data to be managed, which are the array of integers: `'void(int64[:,:], int64[:,:], int64[:,:])'`

▸ The last argument of `@guvectorize` specifies how to manipulate the matrix dimensions: `'(m,n),(n,p)->(m,p)'`

```
@guvectorize(['void(int64[:,:], int64[:,:], int64[:,:])'],
             '(m,n),(n,p)->(m,p)')
```

In the subsequent code, we define the `matmul(A, B, C)` operation. It accepts the two input matrix A and B and produces a C output matrix. According to the `gufunc` signature, we should have:

```
A(m,n)* B(n,p) = C(m,p) where m,n,p are the matrix dimensions.
```

The matrix product is simply performed via three `for` loops along with the matrix indices:

```
for i in range(m):
        for j in range(p):
            C[i, j] = 0
            for k in range(n):
                C[i, j] += A[i, k] * B[k, j]
```

The Numpy's function `randint` is used to build integers from random matrices:

```
dim = 10
A = np.random.randint(dim,size=(dim, dim))
B = np.random.randint(dim,size=(dim, dim))
```

Finally, the `matmul` function is called with these matrices with arguments, and the resultant matrix is printed out:

```
C = matmul(A, B)
print("RESULT MATRIX C = A*B")
        print(":\n%s" % C)
```

Using GPU-accelerated libraries with NumbaPro

NumbaPro provides a Python wrap for CUDA libraries for numerical computing. Each code using these libraries will get a significant speedup without writing any GPU-specific code. The libraries are explained as follows:

- ▶ **cuBLAS**: This is a library developed by NVIDIA that provides the main functions of linear algebra to run on a GPU. Like the **Basic Linear Algebra Subprograms** (**BLAS**) library that implements the functions of linear algebra on the CPU, the cuBLAS library classifies its functions into three levels:
    - ❏ **Level 1**: Vector operations
    - ❏ **Level 2**: Transactions between a matrix and vector
    - ❏ **Level 3**: Operations between matrices

The division of these functions in the three levels is based on the number of nested loops that are needed to perform the selected operation. More precisely, the operations of the level are essential cycles that are geared to complete the execution of the selected function.

- **cuFFT**: This provides a simple interface to calculate the **Fast Fourier Transform** (**FFT**) in a distributed manner on an NVIDIA GPU, enabling you to exploit the parallelism of the GPU without having to develop your own implementation of the FFT.

- **cuRAND**: This library provides the creation of quasirandom numbers. A quasirandom number is a random number generated by a deterministic algorithm.

- **cuSPArse**: This provides a set of functions for the management of sparse matrices. Unlike the previous case, its functions are classified into four levels:

  - **Level 1**: These are operations between a vector that is stored in a shed and a vector that is stored in a dense format.

  - **Level 2**: These are the transactions between a matrix format stored in a shed and a vector stored in the dense format.

  - **Level 3**: These are the operations in a matrix format that are stored in a shed and set of vectors that are stored in a dense format (this set can be considered as one large dense matrix.)

  - **Conversion**: These are operations that allow the conversion between different storage formats.

How to do it...

In this example, we present an implementation of **GEneral Matrix Multiply** (**GEMM**), which is a routine to perform matrix-matrix multiplication on NVIDIA GPUs. The sequential version using the NumPy Python module and the parallel version using the cuBLAS library will be reported. Also, a comparison of the execution time will be made between the two algorithms.

The code for this is as follows:

```
import numbapro.cudalib.cublas as cublas
import numpy as np
from timeit import default_timer as timer

dim = 10

def gemm():
    print("Version 2".center(80, '='))

    A = np.random.rand(dim,dim)
    B = np.random.rand(dim, dim)
```

```
            D = np.zeros_like(A, order='F')

            print("MATRIX A :")
            print A
            print("VECTOR B :")
            print B

            # NumPy
            start = timer()
            E = np.dot(A, B)
            numpy_time = timer() - start
            print("Numpy took %f seconds" % numpy_time)

            # cuBLAS
            blas = cublas.Blas()

            start = timer()
            blas.gemm('T', 'T', dim, dim, dim, 1.0, A, B, 1.0, D)
            cuda_time = timer() - start
            print ("RESULT MATRIX EVALUATED WITH CUBLAS")
            print D
            print("CUBLAS took %f seconds" % cuda_time)
            diff = np.abs(D - E)
            print("Maximum error %f" % np.max(diff))


        def main():

            gemm()

        if __name__ == '__main__':
            main()
```

The output obtained for this will be as follows:

```
MATRIX A :
[[ 0.79582178   0.95671563   0.69251157   0.85600979   0.32826726   0.72861569
   0.20724061   0.55065641   0.2257875    0.90146437]
 [ 0.6742022    0.43449657   0.04862685   0.9023226    0.87598306   0.20774405
   0.15774015   0.2847742    0.81601615   0.34114773]
 [ 0.61500219   0.65982283   0.73493152   0.21913261   0.80862566   0.73982082
   0.84005388   0.38745489   0.676947     0.31530397]
```

```
[ 0.60694411   0.65138528   0.63773284   0.06589098   0.49177294   0.02029247
  0.9064746    0.93419845   0.14609622   0.28317855]
[ 0.60166404   0.41423776   0.09938464   0.19315303   0.07374789   0.45335697
  0.2912572    0.81481984   0.65222424   0.0670377 ]
[ 0.32192297   0.30244072   0.86595209   0.37701833   0.79095644   0.11518194
  0.88491826   0.98290063   0.62965353   0.38323725]
[ 0.21512101   0.64731098   0.4079146    0.8371392    0.01398673   0.85945652
  0.0586854    0.48812094   0.3625991    0.58142603]
[ 0.77378663   0.43994483   0.5620805    0.70350504   0.60589009   0.09605428
  0.25423268   0.06869655   0.13642323   0.00221422]
[ 0.77808301   0.47386303   0.54323866   0.42010733   0.80652762   0.05903843
  0.63316824   0.58479485   0.45141828   0.46231481]
[ 0.97122802   0.53723365   0.68688748   0.54315409   0.00883411   0.9855186
  0.53542786   0.83478941   0.27459888   0.21024639]]
VECTOR B :
[[ 0.17084153   0.44546677   0.21551063   0.39731923   0.00102686   0.81069924
   0.00681474   0.01126972   0.13769525   0.63437229]
 [ 0.81913609   0.97583768   0.52579565   0.20179695   0.24066758   0.18154282
   0.75033104   0.41878918   0.96892428   0.54358419]
 [ 0.10071768   0.3090773    0.94185921   0.70550442   0.10651627   0.62659408
   0.23255164   0.96166165   0.65615938   0.16991118]
 [ 0.84163163   0.59296382   0.12281989   0.32851275   0.78716318   0.02568872
   0.02367708   0.65485736   0.79834789   0.76747705]
 [ 0.90406949   0.03424157   0.01519989   0.5011444    0.63175281   0.17705116
   0.16257016   0.81357471   0.58567631   0.24503327]
 [ 0.62989968   0.47944669   0.86860435   0.94086568   0.24312278   0.13450463
   0.16352136   0.42323191   0.46907905   0.97772097]
 [ 0.44608094   0.19969488   0.01035155   0.69528549   0.07219375   0.91454669
   0.18330497   0.76095336   0.12880003   0.24301603]
 [ 0.37860881   0.33079438   0.19275564   0.58316669   0.35753971   0.63697732
   0.72063491   0.42698316   0.53811423   0.83682958]
 [ 0.42135462   0.89413827   0.00620849   0.63770542   0.29376823   0.68415057
   0.71826696   0.9748898    0.9086774    0.7084634 ]
 [ 0.08020851   0.47789158   0.45538401   0.26468263   0.84960276   0.1108932
   0.0407631    0.41811299   0.2539022    0.73346706]]
```

```
Numpy took 1.167435 seconds
```

RESULT MATRIX EVALUATED WITH CUBLAS

```
[[ 2.93393517   3.22653293   2.58999843   2.97688025   2.40723642   2.22561846
    1.71083261   3.20145366   3.4654546    3.9246803 ]
 [ 2.70759988   2.42236864   0.94108333   2.20715685   2.06739391   1.78390442
    1.37381915   2.80760808   2.87826551   2.88739456]
 [ 2.93301949   2.70921232   2.08465713   3.39447429   1.76684939   2.84034554
    1.8600905    3.70096673   3.21368161   3.20257798]
 [ 2.05665894   1.92477247   1.42646422   2.45288009   1.27576149   2.65682509
    1.68187918   2.6942483    2.30742661   2.35163885]
 [ 1.68553937   1.98030198   1.05436088   2.03107385   0.98066787   1.94328559
    1.54050405   1.8876191    2.04514196   2.49719893]
 [ 2.55782414   2.2600454    1.57942935   3.11991574   1.91570669   2.93236718
    1.92525406   3.76932667   3.03618471   2.87628333]
 [ 2.27705425   2.53777179   1.98218876   2.30511984   1.85547257   1.36423334
    1.39131705   2.43879465   2.75148098   3.14994564]
 [ 1.94662205   1.62822264   1.12425671   1.72230283   1.21131853   1.56748417
    0.79113948   2.08449619   2.05742732   1.82536594]
 [ 2.42686338   2.22641127   1.3762425    2.57727754   1.80747335   2.53040609
    1.51847658   3.05078902   2.68199133   2.72340269]
 [ 2.44854528   2.69315101   2.3255071    3.17886105   1.47260987   2.69597578
    1.65043895   2.79595207   2.82714486   3.58489296]]
```

CUBLAS took 0.004226 seconds

Maximum error 0.000000

The result obtained confirms the effectiveness of the cuBLAS library.

How it works...

In order to make a comparison between a NumPy and cuBLAS implementation of a matrix product, we import all the required libraries:

```
import numbapro.cudalib.cublas as cublas
import numpy as np
```

Also, we define the matrix dimension:

```
dim = 10
```

The core algorithm is the `gemm()` function. First, we define the input matrices:

```
A = np.random.rand(dim,dim)
B = np.random.rand(dim,dim)
```

Here, `D` will contain the output of the cuBLAS implementation:

```
D = np.zeros_like(A, order='F')
```

In this example, we compare the calculation done with NumPy and cuBLAS. The NumPy evaluation is: `E = np.dot(A,B)`, where the matrix `E` will contain the dot product.

Finally, the cuBLAS implementation is as follows:

```
blas = cublas.Blas()
    start = timer()
    blas.gemm('T', 'T', dim, dim, dim, 1.0, A, B, 1.0, D)
    cuda_time = timer() - start
```

The `gemm()` function is a cuBLAS level 3 function:

```
numbapro.cudalib.cublas.Blas.gemm(transa, transb, m, n, k, alpha,
                                  A, B,beta, C)
```

It realizes a matrix-matrix multiplication in the following form:

```
C = alpha * op(A) * op(B) + beta * C where op is transpose or not.
```

At the end of the function, we compare the two results and report the execution time (`cuda_time`):

```
print("CUBLAS took %f seconds" % cuda_time)
    diff = np.abs(D - E)
    print("Maximum error %f" % np.max(diff))
```

There's more...

In this example, we saw an application of the cuBLAS library. For more complete references, refer to `http://docs.nvidia.com/cuda/cublas/index.html` and `http://docs.continuum.io/numbapro/cudalib` for a complete list of CUDA function libraries wrapped with NumbaPro.

Using the PyOpenCL module

Open Computing Language (**OpenCL**) is a framework used to develop programs that work across heterogeneous platforms, which can be made either by the CPU or GPU that are produced by different manufacturers. This platform was created by Apple, but has been developed and maintained by a non-profit consortium called the Khronos Group. This framework is the main alternative for the CUDA execution of software on a GPU, but has a point of view that is diametrically opposed. However, CUDA makes specialization its strong point (produced, developed, and compatible with NVIDIA), ensuring excellent performance at the expense of portability. OpenCL offers a solution compatible with nearly all devices on the market. Software written in OpenCL can run on processor products from all major industries, such as Intel, NVIDIA, IBM, and AMD. OpenCL includes a language to write kernels based on C99 (with some restrictions), allowing you to use the hardware available directly in the same way as with CUDA-C-Fortran or CUDA. OpenCL provides functions to run highly parallel and synchronization primitives, such as indicators for regions of memory and control mechanisms for the different platforms of execution. The portability of OpenCL programs, however, is limited to the ability to run the same code on different devices, and this ensures that the performance is equally reliable. To get the best performance possible, it is fundamental that you refer to the execution platform, optimizing the code based on the characteristics of the device. In the following recipes, we'll examine the Python implementation of OpenCL called PyOpenCL.

Getting ready

PyOpenCL is to OpenCL what PyCUDA is to CUDA: a Python wrapper to those GPGPU platforms (PyOpenCL can run alternatively on both NVIDIA and the AMD GPU card.) It is developed and maintained by Andreas Klöckner. Installing PyOpenCL on Windows is easy when using the binary package provided by Christoph Gohlke. His webpage contains Windows binary installers for the most recent versions of hundreds of Python packages. It is of invaluable help for those Python users that use Windows.

With these instructions, you will build a 32-bit PyOpenCL library for a Python 2.7 distro on a Windows 7 machine with a NVIDIA GPU card:

1. Go to `http://www.lfd.uci.edu/~gohlke/pythonlibs/#pyopencl` and download the file from `pyopencl-2015.1-cp27-none-win32.whl` (and the relative dependencies if required).

2. Download and install the Win32 OpenCL driver (from Intel) from `http://registrationcenter.intel.com/irc_nas/5198/opencl_runtime_15.1_x86_setup.msi`.

3. Finally, install the `pyOpenCL` file from Command Prompt with the command:

```
pip install pyopencl-2015.1-cp27-none-win32.whl
```

How to do it...

In this first example, we verify that the PyOpenCL environment is correctly installed.

So, a simple script that can enumerate all major hardware features using the OpenCL library is presented as:

```python
import pyopencl as cl


def print_device_info() :
    print('\n' + '=' * 60 + '\nOpenCL Platforms and Devices')
    for platform in cl.get_platforms():
        print('=' * 60)
        print('Platform - Name:  ' + platform.name)
        print('Platform - Vendor:  ' + platform.vendor)
        print('Platform - Version:  ' + platform.version)
        print('Platform - Profile:  ' + platform.profile)

        for device in platform.get_devices():
            print('    ' + '-' * 56)
            print('    Device - Name:  ' \
                + device.name)
            print('    Device - Type:  ' \
                + cl.device_type.to_string(device.type))
            print('    Device - Max Clock Speed:  {0} Mhz'\
                .format(device.max_clock_frequency))
            print('    Device - Compute Units:  {0}'\
                .format(device.max_compute_units))
            print('    Device - Local Memory:  {0:.0f} KB'\
                .format(device.local_mem_size/1024.0))
            print('    Device - Constant Memory:  {0:.0f} KB'\
                .format(device.max_constant_buffer_size/1024.0))
            print('    Device - Global Memory: {0:.0f} GB'\
                .format(device.global_mem_size/1073741824.0))
            print('    Device - Max Buffer/Image Size: {0:.0f} MB'\
                .format(device.max_mem_alloc_size/1048576.0))
            print('    Device - Max Work Group Size: {0:.0f}'\
                .format(device.max_work_group_size))
    print('\n')

if __name__ == "__main__":
    print_device_info()
```

The output that shows the main characteristics of the CPU and GPU card that is installed should be like this:

```
C:\Python CookBook\Chapter 6 - GPU Programming with Python\>python
PyOpenCLDeviceInfo.py


================================================================
OpenCL Platforms and Devices
================================================================
Platform - Name:  NVIDIA CUDA
Platform - Vendor:  NVIDIA Corporation
Platform - Version:  OpenCL 1.1 CUDA 6.0.1
Platform - Profile:  FULL_PROFILE
        ----------------------------------------------------------
    Device - Name:  GeForce GT 240
    Device - Type:  GPU
    Device - Max Clock Speed:  1340 Mhz
    Device - Compute Units:  12
    Device - Local Memory:  16 KB
    Device - Constant Memory:  64 KB
    Device - Global Memory: 1 GB




================================================================
Platform - Name:  Intel(R) OpenCL
Platform - Vendor:  Intel(R) Corporation
Platform - Version:  OpenCL 1.2
Platform - Profile:  FULL_PROFILE
        ----------------------------------------------------------
    Device - Name:  Intel(R) Core(TM)2 Duo CPU      E6550   @ 2.33GHz
    Device - Type:  CPU
    Device - Max Clock Speed:  2330 Mhz
    Device - Compute Units:  2
    Device - Local Memory:  32 KB
    Device - Constant Memory:  128 KB
    Device - Global Memory: 2 GB
```

How it works...

The code is very simple. In the first line, we import the `pyopencl` module:

```
import pyopencl as cl
```

Then, the `platform.get_devices()` method is used to get a list of devices. For each device, the set of its main features are printed on the screen:

- ▸ The name and device type
- ▸ Max clock speed
- ▸ Compute units
- ▸ Local/constant/global memory

How to build a PyOpenCL application

As for programming with PyCUDA, the first step to build a program for PyOpenCL is the encoding of the host application. In fact, it is performed on the host computer (typically, the user's PC) and then it dispatches the kernel application on the connected devices (GPU cards).

The host application must contain five data structures:

- ▸ **Device**: This identifies the hardware where the kernel code must be executed. A PyOpenCL application can be executed on CPU and GPU cards but also in embedded devices, such as **Field Programmable Gate Array** (**FPGA**).
- ▸ **Program**: This is a group of kernels. A program selects the kernel that must be executed on the device.
- ▸ **Kernel**: This is the code to be executed on the device. A kernel is essentially a C-like function that enables it to be compiled for execution on any device that supports OpenCL drivers. A kernel is the only way the host can call a function that will run on a device. When the host invokes a kernel, many work items start running on the device. Each work item runs the code of the kernel, but works on a different part of the dataset.
- ▸ **Command queue**: Here, each device receives kernels through this data structure. A command queue orders the execution of kernels on the device.

▶ **Context**: This is a group of devices. A context allows devices to receive kernels and transfer data.

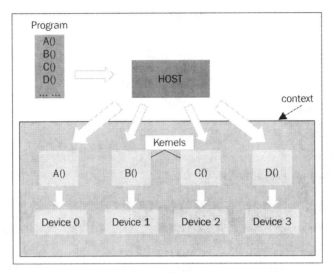

PyOpenCL programming

The preceding figure shows how these data structures can work in a host application. Note that a program can contain multiple functions to be executed on the device, and each kernel encapsulates only a single function from the program.

How to do it...

In this example, we show you the basic steps to build a PyOpenCL program. The task here is to execute the parallel sum of two vectors. In order to maintain a readable output, let's consider two vectors each from the 100 elements. The resulting vector will be for each *i*th element, which is the sum of the *i*th element `vector_a` and `vector_b`.

Of course, to be able to appreciate the parallel execution of this code, you can also increase some orders whose magnitude is of the size of the `vector_dimension` input:

```
import numpy as np
import pyopencl as cl
import numpy.linalg as la

vector_dimension = 100

vector_a = np.random.randint(vector_dimension, size=vector_dimension)
vector_b = np.random.randint(vector_dimension, size=vector_dimension)
```

```
platform = cl.get_platforms()[0]
device = platform.get_devices()[0]

context = cl.Context([device])
queue = cl.CommandQueue(context)

mf = cl.mem_flags
a_g = cl.Buffer(context, mf.READ_ONLY | mf.COPY_HOST_PTR,
hostbuf=vector_a)
b_g = cl.Buffer(context, mf.READ_ONLY | mf.COPY_HOST_PTR,
hostbuf=vector_b)

program = cl.Program(context, """
__kernel void vectorSum(__global const int *a_g, __global const int
*b_g, __global int *res_g) {
  int gid = get_global_id(0);
  res_g[gid] = a_g[gid] + b_g[gid];
}
""").build()

res_g = cl.Buffer(context, mf.WRITE_ONLY, vector_a.nbytes)
program.vectorSum(queue, vector_a.shape, None, a_g, b_g, res_g)

res_np = np.empty_like(vector_a)
cl.enqueue_copy(queue, res_np, res_g)

print ("PyOPENCL SUM OF TWO VECTORS")
print ("Platform Selected = %s" %platform.name )
print ("Device Selected = %s" %device.name)
print ("VECTOR LENGTH = %s" %vector_dimension)
print ("INPUT VECTOR A")
print vector_a
print ("INPUT VECTOR B")
print vector_b
print ("OUTPUT VECTOR RESULT A + B ")
print res_np

assert(la.norm(res_np - (vector_a + vector_b))) < 1e-5
```

The output from Command Prompt should be like this:

```
C:\Python CookBook\ Chapter 6 - GPU Programming with Python\Chapter 6 -
codes>python PyOpenCLParallellSum.py
```

```
Platform Selected = NVIDIA CUDA
Device Selected = GeForce GT 240
```

```
VECTOR LENGTH = 100
INPUT VECTOR A
```

```
[ 0 29 88 46 68 93 81  3 58 44 95 20 81 69 85 25 89 39 47 29 47 48 20 86
59 99  3 26 68 62 16 13 63 28 77 57 59 45 52 89 16  6 18 95 30 66 19 29
31 18 42 34 70 21 28  0 42 96 23 86 64 88 20 26 96 45 28 53 75 53 39 83
85 99 49 93 23 39  1 89 39 87 62 29 51 66  5 66 48 53 66  8 51  3 29 96
67 38 22 88]
```

```
INPUT VECTOR B
```

```
[98 43 16 28 63  1 83 18  6 58 47 86 59 29 60 68 19 51 37 46 99 27  4 94
5 22  3 96 18 84 29 34 27 31 37 94 13 89  3 90 57 85 66 63  8 74 21 18 34
93 17 26  9 88 38 28 14 68 88 90 18  6 40 30 70 93 75  0 45 86 15 10 29
84 47 74 22 72 69 33 81 31 45 62 81 66 69 14 71 96 91 51 35  4 63 36 28
65 10 41]
```

```
OUTPUT VECTOR RESULT A + B
```

```
[ 98  72 104  74 131  94 164  21  64 102 142 106 140  98 145  93 108  90
  84  75 146  75  24 180  64 121   6 122  86 146  45  47  90  59 114 151
  72 134  55 179  73  91  84 158  38 140  40  47  65 111  59  60  79 109
  66  28  56 164 111 176  82  94  60  56 166 138 103  53 120 139  54  93
 114 183  96 167  45 111  70 122 120 118 107  91 132 132  74  80 119 149
 157  59  86   7  92 132  95 103  32 129]
```

How it works...

In the first line of the code after the required module import, we defined the input vectors:

```
vector_dimension = 100
vector_a = np.random.randint(vector_dimension, size= vector_dimension)
vector_b = np.random.randint(vector_dimension, size= vector_dimension)
```

Each vector contains 100 integers items that are randomly selected thought the NumPy function np.random.randint(max integer , size of the vector).

Then, we must select the device to run the kernel code. To do this, we must first select the platform using the PyOpenCL's get_platform() statement:

```
platform = cl.get_platforms()[0]
```

This platform, as you can see from the output, corresponds to the NVIDIA CUDA platform. Then, we must select the device using the platform's `get_device()` method:

```
device = platform.get_devices()[0]
```

In the following code, the context and queue are defined. PyOpenCL provides the method context (device selected) and queue (context selected):

```
context = cl.Context([device])
queue = cl.CommandQueue(context)
```

To perform the computation in the device, the input vector must be transferred to the device's memory. So, two input buffers in the device memory must be created:

```
mf = cl.mem_flags
a_g = cl.Buffer(context, mf.READ_ONLY | mf.COPY_HOST_PTR,
hostbuf=vector_a)
b_g = cl.Buffer(context, mf.READ_ONLY | mf.COPY_HOST_PTR,
hostbuf=vector_b)
```

Also, we prepare the buffer for the resulting vector:

```
res_g = cl.Buffer(context, mf.WRITE_ONLY, vector_a.nbytes)
```

Finally, the core of the script, that is, the kernel code is defined inside `program`:

```
program = cl.Program(context, """
__kernel void vectorSum(__global const int *a_g, __global const int
*b_g, __global int *res_g) {
  int gid = get_global_id(0);
  res_g[gid] = a_g[gid] + b_g[gid];
}
""").build()
```

The kernel's name is `vectorSum`, while the parameter list defines the data types of the input arguments (vectors of integers) and output data type (a vector of the integer).

In the body of the kernel function, the sum of two vectors is defined as follows:

- **Initialize the vector index**: `int gid = get_global_id(0)`
- **Sum up the vector's components**: `res_g[gid] = a_g[gid] + b_g[gid];`

In OpenCL and PyOpenCL, buffers are attached to a context and are only moved to a device once the buffer is used on that device. Finally, we execute `vectorSum` in the device:

```
program.vectorSum(queue, vector_a.shape, None, a_g, b_g, res_g)
```

To visualize the results, an empty vector is built:

```
res_np = np.empty_like(vector_a)
```

Then, the result is copied into this vector:

```
cl.enqueue_copy(queue, res_np, res_g)
```

Finally, the results are displayed:

```
print ("VECTOR LENGTH = %s" %vector_dimension)
print ("INPUT VECTOR A")
print vector_a
print ("INPUT VECTOR B")
print vector_b
print ("OUTPUT VECTOR RESULT A + B ")
print res_np
```

To check the result, we use the `assert` statement. It tests the result and triggers an error if the condition is `false`:

```
assert(la.norm(res_np - (vector_a + vector_b))) < 1e-5
```

Evaluating element-wise expressions with PyOpenCl

Similar to PyCUDA, PyOpenCL provides the functionality in the `pyopencl.elementwise` class that allows us to evaluate the complicated expressions in a single computational pass. The method that realized this is:

```
ElementwiseKernel(context, argument, operation, name,",",",
                        optional_parameters)
```

Here:

- `context`: This is the device or the group of devices on which the element-wise operation will be executed
- `argument`: This is a C-like argument list of all the parameters involved in the computation
- `operation`: This is a string that represents the operation that is to be performed on the argument list
- `name`: This is the kernel name associated with `ElementwiseKernel`
- `optional_parameters`: These are not important for this recipe.

How to do it...

In this example, we will again consider the task of adding two integer vectors of 100 elements. The achievement, of course, changes because we use the `ElementwiseKernel` class, as shown:

```python
import pyopencl as cl
import pyopencl.array as cl_array
import numpy as np

context = cl.create_some_context()
queue = cl.CommandQueue(context)

vector_dimension = 100
vector_a = cl_array.to_device(queue,  np.random.randint(vector_
dimension, size=vector_dimension))
vector_b = cl_array.to_device(queue,  np.random.randint(vector_
dimension, size=vector_dimension))
result_vector = cl_array.empty_like(vector_a)

elementwiseSum = cl.elementwise.ElementwiseKernel(context, "int *a,
int *b, int *c", "c[i] = a[i] + b[i]", "sum")
elementwiseSum(vector_a, vector_b, result_vector)

print ("PyOpenCL ELEMENTWISE SUM OF TWO VECTORS")
print ("VECTOR LENGTH = %s" %vector_dimension)
print ("INPUT VECTOR A")
print vector_a
print ("INPUT VECTOR B")
print vector_b
print ("OUTPUT VECTOR RESULT A + B ")
print result_vector
```

The output of this code is as follows:

```
C:\Python CookBook\Chapter 6 - GPU Programming with Python\>python
PyOpenCLElementwise.py


Choose platform:
[0] <pyopencl.Platform 'NVIDIA CUDA' at 0x2cc6c40>
[1] <pyopencl.Platform 'Intel(R) OpenCL' at 0x3cf440>
Choice [0]:0
Set the environment variable PYOPENCL_CTX='0' to avoid being asked again.
```

PyOpenCL ELEMENTWISE SUM OF TWO VECTORS

VECTOR LENGTH = 100

INPUT VECTOR A

```
[70 95 47 53 71 52 15 10 95  5 76 40 55 87  7 18 44 72  2 42 47 86 58 87
 64 79 44 94  5 54 92 21 60 67 43 92 38 49 97 14 17 35 87 94  3 17 87 24
 50 43 39 71 84  7 64 60 29 74 65 82 42 35 96 80 94 57 21 56 94  8  3 94
 30 64 44 34 79  5 88 80 98 88  5  2 77 57  7 93 49 42 56 19 81 36 19 24
 27 18  1 40]
```

INPUT VECTOR B

```
[82 32 72  9 29 29 92  2 20 44 31 91 63 97 86 37 39 41 19 78 60 30 21 69
 29 38 56 49 97 18 44 84 27 73 73 14 67 43 17 58 81 52 89 84 80 96 58 80
 20 91 20 61 92 46 34 98 21 82 52 34 81 45 35 28 23 59 21 89 47 75 49 43
 92 91 84 59 35 61 42 12 69 15 98 85 12 36 64 89 76 29  8 81 62  5 58 13
 46 82 12 66]
```

OUTPUT VECTOR RESULT A + B

```
[152 127 119  62 100  81 107  12 115  49 107 131 118 184  93  55  83 113
  21 120 107 116  79 156  93 117 100 143 102  72 136 105  87 140 116 106
 105  92 114  72  98  87 176 178  83 113 145 104  70 134  59 132 176  53
  98 158  50 156 117 116 123  80 131 108 117 116  42 145 141  83  52 137
 122 155 128  93 114  66 130  92 167 103 103  87  89  93  71 182 125  71
  64 100 143  41  77  37  73 100  13 106]
```

How it works...

In the first line of the script, we import all the requested modules:

```
import pyopencl as cl
import pyopencl.array as cl_array
import numpy
```

To initialize the context, we use the `cl.create_some_context()` method. It asks the user which context must be used to perform the calculation:

```
Choose platform:
[0] <pyopencl.Platform 'NVIDIA CUDA' at 0x2cc6c40>
[1] <pyopencl.Platform 'Intel(R) OpenCL' at 0x3cf440>
```

Then, we instantiate the queue that will receive `ElementwiseKernel`:

```
queue = cl.CommandQueue(context)
```

The input vectors and the result vector are instantiated:

```
vector_dimension = 100
vector_a = cl_array.to_device(queue,  np.random.randint(vector_
dimension, size=vector_dimension))
vector_b = cl_array.to_device(queue,  np.random.randint(vector_
dimension, size=vector_dimension))
result_vector = cl_array.empty_like(vector_a)
```

The input vectors `vector_a` and `vector_b` are integer vectors of random values that are obtained using the NumPy's `random.radint` function. The inputs vectors are defined and copied into the device using the PyOpenCL statement:

```
cl.array_to_device(queue,array)
```

Finally, the `ElementwiseKernel` object is created:

```
elementwiseSum = cl.elementwise.ElementwiseKernel(context,  "int *a,
int *b, int *c", "c[i] = a[i] + b[i]", "sum")
```

In this code:

▸ All the arguments are in the form of a string formatted as a C argument list (they are all integers)

▸ A snippet of C carries out the operation, which is the sum of the vector components

▸ The function's name is used to compile the kernel ^s

Then, we can call the `elementwiseSum` function with the arguments defined previously:

```
elementwiseSum(vector_a, vector_b, result_vector)
```

The example ends by printing the input vectors and the result is obtained:

```
print vector_a
print vector_b
print result_vector
```

Testing your GPU application with PyOpenCL

In this chapter, we comparatively tested the performance between a CPU and GPU. Before you begin the study of the performance of algorithms, it is important to keep in mind the platform of execution on which the tests were conducted. In fact, the specific characteristics of these systems interfere with the computational time and they represent an aspect of primary importance.

To perform the tests, we used the following machines

- ▸ **GPU**: GeForce GT 240
- ▸ **CPU**: Intel Core2 Duo 2.33 Ghz
- ▸ **RAM**: DDR2 4 Gb

How to do it...

In this test, the computation time of a simple mathematical operation, that is, the sum of two vectors with elements expressed in a floating point will be evaluated and compared. To make a comparison, the same operation was implemented in two separate functions.

The first one uses only the CPU, while the second is written using PyOpenCL and makes use of the GPU for calculation. The test is performed on vectors of a dimension equal to 10,000 elements.

The code for this is as follows:

```python
from time import time  # Import time tools

import pyopencl as cl
import numpy as np
import PyOpeClDeviceInfo as device_info
import numpy.linalg as la

#input vectors
a = np.random.rand(10000).astype(np.float32)
b = np.random.rand(10000).astype(np.float32)

def test_cpu_vector_sum(a, b):
    c_cpu = np.empty_like(a)
    cpu_start_time = time()
    for i in range(10000):
            for j in range(10000):
                    c_cpu[i] = a[i] + b[i]
    cpu_end_time = time()
    print("CPU Time: {0} s".format(cpu_end_time - cpu_start_time))
    return c_cpu

def test_gpu_vector_sum(a, b):
    #define the PyOpenCL Context
    platform = cl.get_platforms()[0]
    device = platform.get_devices()[0]
    context = cl.Context([device])
```

```
    queue = cl.CommandQueue(context, \
                properties=cl.command_queue_properties.PROFILING_
ENABLE)

#prepare the data structure
    a_buffer = cl.Buffer\
                (context, \
                cl.mem_flags.READ_ONLY \
                | cl.mem_flags.COPY_HOST_PTR, hostbuf=a)
    b_buffer = cl.Buffer\
                (context, \
                cl.mem_flags.READ_ONLY \
                | cl.mem_flags.COPY_HOST_PTR, hostbuf=b)
    c_buffer = cl.Buffer\
                (context, \
                cl.mem_flags.WRITE_ONLY, b.nbytes)
    program = cl.Program(context, """
    __kernel void sum(__global const float *a,
                      __global const float *b,
                      __global float *c)
    {
        int i = get_global_id(0);
        int j;
        for(j = 0; j < 10000; j++)
        {
            c[i] = a[i] + b[i];
        }
    }""").build()
    #start the gpu test
    gpu_start_time = time()
    event = program.sum(queue, a.shape, None, \
                        a_buffer, b_buffer, c_buffer)
    event.wait()
    elapsed = 1e-9*(event.profile.end - event.profile.start)
    print("GPU Kernel evaluation Time: {0} s".format(elapsed))
    c_gpu = np.empty_like(a)
    cl.enqueue_read_buffer(queue, c_buffer, c_gpu).wait()
    gpu_end_time = time()
    print("GPU Time: {0} s".format(gpu_end_time - gpu_start_time))
    return c_gpu

#start the test
if __name__ == "__main__":
    #print the device info
```

```
       device_info.print_device_info()
       #call the test on the cpu
       cpu_result = test_cpu_vector_sum(a, b)
       #call the test on the gpu
       gpu_result = test_gpu_vector_sum(a, b)
       #
       assert (la.norm(cpu_result - gpu_result)) < 1e-5
```

The output of the test is as follows, where the device information with the execution time is printed out:

```
C:\Python Cook\Chapter 6 - GPU Programming with Python\Chapter 6 -
codes>python PyOpenCLTestApplication.py


===============================================================
OpenCL Platforms and Devices
===============================================================
Platform - Name:  NVIDIA CUDA
Platform - Vendor:  NVIDIA Corporation
Platform - Version:  OpenCL 1.1 CUDA 6.0.1
Platform - Profile:  FULL_PROFILE
       ----------------------------------------------------------
    Device - Name:  GeForce GT 240
    Device - Type:  GPU
    Device - Max Clock Speed:  1340 Mhz
    Device - Compute Units:  12
    Device - Local Memory:  16 KB
    Device - Constant Memory:  64 KB
    Device - Global Memory: 1 GB
    Device - Max Buffer/Image Size: 256 MB
    Device - Max Work Group Size: 512
===============================================================
Platform - Name:  Intel(R) OpenCL
Platform - Vendor:  Intel(R) Corporation
Platform - Version:  OpenCL 1.2
Platform - Profile:  FULL_PROFILE
       ----------------------------------------------------------
    Device - Name:  Intel(R) Core(TM)2 Duo CPU      E6550  @ 2.33GHz
    Device - Type:  CPU
```

```
Device - Max Clock Speed:   2330 Mhz
Device - Compute Units:   2
Device - Local Memory:   32 KB
Device - Constant Memory:   128 KB
Device - Global Memory: 2 GB
Device - Max Buffer/Image Size: 512 MB
Device - Max Work Group Size: 8192
```

```
CPU Time: 71.9769999981 s
GPU Kernel Time: 0.075756608 s
GPU Time: 0.0809998512268 s
```

Even if the test is not computationally expansive, it provides useful indications of the potential of a GPU card.

How it works...

As explained in the preceding section, the test consists of two parts. The code that runs on the CPU and the code that runs on the GPU. Both were taken to the execution time.

Regarding the test on the CPU, the test_cpu_vector_sum function has been implemented. It consists of two loops on 10,000 vectors elements:

```
cpu_start_time = time()
    for i in range(10000):
                for j in range(10000):
            c_cpu[i] = a[i] + b[i]
    cpu_end_time = time()
```

The sum operation of the *i*th vector components is executed 1,000,000,000 times, and it will be computationally expensive.

The total CPU time will have the following difference:

```
CPU Time = cpu_end_time - cpu_start_time
```

To test the GPU time, we implemented the regular definition schema of an application for PyOpenCL:

- ▸ We established the definition of the device and context
- ▸ We set up the queue for execution

- ▶ We created memory areas to perform the computation on the device (three buffers defined as `a_buffer, b_buffer, c_buffer`)
- ▶ We built the kernel
- ▶ We evaluated the kernel call and GPU time:

```
gpu_start_time = time()
            event = program.sum(queue, a.shape, None, \
                          a_buffer, b_buffer, c_buffer)

              cl.enqueue_read_buffer(queue, c_buffer, c_gpu).wait()
      gpu_end_time = time()
```

Here, `GPU Time = gpu_end_time - gpu_start_time`.

Finally, in the main program we call the testing function and `print_device_info()` that we defined previously:

```
if __name__ == "__main__":
    device_info.print_device_info()
    cpu_result = test_cpu_vector_sum(a, b)
    gpu_result = test_gpu_vector_sum(a, b)
    assert (la.norm(cpu_result - gpu_result)) < 1e-5
```

To check the result, we used the `assert` statement that verifies the result and triggers an error if the condition is `false`.

Index

J

Just-in-time (JIT) compiler 202

K

kernel
  about 203
  invoking, with GPUArray 218-220

L

load balancing cluster 12
lock
  used, for thread synchronization 41-45

M

map functions
  handling, with SCOOP 163-166
mapping
  about 18
  dynamic mapping 18
MapReduce
  Map 190
  operation, performing with PyCUDA 225-228
  Reduce 190
  used, with Disco 190-195
memory access
  cache only memory access (COMA) 9
  non-uniform memory access (NUMA) 9
  no remote memory access (NORMA) 9
  uniform memory access (UMA) 9
memory architecture
  about 3
  multiple instruction, multiple data (MIMD) 6
  multiple instruction, single data (MISD) 5
  single instruction, multiple data (SIMD) 5
  single instruction, single data (SISD) 3, 4
memory organization
  about 6, 7
  distributed memory 10, 11
  shared memory 8, 9
message passing model 15
mpi4py Python module
  URL 98
  using 97-100

multithread applications
  performance, evaluating 66-72
multithreaded programming 34
multithread model 15

N

non-uniform memory access (NUMA) 9
no remote memory access (NORMA) 9
NumbaPro
  about 229
  GPU-accelerated libraries, using 234-239
  used, for GPU programming 229-233
NVIDIA CUDA Development Driver
  URL 204
NVIDIA GPU Computing SDK
  URL 204

O

objects
  chaining, with Pyro4 171-177
  exchanging, between process 84
  exchanging, pipes used 88-90
  exchanging, queue used 84-87
ØMQ package 158
Open Computing Language (OpenCL) 240
Open Telecom Platform (OTP) 153

P

parallel computing
  memory architecture 3
parallel program
  agglomeration 17
  designing 16
  mapping 18
  performance, evaluating 19
  task assignment 17
  task decomposition 17
parallel programming models
  about 14
  data parallel model 16
  message passing model 15
  multithread model 15
  shared memory model 14

Thank you for buying
Python Parallel Programming Cookbook

About Packt Publishing

Packt, pronounced 'packed', published its first book, *Mastering phpMyAdmin for Effective MySQL Management*, in April 2004, and subsequently continued to specialize in publishing highly focused books on specific technologies and solutions.

Our books and publications share the experiences of your fellow IT professionals in adapting and customizing today's systems, applications, and frameworks. Our solution-based books give you the knowledge and power to customize the software and technologies you're using to get the job done. Packt books are more specific and less general than the IT books you have seen in the past. Our unique business model allows us to bring you more focused information, giving you more of what you need to know, and less of what you don't.

Packt is a modern yet unique publishing company that focuses on producing quality, cutting-edge books for communities of developers, administrators, and newbies alike. For more information, please visit our website at www.packtpub.com.

About Packt Open Source

In 2010, Packt launched two new brands, Packt Open Source and Packt Enterprise, in order to continue its focus on specialization. This book is part of the Packt open source brand, home to books published on software built around open source licenses, and offering information to anybody from advanced developers to budding web designers. The Open Source brand also runs Packt's open source Royalty Scheme, by which Packt gives a royalty to each open source project about whose software a book is sold.

Writing for Packt

We welcome all inquiries from people who are interested in authoring. Book proposals should be sent to author@packtpub.com. If your book idea is still at an early stage and you would like to discuss it first before writing a formal book proposal, then please contact us; one of our commissioning editors will get in touch with you.

We're not just looking for published authors; if you have strong technical skills but no writing experience, our experienced editors can help you develop a writing career, or simply get some additional reward for your expertise.

Parallel Programming with Python

ISBN: 978-1-78328-839-7   Paperback: 128 pages

Develop efficient parallel systems using the robust Python environment

1. Demonstrates the concepts of Python parallel programming.

2. Boosts your Python computing capabilities.

3. Contains easy-to-understand explanations and plenty of examples.

Python High Performance Programming

ISBN: 978-1-78328-845-8   Paperback: 108 pages

Boost the performance of your Python programs using advanced techniques

1. Identify the bottlenecks in your applications and solve them using the best profiling techniques.

2. Write efficient numerical code in NumPy and Cython.

3. Adapt your programs to run on multiple processors with parallel programming.

Please check **www.PacktPub.com** for information on our titles

[PACKT] open source✧
community experience distilled

PUBLISHING

Python Testing Cookbook

ISBN: 978-1-84951-466-8 Paperback: 364 pages

Over 70 simple but incredibly effective recipes for taking control of automated testing using powerful Python testing tools

1. Learn to write tests at every level using a variety of Python testing tools.

2. The first book to include detailed screenshots and recipes for using Jenkins continuous integration server (formerly known as Hudson).

3. Explore innovative ways to introduce automated testing to legacy systems.

4. Written by Greg L. Turnquist – senior software engineer and author of Spring Python 1.1.

Mastering Python [Video]

ISBN: 978-1-78398-896-9 Duration: 02:35 hours

Get to grips with Python best practices and advanced tools to design, distribute, and test your programs

1. Explore the immense Python libraries to write efficient, reusable code.

2. Create adaptable programs that run on multiple processors with parallel programming.

3. Become a Python expert with the help of detailed discussions, illustrated with concrete examples.

Please check **www.PacktPub.com** for information on our titles

CPSIA information can be obtained at www.ICGtesting.com
Printed in the USA
LVOW09s0102290416

485871LV00007B/34/P